Working with

Subtle Energies

David Spangler

ALSO BY DAVID SPANGLER

WORKING WITH SUBTLE ENERGIES

Edited by Aidan Spangler and Julia Spangler
Book Design by Jeremy Berg

Published by Lorian Press
6592 Peninsula Dr
Traverse City, MI 49686

ISBN: 978-0-936878-78-2

Spangler/David
Working With Subtle Energies/David Spangler

First Edition February 2016

Printed in the United States of America

0 9 8 7 6 5 4 3 2 1

www.lorian.org

DEDICATION

I dedicate this book to all those who work to create partnership and collaboration with the subtle dimensions of Earth in order to foster wholeness in our world.

ACKNOWLEDGEMENTS

In my work exploring the subtle environment and the ways we may engage with subtle energies, I have been encouraged and supported by wonderful friends and colleagues, including especially my fellow Lorians, and by the many people who honored me by attending the classes in which much of the material in this book was developed. Thank you all! I also thank as always my wife Julia and my children whose support has made my work possible.

TABLE OF CONTENTS

PREFACE

This book is the second in a trilogy of books describing my insights and experiences with the non-physical dimensions of the Earth. I call these dimensions the *Subtle Worlds*. The first book in this trilogy is *Subtle Worlds: An Explorer's Field Notes*. It provides an overview of these non-physical dimensions and the beings that inhabit and work within them. The third book is *Collaborating with Subtle Worlds*. It is a more detailed look at the nature of subtle beings and how to safely engage and work with them. This book covers the middle ground. It is neither an overview nor is it about subtle beings themselves. It is about what I call *subtle energies*, qualities and forces that fill the non-physical world the way sunlight fills the physical air around us. It is about *energy hygiene*, methods and techniques for working with these non-physical forces. As such, it takes a specific part of the subtle worlds—the subtle environment—and explores it in more detail than in the first book of this trilogy. It provides a foundation on which the material and techniques described in the third book are based.

All three books are part of a larger body of thought, teaching and practice called *Incarnational Spirituality*. The essence of this approach is this: we are born into this world not as exiles from our "true home", not as students seeking to learn and then graduate to a better place, not as debtors working to pay off past obligations, but as generative sources of life, Light, and sacredness. We incarnate into a whole world that is both physical and non-physical. We can relate lovingly, creatively, and collaboratively with both these aspects of the world out of the power and presence of our generative nature. We are caretakers of this world and help foster its wholeness and emerging potentials. We are incubators of the world as a living, evolving, soul-filled organism.

This book and its two companion books in the Subtle World Trilogy deal with how we can relate "lovingly, creatively, and collaboratively" with the non-physical aspects of the world as an integral part of fostering the wholeness of the world.

If you'd like to know my personal story and how I've come to work with the subtle worlds as I have, you can read my memoir, *Apprenticed to Spirit*. If you are interested in Incarnational Spirituality itself, then to start, I recommend the following books I've authored in this order: *An Introduction to Incarnational Spirituality, Journey into Fire, The Call of the World*, and *Partnering with Earth*. You may also wish to look at *The Gathering Light*, by Jeremy Berg. These provide the overarching context in which the ideas explored in the Subtle World Trilogy are placed. For in-depth, further study, there are other books along with classes and study materials that are available. Complete information can be found in the Lorian Bookstore on the Lorian website, www.Lorian.org.

I want to offer a word about the material in this book. There is nothing new or revolutionary about perceiving and engaging with subtle energies. For millennia, people have known about, sensed and worked with non-physical energies for good or ill. As science and technology developed along with a corresponding materialist worldview in Western society, this knowledge of the subtle worlds has largely been forgotten or relegated to religion or simply to superstition. But this is changing as science itself reveals more and more about the energy fields surrounding and interpenetrating not only the physical body but everything within the environment. New fields like bioenergetics and new organizations such as the Association for Comprehensive Energy Psychology are expanding public and professional awareness that our planet is an ecosystem embracing both physical and non-physical reality. We all participate in and are affected by the subtle energetic side of things. Learning how to work with such subtle energies has many benefits.

This book is not a comprehensive survey of this field, however. It is instead, like the other two books in this series, a set of "field notes" based on my personal experience. This is working with the subtle worlds and subtle energies as I have perceived and experienced them. Other people could well have different experiences and consequently different perspectives. I think of this book as an introduction to the subject and as a basis for further research and exploration. We all inhabit the subtle dimensions of life all the time. Learning to inhabit them well is an important and much needed skill for our future.

INTRODUCTION

For the better part of seventy years, I've been aware of a non-physical aspect to the world around us. As a child, this usually took the form of perceiving a radiance or emanation of energy surrounding the things around me. My earliest memories are of a world in which everything is alive. It was obvious to me that there was a difference between the life I saw manifested in the plants and animals, as well as the people, that made up my everyday world and an energy of life I felt present in things like stones, chairs, tables, my bed, my toys, and even whole buildings. The life of the inorganic world didn't manifest itself outwardly, but it was present inwardly nonetheless in some manner or in some dimension I could not explain. And I was aware of it, sometimes acutely as when certain places or individuals radiated distinctly unpleasant and disturbing qualities, or when, just the opposite, they glowed with love and vitality.

From time to time, I even observed beings—sometimes human, sometimes not—who would appear and disappear seemingly at random. I have a particularly vivid memory from when I was six years old of playing on the kitchen floor and looking up to see a chubby, smiling figure dressed in overalls standing over me. I had no idea where this person had come from as one minute he had not been there and the next minute he was. I felt a wave of interest and love towards me. He seemed perfectly solid, yet as I looked at him, he faded away and disappeared. I had no idea who he was, but some years later, my grandmother was showing me an album of pictures and there in one of the photos was this same man, wearing the same overalls. It was my grandfather who had died some years before I was born and who, though an engineer and an inventor by profession, had owned a farm where on weekends he would put on the overalls to do work around his land.

All these experiences were fairly passive on my part. I didn't initiate them, nor did I try to interact with any of the energies I felt or saw. On those occasions when a being would show up, I would acknowledge it but that was all. Whatever this invisible world was, I felt comfortable with it but I didn't know what to do with it. So I basically left it alone to put all my attention on the physical world that was so engaging.

When I was in college, though, this somewhat passive relationship to the non-physical side of the world began to change, so much so that I realized my work wasn't in the field of molecular biology, which is what I was studying, but in some way with the phenomena represented by these inner dimensions. The result of this was that I left college and moved to Los Angeles where I had been invited to come give some lectures by some close friends who ran a metaphysical center. They knew of my non-physical perceptions and felt that the people they attracted would be interested in hearing from me about my experiences.

I had been in Los Angeles for about a week when I was visited one morning by an unusually strong and energetically radiant spirit who said we had a work to do together. I called him "John," and we entered into a collegial partnership that lasted for nearly thirty years. All of this I relate in detail in my book *Apprenticed to Spirit*.

For the first five years of our association, John was a mentor and teacher as well as a friend and colleague. It was he who taught me how to transform what had been a passive awareness into a set of active tools with which I could mindfully engage with subtle energies.

I was twenty when I met John fifty years ago. The material in this book is a distillation of the lessons and training I received from him and from other non-physical colleagues as well as of the fruits of these past fifty years of experience. The "field notes" I'm sharing with you here are certainly not the only way to go about perceiving or engaging with the non-physical or "subtle" dimensions, but they are how I was trained. They have served me well. I offer them in the hopes that you will find insights and practices of value here for you as well.

There are four important ideas that I wish to affirm at the outset. The first is this: **IN ENGAGING THE SUBTLE WORLDS, LOVE AND TRUST YOURSELF AND HAVE NO FEAR.**

Between horror novels and spooky movies, not to mention some religious traditions, we are encouraged to be afraid when it comes to the non-physical worlds and the forces within them. Fear, though, makes working with subtle energies more difficult and can, in fact, create danger where otherwise none would exist.

Many things in our world can potentially be harmful or dangerous. The electricity that lights my home can just as easily kill me if I engage with it recklessly. Used properly and with understanding, however, it is a blessing that brings me light in the darkness and powers the tools that make my life easier. The same is true for subtle energies. There is nothing inherently to fear. They are natural phenomena, the same as the wind, sunlight, or electricity. What you will learn in this book will give you a safe foundation for engaging with them.

Most importantly, you want to be able to honor and trust yourself, to love who you are and what you can become. For reasons I will make clear from the outset, you want to "stand" solidly on the inner "land" of your own being, attuned to your own identity and its sovereignty. When you do this, it creates a powerful inner presence which determines how you will engage with subtle forces and how they will respond to you.

The second important idea we need to affirm is this: **YOU DO NOT HAVE TO BE "PSYCHIC" TO WORK WITH SUBTLE ENERGIES**.

Awareness of the subtle realms needs no special talents or abilities. What it does require is your attention, your intention, and your patient discernment. Working with subtle energies is a bit like tending a garden: initially the seeds are invisible and you can't see what's going on, but in time, shoots begin to poke through the soil and the process of growth becomes visible. This happens when developing the capacities to engage and work with subtle energies as well

I do not need to be an electrician or an electrical engineer to turn on the lights in my room; I just need to know where the switch is. Similarly, you do not need to be a mystic, an occultist, or a psychic to connect with subtle energies; you just need to know where your internal switch is. This is what you'll learn in this book.

The third important idea is this: **SUBTLE ENERGIES ARE NOT FORCES TO BE MANIPULATED BUT LIVING PROCESSES WITH WHICH YOU ENTER INTO A RELATIONSHIP. EACH SUCH RELATIONSHIP WILL BE UNIQUE WITH EACH PERSON.**

Although I will be presenting suggestions on how to engage with subtle energies, remember that you are a unique individual and that this engagement will be shaped and influenced by who you are. No two people perceive or connect with subtle energies in exactly the same way; there can be many similarities, but in the end, you need to discover and honor your unique way of engaging with the subtle worlds. Just as no two relationships between people are exactly alike, so your relationship with these living energies will not be like anyone else's, even when there are similarities.

The fourth important idea is this: **YOU WILL PERCEIVE SUBTLE ENERGIES IN YOUR OWN UNIQUE WAY WHICH MAY HAVE NOTHING AT ALL TO DO WITH "SEEING" OR "HEARING."**

It's not at all uncommon for a person who's trying to perceive subtle energies to feel he or she is failing if he or she doesn't see or hear anything. We are accustomed to receiving information through our five physical senses, information that is visual, auditory, tactile, and so forth. But we have subtle senses, too, and the way they perceive subtle energies often is not at all like sight or hearing. I'll write about this at some length later in this book. For now, just know that whether or not you "see" or "hear" something when trying to tune into subtle energies is not a measure of your success.

A WORD ABOUT THE EXERCISES

DOING EXERCISES OR EXPERIMENTS ("EXPERICISES")

At the end of each chapter, you will find one or more exercises. I think of these exercises as lenses to allow you a clearer focus on the topics covered in the chapter. If a particular exercise doesn't work for you—if, metaphorically, the lens is out of focus for you—then feel free to change or adapt it as long as such changes are in keeping with the objective. In other words, if you wanted to magnify and see a skin cell on your hand but the microscope you're using is out of focus, you don't want to trade it in for a telescope in order to look at the planet Venus. Just find a microscope that works for you but keep the objective in mind.

I think of these exercises as experiments because that is really what they are. There is nothing magical about them; they are not carved in stone. They truly are experiments in evoking, invoking, or in some manner arriving at a particular experience, usually a *felt sense* of the central topic covered in the preceding chapter. Because they are experiments, they may work for you or they may not. An experiment that doesn't work conveys important information, too, and helps you redesign the experiment (or exercise) in a way that hopefully will accomplish the purpose. By thinking of them as experiments, you are not bound to them nor will you think of them as "sacred processes" that cannot be changed or adapted to your unique style and nature. Experiments are adventures and open us to new knowledge. They are servants of discovery. Have fun with the exercises and let them serve your discovery of yourself and of the subtle energies that make up your life.

FELT SENSE

In the various exercises (experiments) and practices of Incarnational Spirituality, you'll find that in the instructions, you are often asked to discern the felt sense of a particular attunement or state of consciousness that is the object of the exercise or practice. This felt sense is a blending of physical sensations as well as mental and emotional states (such as moods or feelings).

Suppose you're angry at someone and I say to you, "What does this anger feel like in your body?" Turning your attention to your body, you might feel a pressure in your gut or tightness in your back. Your face may feel flushed. You may feel your hands clenching and unclenching. All of these things contribute to the felt sense of the anger.

Or imagine seeing a glorious sunset with the sky filled with rich colors. How does that feel in your body? Your mind? Your emotions? When I see something like that and feel the awe and wonder of it, I can feel as if my body is opening out and becoming larger. I feel more spacious. That is part of the felt sense of the sunset.

Felt sense is like a body language telling you what is going on at an unconscious, preverbal level. By paying attention to the body sensations—to the felt sense—you may find your body giving you information about yourself and your experiences that is healing or at least helpful.

A felt sense can be subtle and not quickly or easily discerned. It may take time just sitting with the body and listening to it, paying attention to it, as you think about or contemplate something about which you'd like the body's response. Felt sense is information, the body talking to you. As I use the term, it's also the unconscious yet deeply aware parts of your mind and heart talking to you as well. It's a communication that you *feel* in yourself, which is why it's a *felt* sense.

Once you have this felt sense committed to memory—the "thought-memory" of your mind, the "feeling-memory" of your emotions, and the "muscle-memory" or "physiological-memory" of your body—you can dispense with the exercise itself. In effect, once you have seen and experienced that inner quality or presence for which the exercise/experiment is a lens so that you can recall it when needed, you don't need the exercise itself. The experiment has paid off.

PART 1
FUNDAMENTALS

CHAPTER ONE
Three to Start

How often do you walk into a room and sense its "atmosphere" or mood. You know without knowing why that something pleasant or unpleasant has happened there. You may feel welcomed and at ease in the room or you may feel like you immediately want to turn around and walk out of it. Nothing outwardly may be the obvious cause of your reaction. It's a response to something existing in a non-physical environment.

Or you may meet someone for the first time, and for no apparent reason, you feel an immediate liking or disliking for the person. You may feel strongly attracted or strongly repelled. It has nothing to do with how that person is dressed, with his or her looks, with the sound of his or her voice, or with any outward manifestation. You may intellectually identify something about that person's appearance or mannerisms as a way of rationally explaining to yourself why you feel the way you do, but intuitively you know it's not the reason. Something else, something deeper, is at work.

What is happening is that you are sensing *subtle energies*. Subtle energies are a natural complement to the physical world. They are part of what I think of as "Earth's other half," the planet's non-physical ecology, and are so-called because they exist and manifest in ways that are usually too subtle for our normal physical senses to register. Yet on some level of our awareness, we do perceive and respond to them.

Let me be clear from the outset. One does not have to be a psychic or a clairvoyant to experience or work with the subtle dimensions both of ourselves and of the world around us. With attention, intention, some practice, and some patience, they can be part of our everyday awareness. When this happens, we find ourselves engaging with the world in a broader and more holistic way.

However, changes may be needed in how we see the world. We need to make some fundamental shifts in our thinking if we wish to attune to and work with subtle energies in an effective and holistic fashion. In particular, there are three concepts it's important to understand.

The Living Universe

The first of these concepts is this: the universe is alive and subtle energies are an expression of this life.

This is in my experience the one crucial idea underlying all attempts to engage with subtle energies and the non-physical dimensions of which they are a manifestation. We are part of a living universe.

The familiar consensual reality in which most of us live on a daily basis divides the world up into the living and the non-living, the organic and the inorganic. The minerals, metals, plastics, ceramics, and other materials that make up our "built world," the world of our artifacts and technologies, are considered to be without life or consciousness of any kind; they are blind, inert substances that we can mold and create as we wish. They are made up of what we like to call "dead matter." This is also true of the various energies we encounter. Electricity, for instance, though vibrantly active, is not considered living. We see it as an impersonal force, a manifestation of chemical and physical properties and relationships.

Although we take this way of seeing the world for granted, historically it's a relatively recent development, one that our ancestors would not have shared prior to the Age of Reason and the Industrial Revolution. Even today, many indigenous peoples around the world do not divide the world up in this way between what is alive and what is not. A stone may be considered just as alive, though in a different way, as the tree that it's lying beside. Both are considered by those who discern this life to have a consciousness to which a human being may relate.

Once we begin to work with subtle energies and with the non-physical dimensions of the world, we step into this different reality. We discover ourselves in a universe in which everything is alive and sentient in ways that transcend and defy our familiar categories. We may feel like Alice after she plunged down the rabbit hole into Wonderland, at least until we become used to the idea. Then we begin to discover just how much of a wonderland the world really is!

I've been aware of subtle energies for almost seventy years. Some of my earliest memories from when I was five and six are of perceiving an energetic emanation around people, places and things. This emanation always felt alive to me, like a presence in itself, though obviously connected to the source from which it was radiating. Life was everywhere irrespective of whether the form from which it emanated was organic or inorganic. This was my experiential introduction to the livingness of the universe around me.

I may control electricity on the physical level (at least as long as its safely contained within the wiring of my house and not loose in the world as lightning), but I don't control subtle forces. When I encounter a subtle energy, it's almost always as if I'm encountering a living creature. As a consequence, rather than control, I seek cooperation.

This is where the term "subtle energy" can be misleading. We consider physical energies like electricity to be blind forces possessing no awareness and thus caring nothing about how we think of them or feel about them. We can manipulate and use them because we do not conceive that they could have any perception of being used or manipulated. In the materialist view, electricity could care less whether we love it, honor it, value it, or cooperate with it.

Subtle energies, though, do have awareness, and thus our attitudes can make a difference in how they respond to us and what they can accomplish on our behalf. If we engage with them with love, honor, and respect, just as we would with a person whose friendship we valued and desired, they will respond more fully than they would otherwise.

We'll be exploring this much more fully as we go on in this book. My point here is to say that working successfully with subtle energies requires a change in how we understand ourselves and the universe in which we live. At the heart of this change is a willingness to shift our perspectives from those of dominance and control to those of respect and cooperation. It's a willingness to see the world in terms of a partnership cosmology.

Many qualities go into creating a positive relationship. In working with subtle energies, it's been my experience that appreciation and gratefulness are two of the most powerful and effective. I bring to the engagement an appreciation of the subtle force with which I'm seeking to collaborate, an appreciation of its nature, its purposes, its qualities or conditions, and its life. This falls into the category of honoring one's partner. I appreciate it for what it can offer to me in helping me achieve a goal and for what it brings that I might not be able to provide myself. I am grateful for it and its collaboration with me. There's an implicit "thank you" in the way I approach subtle energies just as there would be in working with a human partner.

Of course, seeing the world as living and sentient in this way affects more than just our engagement with subtle energies. It affects how we deal with everything in our life: the people we know and meet, the things we use, the places we occupy or visit. The world ceases to be divided between the living and the non-living, the sentient and the non-sentient. When this happens, then the quality of the relationships that I form become ever more important. If I consider that a rock is just "dead matter," then why should I care how I treat it? It can't think or feel anything, so it doesn't matter what I do to it or with it. I don't have a relationship with it in the way I would a fellow human being. But if I accept that at some level, in some manner, the rock is alive and sentient, then the attitude I have while engaging with it does matter. It can make a difference, and this difference spreads out into the entirety of my life.

Once I had to make a month-long trip overseas. I felt it would be nice to have a talisman to bring with me to energetically connect me with my home. I felt a small stone from my yard would be ideal, something I could carry in my pocket. So I set about to find a suitable stone, looking around my front and back yards. Because for me a stone is not just a thing but a living presence, a "thou", I felt I couldn't just pick a stone and take it with me. I wanted to attune to how the stone might feel at being taken out of the energy field of land on which my house is built. After all, energetically, this land was home to all the stones upon and within it.

In this quest, I picked up and held several small, pocket-sized stones. I greeted each one as if it were a living person and held it in my hand in a loving and attentive way. To each stone I asked the question, "Would you be willing to leave this land and travel with me, acting as an ally to keep me in touch with the energies here?" Interestingly, the first four stones I picked up said, "No." They didn't want to leave the land. It was a small pebble I found near my front door that said "Yes" and subsequently did travel with me as an excellent point of energetic connection.

I should add here that these communications were not in words, though I'm repeating them as if they were. Most subtle communications I have aren't. I supply the words later as I translate the impressions and patterns that I experienced into a verbal interpretation. In this instance, when the response to my question was "no," what I felt was a sudden resistance around the stone, as if its energy were reaching back to the soil from which I had picked it up; the stone felt heavier in my hand. I also experienced what felt like sticky threads of energy — akin, perhaps, to the sticky feeling one has with spider webs — rising up from the ground to tug on the energy field of the stone as well. Through such impressions, it was abundantly clear that the web of energies that connected the stone to the ecosystem of my backyard didn't want to let go. When I picked up the final stone, though, I felt none of this. Instead, I felt a surge of energy towards me and a kind of joyous excitement at the prospect of travel.)

When I returned home a month later, I put the pebble back where I found it with my thanks and felt it "snuggle" in energetically to the energy web of the land around it, but now it brought back to the land around my house a rich impression of the different energies to which it had been exposed during my travels. A win/win all the way around!

This is a small example of approaching the realms of subtle energies with an attitude of forming a relationship rather than just expressing dominance and control over some blind and uncaring force. It may seem challenging (or silly) at first to think in this way, but after a time, it becomes habitual, a "new normal" for how you engage the world around you in more aware, caring, and respectful ways. I have found it a way of thinking and acting that pays rich dividends in all areas of my life.

Being part of a living universe is at the heart of learning to work with subtle energies. This idea will inform all the material that I have to offer you in this book. Working with subtle energies is working with subtle life. If you remember this, you will be putting your best foot forward in this endeavor, and creative relationships will follow.

The Whole Person

The second important concept is to learn to think in terms of wholes, particularly with respect to ourselves. We are taught to think in terms of categories. We say, "this is my body," "this is my soul," "this is the physical world," "this is the subtle world." These are important distinctions, but they do not tell the entire store and in fact can blind us to the deeper wholeness both of our own being and of the world around us.

Some years ago, one of the non-physical individuals I think of as my subtle colleagues asked me to stop thinking of him as a subtle being. "You are establishing," he said, "a category of limited usefulness. To call me a "subtle being" is simply a projection of your perspective since you see yourself as solid and me as being insubstantial. From my point of view, however, you are insubstantial and subtle and I am the solid one. Likewise when you think of yourself as inhabiting the physical world and I as belonging to a non-physical one. Again this is a matter of perspective. The world I experience is solid and real to my senses while to me your world is wispy and without substance. So which of us is a subtle being in a subtle world?"

I had to agree with him that it was a matter of perspective but that these were still useful concepts. "Yes," he said, "they are up to a point, but you should not define yourself or me by them. We are each in our own way whole beings. You are both physical and non-physical in your nature. Is one part of you more real than the other? No, not if you wish to know yourself as a whole being or the world as a whole world. You can identify your parts, but as you would say, don't let the trees blind you to the forest. Don't lose sight of the whole you in the process, for it is the whole you who can best engage with the realms beyond the physical."

In this book, we will be working with a five-fold description of ourselves, as illustrated in Figure 1. Broadly speaking, we have a physical body, a psyche made up of mind and emotions which can engage both physical and non-physical worlds, a subtle energy body, and a soul or spiritual presence. The quality of our connectedness is a fifth aspect of ourselves, one that is sometimes overlooked. Our connections and relationships, however, definitely contribute to who we are and hopefully to our wholeness.

I'll be defining what these are as we go along, and at different times, I'll be focusing on one or another of these five in order to illuminate the processes and concepts I wish to present. But in the back of our minds, we need to remember that we are not one of these elements, we are a whole, integrated system combining all five, body, mind, energy, soul, and connections. We are each a whole person, a definition that supersedes whether we are physical or non-physical.

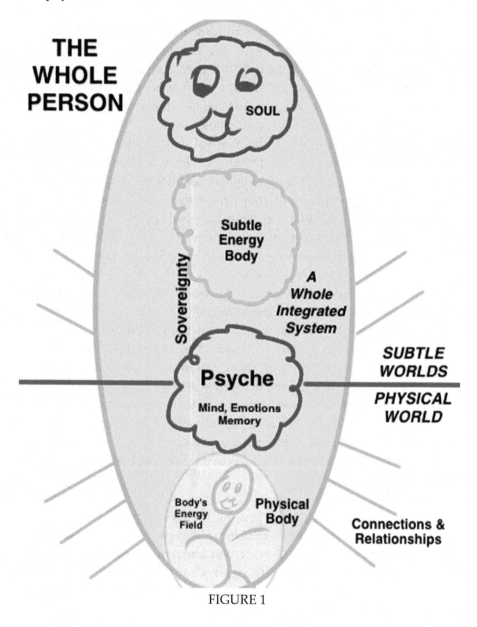

THE WHOLE PERSON

SOUL

Subtle Energy Body

Sovereignty

A Whole Integrated System

Psyche

Mind, Emotions Memory

SUBTLE WORLDS

PHYSICAL WORLD

Body's Energy Field

Physical Body

Connections & Relationships

FIGURE 1

It's not always easy to remember this. It's far simpler and more familiar to think of ourselves as physical people *here* engaging with a whole other place, the subtle worlds, out there. And obviously there are very real differences between these two domains. In one sense, we are physical individuals learning to engage with a non-physical or subtle reality. But I have learned over the years just how useful and important it can be to think of myself as a whole person living in a whole universe when it comes to dealing with subtle phenomena.

Put another way, I want to recognize the differences, but I don't want to elevate them to the status of obstacles and barriers. My wife and I are different genders. She's a woman, I'm a man, and we definitely see many things differently because of this. But we are also both human beings which gives us many common and shared insights as well. Our humanness connects us.

Working with the subtle worlds is all about connectedness. In effect, my subtle colleague was saying, don't see me as a category, especially one that divides us. See me as a fellow person, for then we experience our unity and the connections can flow more easily between us. When we think of ourselves as whole people living in a whole universe, we emphasize the connections in our minds and hearts rather than the differences that separate us. In dealing with the subtle worlds, this really can make a difference that matters. Whatever you do to foster your wholeness will have positive benefits on any work you do with the subtle worlds.

A Place to Stand

The Greek philosopher Archimedes said "Give me a lever and a place to stand, and I can move the world." In working with subtle energies, you learn how to use the "lever" of your own will, attention, love, and connectedness to influence and shape—to move into new patterns—the flow of the living currents of the universe that surround you. To do so, you need a place on which you can stand with surety, safety, strength, and power. I think of this place as your "inner land." It is the land of the wholeness that emerges from your connectedness to yourself and to the world around you. I suggest this in Figure 2.

A PLACE TO STAND

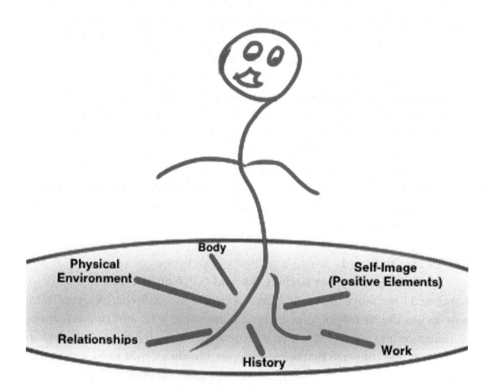

Your Inner "Land"

FIGURE 2

Your inner "land" is a state of mind and heart in which you experience a sense of the inner support that comes to you from different aspects of your life. It is an attunement to the things that make you *you* and differentiate you from everyone else. It is the "land" of your identity, a concept we'll be encountering many times in this book. In effect, you are standing on the bedrock of yourself as a whole person.

I don't know what your land is for you, but here are some suggestions as illustrated in Figure 2. Your land can be a condition of arising from your connectedness and love for the immediate physical environment—the actual, physical place and land—around you where you live; your relationships with others and the strengths they give you; the positive elements of your self-image; your history and autobiography; your body, and your sense of accomplishment in your work or your craft (the things you do that help you feel productive in the world).

For example, my inner land would include my family (Julie and my kids), my work as a teacher and researcher, my love of games and movies, the land of the Pacific Northwest where I live (its mountains, rivers, lakes, volcanoes, and evergreen forests), my physical home and its property, the strength and support of my physical body, my history (such as my time as a co-director of the Findhorn Foundation Community in northern Scotland, my early training in biology, and my childhood growing up on an American air base in Morocco), and my connections with the subtle worlds. All these things converge to give me a sense of identity and support. These things make me or have made me who I am. They are the bedrock of my unique identity and thus create the inner land I stand on to meet the larger life of the universe beyond the physical.

As I say, I don't know what your land may be for you, but look for it in your felt sense of who you are as a person and in the "strata" that make you up and give you support and strength, however you perceive this.

The living universe, the whole person, the inner land: with these three concepts in the back of our minds to guide us, we are ready to begin our engagement with the subtle worlds.

EXERCISE FOR CHAPTER ONE

Exercise: Your Inner Land

- Take a moment to consider just what contributes to your felt sense of yourself as a source of support and power in your life. What elements in your life would you identify as your strong points, the boulders and bedrock on which you inwardly stand? What elements help you to feel powerful and steady as a person? Once you have a sense of this, proceed to the next step.
- Think about each of the elements you just identified that you feel make up the inner "land" on which you stand. Feel the contribution each makes to your strength and presence, to the "land" of your psyche. What is the felt sense of the inner place that these elements create and foster within you?
- Once you have a felt sense of this inner land, link it energetically through love and imagination with the physical land beneath you and around you. It also holds and supports you and can blend its power with your own. All sacred sites are connected to the land; they do not float in a vacuum. This is true of your inner sacred site as well. So connect your inner land with the outer land of your environment. Allow the power of the one to flow into the other, and vice versa, each blessing the other, land communing with land. What is the felt sense of this?
- When you have a felt sense of this combined land—the land of your heart and mind coupled with the land on which your body stands—through an act of will and mindfulness, invoke blessing upon it. In whatever way feels right to you, consecrate this combined "land", attuning it to the sacred that is at the core of both yourself and the world around you. Ask for blessing upon this "land" that blends your inner being with its outer environment. Hold the felt sense of this blessing and of this act of consecration for as long as feels right to you.
- When you are finished, give thanks. Remember the felt sense of this consecrated land within you. End the exercise in whatever graceful way seems right and appropriate to you so that the felt sense of this land the spirit of this inner land—remains part of you for you to draw upon in the future.

CHAPTER TWO
What Are Subtle Energies?

I define subtle energies as *movements in a sea of life and consciousness.*

Imagine being in a pool of water. Any activity sets up ripples that spread out into the pool; how far they go depends on the kind of activity, the power of the ripples, and so on—there are many variables. For instance, the ripples can be the result of a deliberate action, an intent to "make waves", as I would do if I wanted to playfully splash you with water in the pool. Or they can arise just from normal activity that is not directed towards anyone or anything in particular, like the ripples I would create simply by swimming or moving through the water. Subtle energies are the "ripples" caused by activity within a field (or "pool") of consciousness and life.

I suggest this in Figure 3.

SUBTLE ENERGIES
Ripples in the Pool of Beingness
Emanations of Identity

FIGURE 3

All consciousness and life are emanations and manifestations of Identity, the fundamental activity of being. The Identity of the Sacred, the Generative Mystery, manifests the original subtle energy which gives rise to all creation. In mystical and spiritual traditions, this primal energy is simply called "Light."

We are embedded in, surrounded by, filled with, and created from this Light, as is every other thing from star to atom. This Light is the "field of all being," the ultimate pool within which all existence swims. All other subtle forces, fields, presences, energies, lives, consciousnesses, and beings are ultimately derived from the "ripples" or waves of living energy produced in this pool. And because these waves are generated out of the Being of the Sacred, the subtle energies they manifest are alive and sentient for ultimately they are expressions of the life and consciousness of the Sacred.

We actually "swim" in a great many different "pools" or fields of life and consciousness, in addition to that of the Sacred. If we think of the Light of the Sacred—the "universal pool"—as clear, fresh water, then as other Beings or focal points of life and consciousness evolve and are active in this pool, they add their qualities to it, creating "pools" or fields of their own which are fundamentally fields of Light but "flavored" with their unique additions and contributions. In this way, fields of identity begin to manifest within the greater "fresh-water ocean" of the Sacred.

All the beings living here on earth are swimmers in the pool of life and consciousness that has formed around *Gaia*, the Planetary Soul, a global field "flavored" with Gaia's unique spiritual qualities. Then there are "pools" of energy created by continents, landscapes, ecosystems, nations, cities, neighborhoods, even our own homes. And each of us individually creates such a pool of life and consciousness around our own souls and our own bodies. Activity in any of these "pools" generates ripples, the subtle energies which reflect that particular field of life and consciousness. It's for this reason that I experience subtle energies as being sentient and alive in much the same way that a wave in the ocean is composed of the water that constitutes the ocean itself.

This does not mean that when we encounter subtle energies, we will necessarily be directly encountering a subtle being. Sunlight comes from a specific source, the sun, but we can enjoy and work with sunlight without, thankfully, engaging the sun directly, which would definitely be an all-consuming experience! By the time sunlight reaches us, the energy is vastly diffused compared to the surface of the sun itself. Similarly, Gaia, the Soul of the World, is a specific being whose field of life and consciousness encompasses all within the world, but like sunlight, it does so usually in a diffused fashion. So encountering Gaian energies, which make up most of the subtle energies we will be working with, is not the same as encountering Gaia itself.

Understanding the life and sentiency inherent in subtle energies directly affects how you approach and engage them. As I said in the last chapter, while I can control, manipulate, and use physical energies like electricity as I wish (assuming the technology is there to do so), I treat subtle energies as if they were living beings. Control gives way to honor and respect, and manipulation gives way to partnership and collaboration. In other words, working with subtle energies is a *moral* process. In many ways, love is our most important tool for doing subtle energy work.

The Gaian Pools

Although the term *subtle energy* can be used to refer to any non-physical force, quality, or influence, I'm going to give it a more specific definition. Subtle energies have different characteristics and effects depending on the "pool" of consciousness and life in which they are operating or from which they originate.

Think of a hotel by the beach that has two swimming pools, one filled with fresh water and the other with salt water, as in Figure 4. The water in both pools is chemically the same, it's all H_2O, but it will taste and feel different in one pool from the other.

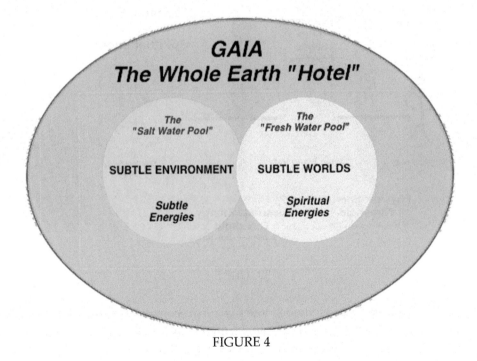

FIGURE 4

The two "pools" of the Earth are the *Subtle Environment* and the *Subtle Worlds*. Both contain non-physical energies, but I will call the energies in the former "subtle energies" and the energies in the latter "spiritual energies."

In making this differentiation, I'm not saying that one is better or "higher" than the other. Both are pools of Light and specifically of Gaian Light or "Earth-

Light" as the Planetary Soul configures it. Speaking generally, *subtle energies* affect our physical bodies and the non-physical energy fields or "subtle bodies" that surround our physical self, whereas *spiritual energies* affect our "Interiority," our inner Self, our Soul. Both are needed, just as we need both food for our bodies and inspiration for our mind, heart, and spirit. All non-physical energies have their place and their roles to fulfill; calling them "subtle" or "spiritual" is merely a convenience for me in being able to differentiate between different effects and characteristics. In this book, we will be considering both.

We can illustrate this difference through the following picture, Figure 5:

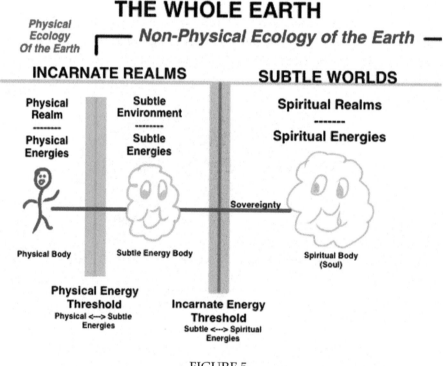

FIGURE 5

I think of the Earth as divided into two great ecologies. One makes up the physical world and all the ecosystems with which we are familiar; the other makes up the non-physical half of our world and is every bit as complex and rich an ecology as anything we will find on the physical earth. Indeed, for all the complexity and interconnectedness of the physical ecosystems that surround us, the ecology of the subtle realms is even more complex, more interwoven and interconnected, and richer with life and activity.

These two ecologies meet and overlap in what I call the Incarnate Realms.

These comprise both the physical world we see around us every day and what I call the *subtle environment*. The latter is part of the non-physical side of the world but one intimately connected to physical life and mirroring its activities.

Beyond the subtle environment lie the *subtle worlds* which have their own divisions and layers—what we may think of as different subtle "ecosystems of consciousness" within the larger whole; for simplicity's sake for this book, I gather all these divisions into a single category: the spiritual realms. If you would like a more detailed exploration and description of these realms, I refer you to the first book in this trilogy, *Subtle Worlds: An Explorer's Field Notes*.

Between these various realms or "ecosystems of consciousness" are distinct energetic thresholds. The most obvious one to all of us is that which separates the physical world from the non-physical dimensions. But as Figure 5 indicates, there is a threshold between the subtle environment and the spiritual realms as well. In my experience, these thresholds in the subtle worlds are not as distinct and dramatic as the one separating the physical and non-physical worlds, but they do represent a shift from one "pool" of life, consciousness, and energy to another. To me, crossing one of these thresholds is like passing from one ecosystem to another; everything feels and behaves differently. There are subtly different organizing principles at work on one side of these thresholds than on another.

As Figure 5 shows, we simultaneously inhabit all three "ecosystems": the physical, the subtle, and the spiritual. In esoteric parlance, we have three bodies, each of which functions in one of these three ecosystems. They are our physical body, our subtle body, and our spiritual body or our soul. They are linked energetically by a stream of life and connection originating in the soul; I call this "spine" of energy our *Sovereignty*. We will be discussing it more fully in Chapter Four as it plays a critical role in all our engagements with the subtle worlds and with subtle energies.

The nature and expression of subtle energies is infinite for all practical purposes. How many different kinds of water are there in the ocean? There is water traveling north in the Gulf Stream, water traveling south in the Canary Current, water flowing from the surface to the ocean bottom as well as currents rising from the bottom to the surface. You have water in layers of temperature. You have swift currents and slow currents, and water circulating within defined boundaries. The salinity and acidity of the water varies from one part of the ocean to another and from one depth to another. All of these phenomena are H_2O, but their individual characteristics are different. The two words "ocean water" thus cover a diversity of manifestations. The same is true for "subtle energies."

Over fifty years of observation, though, I have identified four broad categories of subtle energies. These are energies of pattern and configuration, energies of communication and connection, energies of blessing, and energies in a neutral state that act as a substrate, a medium that supports the other energetic states and can be shaped by them.

Subtle energies of pattern and configuration are those subtle energies that are directly associated with a particular entity and constitute its energy structure or its "energetic flesh." They hold the pattern and configuration of life for that entity. For instance, your own subtle body, which we will cover in more detail later in this book, is made up of subtle energies bound to or emanating from your own Identity. These living energies are uniquely your own. But this is true for inanimate objects as well. My coffee cup has a subtle energy field around it that is uniquely its own as well. For simplicity's sake, I'll call these the energies of self.

Subtle energies of communication and connection are those currents that flow between entities, forming energetic links and bonds. We all form many such links and connections in the course of a day as we interact with people and with the environment. Their intensity and how long they last depends entirely on the strength of connection, attention, intention, resonance, and frequency of contact between ourselves and others. Such links may be very long lasting as in a friendship or may dissipate almost as quickly as they are formed, as in a brief contact with a stranger. Many factors, such as love or hate, can form such links, though with different effects.

Subtle energies of blessing are those subtle energies that convey vitality, nourishment, and empowerment of some nature. I use the term "blessing" very broadly here. A spiritual being may by its very nature and the love it radiates fill an environment with subtle energies that are vitalizing to all the life within that environment. Such a being may or may not be deliberately intending to bless the environment, but its innate emanation of Light has this effect.

I call the fourth category of subtle energies a *substrate*, a term from my past as a biology student. A substrate is any medium that supports the life of something else, providing a "surface" or an environment in which that entity can function. Such energies are neutral but they can be shaped and set into motion by activity from other beings.

This is a complex category. One being's life energies—its energies of self—may provide the substrate for another type of being or likewise provide energies of connection for beings (energies of self) that are contained within its larger field. At the ultimate level, all creation draws its existence from the primal energy—the substrate of Light—that is the life and presence of the Sacred. On the other extreme, our subtle bodies form the substrate from which the trillions of cells that make up our bodies draw their own subtle energy fields. The important things to realize here are that all subtle energies are not the same but at any given instance, a particular subtle energy may be fulfilling more than one role depending on one's perspective and the level at which one is experiencing it.

Though there are important exceptions, in most cases, when I write about "subtle energies" within the Incarnate Realms, these are expressions of Gaian life energy. They are "waves," "ripples," movements within the planetary energetic substrate. Gaia's subtle energies of pattern and configuration—the energies of its life and identity—form the substrate and the surrounding energy field that all of us who are part of this planet live within and for the most part from which we draw our energy. Our subtle bodies, for instance, though they are configured to our individual identities and thus manifest our energies of self are formed from subtle energies provided by the life and energy field of Gaia.

I illustrate this in Figure 6:

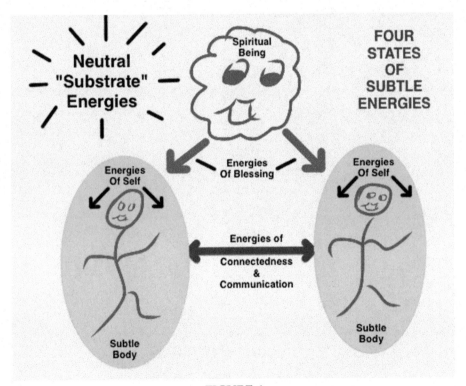

FIGURE 6

This gives an overview of the nature of subtle energies. I'll have much more to say about these phenomena as we go forward in the book. The important idea I wish you to take from this chapter, though, is simply this: that all subtle energies are alive and sentient and thus need to be treated as potential partners with love and respect.

EXERCISES FOR CHAPTER TWO

Exercise: Feeling the Field

This exercise is not original with me. It's a common basic exercise used by many teachers to give a person an experience of the subtle field that exists around their bodies or that their bodies can generate. In this exercise, you are deliberately heightening the subtle energy between your hands to give yourself a tangible experience of its presence. Do the exercise without any expectations or specific images of what you will (or should) experience. Let the experience unfold naturally and without strain.

Rub your hands together quickly and energetically for a few seconds. Extend your arms outward to your sides in a poised but relaxed way. You don't want to tense the muscles in your arms or hands but you want to have a sense of reaching in a calm manner for something to either side. You are thus putting intention into your arms and hands.

Take a few deep breaths and as you do, imagine this breath flowing in and out between your lungs and your hands, as if you are breathing through your hands and arms rather than through your nose or mouth.

After seven or eight breaths, bring your arms and hands forward in front of you and hold them in a relaxed way, your arms slightly bent, as if you were holding a beach ball to your chest. Hold your hands still as you continue to breath in a deep, relaxed manner, not trying to make anything happen.

Now move your hands slowly together (without touching) and then slowly away, contracting and enlarging the space between them as if the beach ball is shrinking and expanding. Do this several times. Be aware of any sensations in your hands as you do so. You may feel a pressure between them as if something invisible is pushing at them, or you may feel a tingling. Pay attention to the felt sense of this sensation. What is this like for you?

When you've had enough, bring your hands together in a swift clap and then let them fall in a relaxed way to the sides of your body. Take a few deep breaths and feel any residual energy in your hands flowing in a harmonious and balanced way back into and through your body.

Exercise: Room Sensing

I'd like you to do this exercise in a fun, easy way. You're not trying to have a psychic experience or engage with subtle energies. Don't strive or strain for any particular effect or experience. Just be aware of whatever you feel in the room as you do the exercise, which in fact may be nothing at all!

Pick a room in your house or apartment where you live. Be aware of your body in this room. Now close your eyes and extend yourself into the space formed by this room, just sensing and feeling it in silence. What is that like? What do you feel? Do you feel any kind of energy in the room? A particular "atmosphere" or "mood?" If so, what is it like? Pay attention in a calm, easy way for as long as it feels comfortable, then open your eyes, ending the exercise.

Now repeat this exercise in another room. How does what you feel and experience in this second room, if anything, differ from the first room? Is one room energetically more powerful or more distinctive than the other?

If you wish, try this again in a third room, again comparing that experience with the ones you had in the other rooms.

CHAPTER THREE
Subtle Self

We can engage with subtle energies because we ourselves are partially subtle beings. Just as the Earth has both physical and non-physical aspects, we do, too, as we saw in Figure 1 We are "amphibious," living and functioning simultaneously in two different realities, one physical, the other non-physical. This is why we can both affect and be affected by subtle energies.

We may justifiably call our subtle aspect our subtle "body" for it functions like a body in providing a means of engagement with the non-physical environment. And like our physical body, it has a complex structure—its own "anatomy" and "physiology"—designed to perform different functions. Because of this complexity, there are many ways of describing or mapping the subtle body. For our purposes, I'm going to offer a simple description since our focus is less on what the subtle body is and more on how we engage with it.

The subtle body is made up of what I called the *energies of self* in the last Chapter. Just as the cells of our body all share the same DNA, so the energies that make up our subtle body share the same vibrational identity. This identity originates from the soul. At the beginning of the incarnational process, the soul impresses its identity and its intentions upon the *substrate Earth energies* of the Incarnate Realm and by blending with these energies, gives them a unique spin, turning them into the necessary incarnational energies of self. I suggest this process in Figure 7. Like a vortex in a lake, this "activity of identity" attracts to itself what it needs to develop, bringing into being an embryonic subtle body.

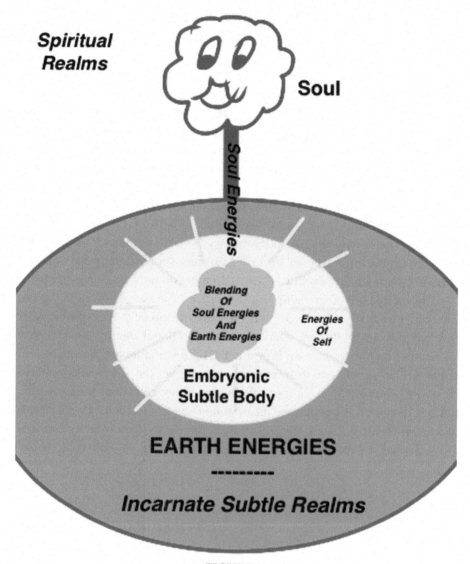

FIGURE 7

In a manner analogous to the development of a zygote in the mother's womb, this embryonic subtle body begins to differentiate into distinct zones of activity, which will continue to evolve throughout the individual's life. I illustrate the most important of these zones in Figure 8. Note that these zones interpenetrate each other in exactly the same way that the various television broadcasts that fill my living room do. My television receives several hundred channels, and the information that each channel contains shares electronic space with the information of all the other channels. Each is being broadcast on its own frequency, but all the frequencies are present in the air around me. This is true of the different parts of the subtle body as well. My skill at drawing can't convey this interpenetration and co-existence, so I'm left with drawing concentric circles. But remember that the reality is more complex and not at all so spacial or hierarchical as I have represented it here.

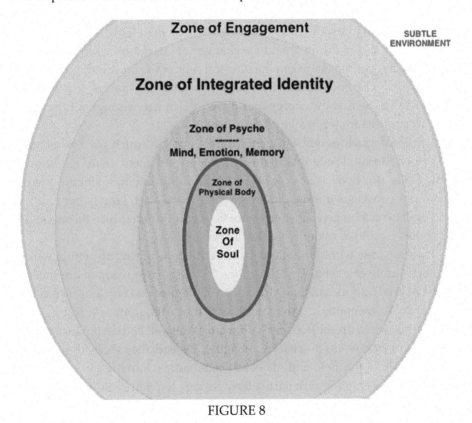

FIGURE 8

The earliest of these zones to come into being is where the new and accumulating energies of the subtle body are most in touch with the energies of the incarnating soul. For now, I'm going to call this the Zone of Soul in keeping with the theme of the picture, but later I'll be calling it our *Interiority* and will have much more to say about it. Suffice it to say that it establishes an incarnational presence of the soul within the subtle realms.

The next zone to differentiate is that which holds the energetic patterns for the development of the physical body. Eventually, as the body develops and is born, this zone will include the electromagnetic and thermal fields that surround us, both of which can be observed through physical means, and a more subtle field of vital energies that is traditionally known as the "etheric body." This mimics its physical counterpart in shape and is a vehicle for the circulation of vitality and life energies throughout the body. Each organ has its own etheric counterpart within this body which affects the health and life of that organ. Consequently, the etheric body and its various components are the focus for a variety of techniques of energy or "vibrational" healing.

The body fields provide the link between the physical and non-physical worlds. These two realms meet in a variety of ways ranging, I believe, from interaction at the quantum level to exchanges of energy between atoms and molecules and perhaps between the physical cells of the body and their subtle counterparts. The body fields also manifest what in the martial arts is called "chi" or"qi" as well as the energy meridians or channels throughout the body used in acupuncture for healing.

The body provides one of the most direct ways in which we can perceive and respond to subtle energies in the invisible environment. Through its own subtle fields, our body is always aware of the subtle environment around us even if our conscious minds remain ignorant of this fact, largely because we don't pay attention or give much credence to—or we misinterpret—the messages our bodies send to us about what they're sensing.

The next zone within the subtle body is the Zone of Psyche, within which develops our *psychic subtle field*. Basically, this is the expression of our mental and emotional activity as shaped by our psychological makeup, our memories, and our daily encounters. We may think that our thoughts and feelings are private and locked up subjectively within our skulls and bodies, but in fact they are not, or at least not as much as we imagine. Instead, they shape the patterns of energy within this field and may even be broadcast into the environment if the thoughts or emotions are particularly strong. If a person is "psychic" and able to pick up on these patterns in the psychic subtle field of another, then they can gain information as to the thoughts and feelings that other person is having. In addition, the psychic subtle field can affect the activity and texture of our subtle body as a whole, influencing how it engages with the subtle environment around it. This becomes an important factor in working with subtle energies.

Our subtle body is as much a living organism as our physical one. Just as our body takes in food, digests it, and turns it into chemicals it can assimilate and make part of itself, the subtle body does something similar with energies it takes in either from the soul or psyche or from the surrounding environment. When this material is assimilated and integrated into our field, then it becomes an expression of our energies of self. It becomes part of our integrated identity. This is the main "body" of our subtle self. When I talk about our subtle field or our subtle body in this book, it is primarily this "zone of integrated identity" to which I'm referring unless I specify otherwise.

Just as our body is covered with skin, so our subtle body has an "outer" layer of subtle energies which is our Zone of Engagement. It is the part of our subtle body that is most exposed to and directly engaged with the subtle worlds and the subtle environment around us. It is the part of us that senses subtle energies in the environment, so in a way it's like a subtle sense organ. Although I draw it as a single field represented by a single circle, it's really a complex system of layers and frequencies.

This is the most fluid part of us as it responds to the stimuli and impacts coming from the various subtle energies and forces presence in the subtle environment (as well as to directive impulses arising from our thinking, feeling, and from our Interiority). It perceives in part by taking on the "shape" or energetic patterns of what it encounters, configuring itself appropriately in ways that generate information in a manner analogous to the information coming from our physical senses. This means that the surface of our subtle body is constantly in motion, unless we direct it otherwise, oscillating and rippling with the effects of the subtle energies that play upon it like the wind upon a lake. I suggest this effect in Figure 9.

This play of energies can have different effects. It can simply provide information about something in our environment. This is a common effect when someone who is psychically sensitive "reads" the subtle information emanating from a person, a place or a situation. Alternatively, the information and energy, particularly if it is nurturing such as the energy of a blessing, can be taken in and assimilated, becoming integrated into our subtle body, turning into an "energy of self." Or it can bounce off our energetic boundaries or be swept away by the currents of our own subtle energy, its impact disappearing like a ripple disappears on the surface of a lake.

Although this Zone of Engagement is composed of the energies of self and is part of the overall Identity of the individual, it holds and presents this identity more loosely, so to speak, in order to have the freedom to effectively configure to and blend with energies of "not-self" in the world around it as part of the process of subtle perception. If the individual's powers of integration and coherency are strong, then this poses no problem. The oscillations of energy take place, information is conveyed, and the subtle body within this Zone bounces back to its native condition in a resilient manner. However, if the individual's overall energy field is itself experiencing incoherency or a lack of integration or for some reason is unable to clearly communicate its identity and energies of self to all parts of its field, then this Zone will retain the imprint and influence of outside energies longer than normal.

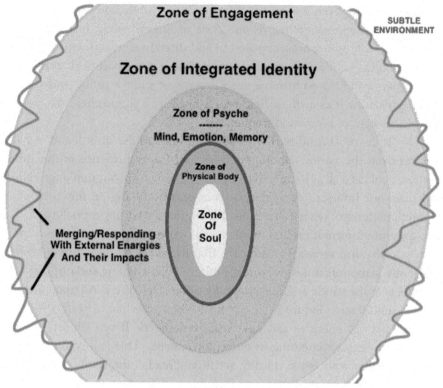

FIGURE 9

When this happens, material we pick up from others and from the world around us impacts us more deeply and with more lasting results, imparting its vectors onto our own energies of self. If the resulting energetic impression in our subtle field is deep enough, it may resist integration, or we might not know how to integrate it.

This can happen with traumatic experiences that leave not only physical memories but energetic traces as well. Such traces can resist being removed by the natural circulation of energy in a healthy subtle body. They can collect and become "locked" within the subtle body in ways analogous to how the effects of trauma can become locked in the muscles and structure of our physical body, as well as in our psyche, persisting over time long after the originating impact.

The challenge with such structures or "cysts" of unintegrated energy in our subtle body is that they can radiate energies that are "not-Self," promoting activities or reactions based on the energetic characteristics of this material rather than on the conscious intentions and presence of our psyche and soul. It's as if they become little centers of will and purpose other than our own, though often without any direction other than to sustain their existence like energy parasites.

I suggest these pockets of unintegrated material in Figure 10.

The challenge with any unintegrated material is that it can become a stuck area where integration breaks down, collecting other energies around them and preventing their assimilation into the wholeness of the self as well. This reminds me of the way the remains of small, dead sea organisms collect to form coral, so I think of these places within us as "coral reefs" within the sea of our subtle body. How extensive or powerful these "reefs" can be depends entirely on the individual and how he or she has dealt with the experiences of his or her life. They can range from energetic material that is temporarily being held "in storage" until he or she can properly process and integrate it, or remove it, to long-lasting patterns of habit and energy that exert a dominating and perhaps even an incapacitating effect on the individual, acting as autonomous centers of will and influence that prevent the person from achieving energetic coherency and wholeness (and psychological wholeness as well).

While traumatic experiences can certainly create a reef, a more common source is from habit and addiction. Part of the challenge of addiction is that in addition to the biochemical and psychological effects in the physical half of us, there can be energy effects that establish themselves in the subtle body as autonomous "cysts" or centers of will that are never properly integrated or assimilated and that compete with the will of the soul or of the incarnate self, affecting our thoughts and feelings within the psyche.

These "coral reefs" can be dissolved by serious inner work, self-knowledge, and love. The help of others is often needed, if only to introduce flowing energy from their fields to help where our energy may be stuck. A therapeutic approach that combined somatic, psychological, interpersonal, and subtle energetic work would be particularly powerful in helping these often stuck and stagnant energies to be melted away and integrated into wholeness. This whole process is even more helped if the healing power of the soul is brought into play as well, for ultimately it is where our wholeness is rooted.

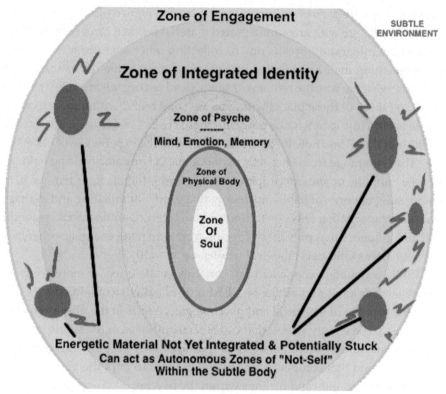

FIGURE 10

These five zones are the primary regions of activity and function that make up our subtle body in this simplified schematic. Our non-physical half could certainly be mapped and described in different ways, and many esoteric traditions do so. However, this model is all we need in this book to give us a foundation for engaging and working with subtle worlds. Our objective here is practical engagement with the living universe around us, not the creation of philosophical and cosmological models. The main point of this chapter is to understand that we are subtle beings as well as physical ones, and it's from the subtle frequencies that make up our incarnation that we have the capability of engaging with the subtle worlds.

EXERCISE FOR CHAPTER THREE

Exercise: Crossing Thresholds

This is a simple exercise for discerning the felt sense of crossing a threshold of energy as directed by your intention. You need a candle as a prop and someplace safe to put the candle. You will also need a box of matches as you will be lighting and extinguishing the candle several times in the course of this exercise.

The idea here is to experience the power of thresholds and the felt sense of shifting from one state of awareness to another and to be able to initiate such a shift at will. However, this exercise does not determine what the nature of that new awareness will be. That is up to you.

The experiment has four parts or "phases."

PHASE ONE

1. Take a moment to reflect on what you are about to do. You are contrasting and experiencing two different states and the passage between them. In its simplest form, one of these states is "Candle Lit" and the other state is "Candle Unlit".

2. Sit for a moment and experience the "Candle Unlit" state. What is its felt sense? Now take a match and light the candle. As you do so, pay attention to any inner shift that may take place within you or in your awareness; you are creating a change, crossing a threshold between one condition and another. What does this feel like?

3. Sit for a moment and experience the "Candle Lit" state. What is its felt sense? Now extinguish the candle. As you do so, pay attention to any inner shift that may take place; you are creating a change, crossing a threshold between one condition and another. What does this feel like?

4. Repeat steps 2 & 3 three or four times, paying attention to the shift itself.

5. Now, imagine that when you light the candle, you are opening a door into the subtle environment around you, and when you extinguish the candle flame, you are closing that door.

6. Light the candle and consciously "open the door" into a subtle realm. What does that feel like? What shift in condition did you feel, if any? Did you feel any difference in energy or power in or around you?

7. Extinguish the candle flame, consciously "closing the door" into a subtle realm. What does that feel like? What shift in condition did you feel, if any? Did you feel any difference in energy or power in or around you?

8. Repeat steps 6 & 7 several times, paying attention to any differences in opening and closing this portal.

Lighting a candle is a universal action representing an invocation of Light or entering into a sacred space. In this step of the exercise, when you light the candle, you are stepping into a sacred, magical space that is invoked around you. When you extinguish the candle, you are stepping out of that space back onto ordinary reality.

The inner state to which I'm suggesting you attune here is one of being aware of the subtle environment (and of your own subtle field). A way to think of it is that in one state you are heightened in your awareness of the physical world around you, but in the other state, you are heightened in the potential of being more aware of subtle forces and energies around you.

In any event, this exercise is focused upon your awareness of making a shift and the felt sense of that shift and threshold, not on the nature or depth of the states into which you are shifting.

PHASE TWO

1. Light the candle. Imagine and feel yourself stepping into or being surrounded by a powerful, empowering, uplifting spiritual and magical space. It is a place of wholeness, connectedness, and balance. Sit for a moment and feel what this is like.

2. Extinguish the candle. Imagine and feel yourself stepping back into the power, connectedness, and balance of your ordinary world. Note that one world is not better than the other; they each manifest some aspect of the sacred. Pay attention instead to the felt sense of the transition between the two.

3. Repeat steps 1 & 2 several times, moving in and out of a state specifically attuned to the inner. Pay attention to the felt sense of this shift.

PHASE THREE

In this phase, set your candle aside unlit. You are going to use only your imagination.

Repeat steps 1 & 2 from Phase Two, but this time, light an imaginary candle in your mind rather than a real candle in the physical world. As before, pay attention to the felt sense of the shift from everyday awareness to a receptive, evocative spiritual awareness. Pay attention to any differences you feel.

PHASE FOUR

In this phase, you also do not use a physical candle, but you don't use an imaginal one either. Instead, imagine YOURSELF as the candle. In this phase, you move between a state of focusing upon your everyday outer world, and a state of expanding your awareness of an invisible subtle environment. You can picture yourself being lit and unlit if you wish, or you can just focus on the threshold within you between these two states (a threshold you have been paying attention to in the previous phases) and imagine moving from one side of it to the other.

Repeat Phase Three above but now with yourself as the candle or the threshold. What does this feel like? Can you experience this threshold? Can you tell the difference?

USING THRESHOLDS

The candle is acting as a gateway or threshold in this exercise. Any threshold can be used in the same way. For example, you can stand on one side of a door and step across the threshold, noting any inner shifts or changes in awareness as you do so. (For that matter, notice just how you feel stepping outdoors from inside and vice versa.) The object is to be aware of inner shifts and gain a capacity to induce them at will so that the gateway or threshold is within you.

With practice, you can learn to stand at your inner threshold and have an awareness that extends comfortably and effectively into both realms, the everyday physical world and an inner world of evocative listening and attunement, intuition and spiritual awareness. In short you can be in both "places" at once.

CHAPTER FOUR
Subtle Awareness

Given that we have a subtle body and we are living simultaneously in both the physical and non-physical worlds, why are we not more aware of the subtle phenomena around us? Well, chances are, if we would consider all the hunches, intuitions, and "feelings" we have about people, places and events, we would discover we are more aware than we thought we were. It's just that most of the time we ignore or dismiss the information that comes from our subtle side because we're just not paying attention, we don't know how to recognize it, or we don't believe in it because it doesn't fit into our familiar frames of reference. Developing subtle awareness isn't necessarily about becoming "psychic" or developing some kind of special clairvoyance. Often it's just a matter of learning to pay attention in new ways to what we're feeling or sensing, allowing a seed of perception a chance to blossom into a flower of information.

Looking at Perception

Let's look at perception itself, whether physical or non-physical. I think of perception as a relationship between four elements, each of which contributes its particular piece. These four are the environment which provides the stimuli; the sensory organ or methodology that receives these stimuli and converts them into information; the brain or organizing instrument that collects, processes and compiles this information; and the mind that interprets that compilation and determines what has been perceived.

For instance, we have a variety of birds that live in the trees around our house and visit our bird feeders on the back porch. My wife Julie will remark about how beautiful their bird song is. In this case, the birds are singing, creating sound waves in the environment which Julie's ears receive and translate into bioelectrical impulses that travel to the brain. There, these signals are transformed into a perception that Julie then interprets as "bird song" or "music."

In my own case, though, this doesn't happen. The birds can be singing and the sound waves impacting my ears, and my ears can be converting the pressure of these sound waves into bioelectric impulses, but there it stops. A bad case of measles when I was six years old left me partly deaf. There's nothing wrong with the actual structure of the ear but many of the nerves that receive and process the bioelectric signals from the ear are dead. There are frequencies of sound that I do not and cannot hear. My brain has lost the ability to process them.

The result of this dysfunction in my brain is that I do not hear most bird song. Julie can be rhapsodizing over how lovely the birds sound, but all I hear is silence, or if I do hear something at the edge of my range, it doesn't sound like music, only like noise. In fact, as far as I'm concerned, if I didn't see the birds, I would not know they are there, and if I were skeptically inclined, I could accuse Julie of making it all up. I could tell her that bird song is just something "in her head," a figment of her imagination.

Which, of course, is what many skeptics say about people like myself who experience subtle perceptions.

From my perspective, everyone has the innate ability to receive information and impulses from the non-physical world; we are doing it all the time, just as my ears are always feeling the pressure of the sound waves caused by birds' singing and other high-pitched frequencies of sound. What most people lack is a way of processing and interpreting this information. My inability to hear birds is a function of actual damage to certain nerves in my brain, but the inability of most people to be aware of subtle perceptions is due more to inactivity and inattention so that the brain areas that link to such perceptions are not developed. This is not entirely a physical issue, either, for attitudes and beliefs play a role here. Our mental and emotional states affect what we perceive, and in the case of subtle perception an unwillingness to accept the possibility of such an awareness or to trust it when it happens can diminish or obstruct its development.

Part of the challenge in developing and using subtle awareness lies in not knowing how to think about it. Our attitudes and expectations, even when we're willing to believe in the possibility of such perception, can affect how smoothly such development can occur.

Here's an example of what I mean. When I'm working with a group discussing subtle perception, invariably someone will say, "Oh, I don't see anything," or "I don't hear anything." There is often a sense of finality about this as if the lack of seeing and hearing closes the door to any kind of awareness of a non-physical reality. But the purpose of a sensory function is to convey information about the environment in which one is embedded so that one may connect and engage with it. Eyes and ears do it one way, but they aren't the only ways that are possible. Consider that in the subtle dimensions, there are no photons of light to excite optic nerves with vision or sound waves to exert pressure upon ear drums to produce the phenomenon of sound. These are physical phenomena, and our physical senses are developed and adapted to them. But if I expect that all sensory information is going to come to me in a manner akin to my physical senses, then I will be less able to recognize such information when it comes in a fashion dictated by the requirements of its own unique environment.

Modes of Perception

We each possess a variety of modes of perception to engage with the world around us, both physically and non-physically. I suggest some of these modes in Figure 11.

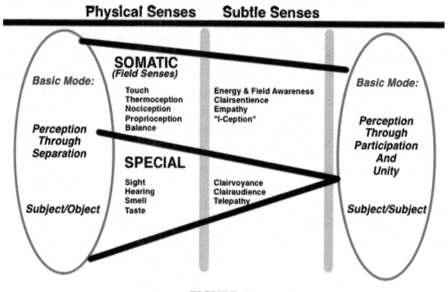

MODES OF PERCEPTION

Physical Senses   Subtle Senses

Basic Mode:

SOMATIC
(Field Senses)

Touch	Energy & Field Awareness
Thermoception	Clairsentience
Nociception	Empathy
Proprioception	"I-Ception"
Balance	

**Perception
Through
Separation**

SPECIAL

Sight	Clairvoyance
Hearing	Clairaudience
Smell	Telepathy
Taste	

Subject/Object

Basic Mode:

**Perception
Through
Participation
And
Unity**

Subject/Subject

FIGURE 11

In the physical world, we actually have nine senses which medical science divides into two categories, special and somatic. The special senses are so-called because they rely on special organs; they include sight, hearing, taste, and smell. The somatic senses, on the other hand, are diffused throughout the whole body, which is to say, they treat the body as a whole field. The body itself is the organ that perceives, rather than some specialized part of it.

These somatic senses include touch, the sensitivity to pressure and vibration; thermoception, the sensitivity to temperature and heat; nociception, the sensitivity to pain; and proprioception, the sensitivity to the body's position and movement in space. A ninth sense is balance, a vestibular sense which some sources think of as a special sense because it functions through the inner ear and others classify as a somatic sense because it is felt throughout the body.

The subtle worlds are environments of energy and consciousness. Our subtle bodies contain modes of perception that are adapted to such environments, and they convey information to our minds in ways that have nothing to do with sight or sound. An important thing to understand about subtle awareness is that I don't have to "see" or "hear" anything in order to perceive into the subtle worlds. I can apprehend what is present around me in other ways.

In my experience, our subtle senses more often than not provide "field" perception; that is, they take in a whole pattern rather than focusing on one part of it at a time. They are more akin to our somatic senses than to our special senses. We may call this perception "clairsentience" or "field awareness" or simply empathy.

I know from my own experience that it's possible to train the brain to be receptive to subtle modes of perception, but to do so, I need to resist the habit of wanting my sensory information to come in familiar packages. I have to go beyond seeing or hearing into other forms of sensitivity.

There is no doubt that people do "see" and "hear" in the subtle realms. In some cases this may actually be due to etheric or subtle sensory organs that mimic these functions, such as the legendary "third eye" of clairvoyance or the inner ear of clairaudience. Telepathy as direct and specific mind to mind communication is also possible. But in many cases, I believe the "sight" or "sound" is due to the interpretive function of perception. I don't have to have light waves hitting my eyes in order to see something. Subtle energies and impulses of thought can trigger visual responses within the mind, resulting in an inner visualization. In fact, this is precisely the use of the imagination as an organ of perception.

We experience this when we read a novel filled with rich descriptions. Visually we are only seeing word symbols on a page, but imaginatively whole worlds arise before our inner eyes, allowing us to see and hear what the author wants us to see and hear. We are taking information in from our environment (the book) to create information in our minds. In the process we can see and hear what isn't there in a physical sense.

Still, if I can free myself of a dependence on using sight and sound as my primary models for sensory perception and thus from expectations built around those models, I will be in a better position to appreciate and learn subtle awareness as a unique experience in its own right and not simply as physical perception in non-physical guise. This comes with practice.

We don't think much about the somatic senses, other than touch, precisely because they are not focused in such a specific way as sight and hearing. They truly are "whole field senses." The information they convey forms the background of our lives for the most part. Yet it's been my experience that the further one moves in consciousness into the subtle environments away from the physical plane, the more one deals with field-like phenomena, and the nature of sensory experience becomes more and more "somatic," involving the whole of one's subtle energy field and less and less focused around a specific perceptual organ. This is a further reason why, in developing subtle perception, it's important to free ourselves of the habit of expecting to "see" and "hear" in the way we do physically. It may happen, but more likely, it will not. You perceive with your whole subtle field, not just with a part of it.

Subtle awareness has one particular characteristic that is very important. Put simply, the subtle body more often than not perceives by becoming that which it is perceiving. It takes on, if only for a short time, the characteristics and "vectors"—i.e. the identity—of that which is vibrationally engaging it. I call this "I-ception," perception through identification and identity. It creates an experience of becoming and sharing an identity with that which is being observed in the subtle realms. This condition of blending can convey a great deal of information in a very short time, but it has consequences. If the impression striking the subtle body is strong, it may take some time for the "energies of self" to reassert their normal pattern; I'll be talking about this in more detail in the next Chapter.

But here's a common example: you enter a room where someone has been venting angry feelings. That person may no longer be there, but his or her angry energies are still present in the subtle environment of the room. Your own subtle body picks up on these energies and temporarily vibrates in resonance with them. The "I-ceptive" aspect of your subtle awareness identifies energetically with this anger in order to perceive it. In the process, you may suddenly feel some discomfort and distress without knowing why. You may even begin to feel angry yourself. If you are familiar with subtle awareness, you can say, "Oh, someone was angry here," and let it go. Your own natural vibrational characteristics reassert themselves, and the anger goes away. But if you aren't aware that this anger is a result of a subtle perception of something in the invisible environment, or you discount it, you may misperceive this anger as coming from within you. You identify with it and personalize it. Your brain tells a story about it, drawing from your past patterns, which enhances its effect within your energy field. At this point, this anger potentially becomes an energetic "coral reef" as I described in the last Chapter, continuing to radiate its angry energy within your system until such time as it is cleared out or assimilated. However, if the anger resonates with angry issues in your own makeup, it can be "fed" by your own anger, giving it a longer life-span within your subtle body than it might have otherwise.

The important insight to have here is that at the physical level, we perceive through separation; we as the perceiving subject are aware of an object separate from ourselves, and our perception maintains this sense of separation. However, the more we move into the subtle worlds and the more we use subtle senses, the more the mode of perception changes to one of perception through participation and a unity of identification. We are a subject blending with another subject. This can be disconcerting until we become used to it, and as I've said, it can seem threatening to our own identities, though as we shall see, it need not be. I'll be discussing this in more detail beginning in the next Chapter.

Body as Foundation

It may seem paradoxical but the place to start in developing subtle awareness is with the physical body. It has an intelligence and wisdom evolved over millions of years, and part of this evolution has been in developing ways of being aware of, responding to and integrating subtle energies through its own body fields. The body is our foundation in dealing with the subtle worlds, especially as it has such a solid "here-and-now" identity that can help anchor our energetic identity.

As I said above, the somatic senses are in some ways closer in function and experience to our subtle senses, so they provide a good place to start. In particular, I want to focus on proprioception, the body's awareness of its boundaries, its position, and its movement through space. This is the somatic sense that creates "body maps." Here's an example. If you drive a car, you know that you come to experience the car as if it were an extension of your body in space. You can feel where the edges of the car are, where the bumpers are, and so forth. You know the position of the car (of "yourself-as-car") in space, and this is invaluable information in driving and avoiding collisions. The dimensions of the car become part of your body map while you are in the car. Part of the challenge in learning to drive a new car comes from the fact that you have to relearn your new "body's" dimensions, which may be quite different from those of the car you're used to driving.

When I traveled to give lectures, I would often rent a car at the airport to get wherever I needed to be. In the process, I got to experience a wide variety of car shapes from very small compacts to, at one time, a fifteen-seater van that was really a small bus. It was always interesting to observe how long it took me to feel comfortable with the new "car-as-my-body". The large van gave me the most problem, but at the end of the week for which I had rented it, I could maneuver it as easily as I did my much smaller compact at home.

Here's a simple experiment: Walk out of your home and walk up and down the block. As you do, pay attention to the feel of your body, its position in space, its movement, and so forth. Then, if you have a car that you regularly use, climb into it and drive around the same block a couple of times. Now what does your body feel like? Can you feel how your "body-map" or your "body-sense" incorporates the car into itself as if the car now is your body? If so, your body-sense has changed its shape, hasn't it? Your car doesn't have two arms, two legs, hands or feet, after all. It has a different shape, and your body-map has adapted to it.

You don't have to have a car to do this experiment. You can do it with an object. If you play golf, it could be a golf club; if you play baseball, it could be a bat. If you're a tennis player, it could be your racquet. I'm sure you can find examples in your own life.

The important point right now is that somatic perception, particularly proprioception, can lead directly into subtle perception. Both types of perception deal with fields. You can expand the sense of your "body map" from your physical self into a sphere of energy surrounding you, that is to say, into your subtle body. In effect, just as you might map your body to a car or a tool, in this case you're mapping your body to your personal subtle field. At this point, you become open to subtle perception — to the impact of subtle energies upon your expanded body map, the felt sense of your subtle field.

Using this approach based on the body and its proprioceptive sense, you can begin to build up an awareness of the subtle energy field surrounding you.

EXERCISES FOR CHAPTER FOUR

Exercise: The Somatic Space

In this exercise, you are going to explore your somatic sense of proprioception. This is the sense that tells you your body's position and movement in space; it helps your brain create a body-map.

If you drive a car, you will have experienced this in the way that the car itself can seem as if it's an extension of your body. Or if you are using a tool regularly, like a hammer or a golf club, it also can feel like an extension of your arm and hand. In effect, the car or the tool expands the felt-sense of your body.

In this exercise you want to experience this expanded sense. There are different ways you can do this. You could, for instance, go for a drive in your car and pay attention to how it feels like an extension of you. Or you could do some work using a tool and pay attention to how it can seem like a part of your body.

But here is an exercise you can do that doesn't require driving around or using a tool. Note that in doing this exercise, your intent is to stay within the physical realm and experience an expanded body sense—that is, an expansion of how your body "maps" itself or senses itself in physical space. You're not trying to attune to anything of a subtle nature here.

To do this exercise, find yourself a comfortable chair to sit in.

- Close your eyes and just let your attention flow throughout your body. Just relax and feel the position of your body in the chair. Feel your shape as you sit. Feel where your arms are...where your hands are...where your fingers are. Feel where your legs are...where your feet are..., where your toes are. Feel your torso. Feel the position of your head. Relax and enjoy being in this position in space.
- Now feel yourself melting into the chair. Feel your torso melting into the back of the chair, becoming the back of the chair. Feel your arms melting into the arms of the chair, becoming the arms of the chair. Feel your legs and feet melting into the chair, becoming the support of the chair. Feel the chair as an extension of your body. The chair is your body. Feel your chair-body resting on the floor of your room. Feel the way being the chair expands the feel of your presence in the room.
- Now feel yourself melting into the room around you, beginning with the floor but expanding into the walls. The floor of the room becomes your feet, the walls your arms and torso, the ceiling your head. You are not filling the space in the room; you are simply extending yourself

into the floor, the walls, and the ceiling. Feel how the room expands your body-sense, your body-map, compared to being in the chair. Feel the room as an extension of your body. The room is your body.

- When you feel ready, bring your body sense back into the chair. Feel yourself flowing back from the walls, the ceiling, the floor into the chair. Your body-sense is contracting. Your somatic space is now the chair again. Relax and feel the chair as your body.

- When you feel ready, bring your body sense back from the chair and into your physical body. Feel yourself flowing back into your arms and hands and fingers, back into your legs and feet and toes, back into your torso, back into your head. You are now only your physical body sitting in the chair. Relax and feel your body once again separate from the chair, separate from the room.

- Stand up and stretch. This helps you re-center yourself in your body.

Exercise: From Soma to Aura

With this exercise, we start expanding our awareness into our subtle field. We can do this because the somatic field to which our sense of proprioception leads us is only a step away from an awareness of our personal subtle etheric field.

So this exercise should be an easy step, but it's an important one. This is truly the opening of the door into subtle perception, something you already explored using the candles and the threshold exercise. Movement of awareness from the somatic field to etheric field can be a foundation for that deeper work.

In this exercise, you are simply expanding your awareness into your own personal subtle energy field or aura. I'd like you to keep this objective and boundary in mind since it may be easy, especially for those of you already familiar with these capacities, to move further out into the subtle environment itself.

Having a well-developed sense of your own energy field is an important skill in its own right. This field is in many ways your primary sensing organ when dealing with the subtle environment. In important ways, this personal energy field is the first subtle realm a person may encounter.

Mostly the object of the exercise is for you to experience that in fact you HAVE a subtle energy field that surrounds you, nothing more. We're just taking a very simple step from somatic field to subtle energy field, from soma to aura.

You begin this exercise exactly as you did the previous one of entering into somatic space. Only this time, instead of melting into the chair you are going to "melt into air" or rather into your subtle field.

- Close your eyes and just let your attention flow throughout your body. Just relax and feel the position of your body. Feel your shape as you sit. Feel where your arms are...where your hands are...where your fingers are. Feel where your legs are...where your feet are... where your toes are. Feel your torso. Feel the position of your head. Relax and enjoy being in this position in space.

- Feel your body melting into the air around you, into the space around you, turning from solid flesh into a fine and luminous mist. This mist expands into a bubble surrounding you. Just let yourself melt and expand into this bubble of light. Your body is changing shape from a solid form into a sphere of energy and light.

- Let your attention focus on this sphere of light and energy surrounding you. What does it feel like? Can you feel its edges? Can you feel its dimensions? What does it contain? Is it undifferentiated? Does it have differentiation with it? Does it have texture? Who are you as this sphere of energy and light? How does it relate to the physical body which it surrounds?

- Remain in this sphere feeling its contours, its characteristics, its nature, its dimensions, its sensitivities for as long as feels comfortable. You're not trying to discern anything outside of this sphere, nor are you trying to use it in any way or make it do anything. You are just relaxing within it and feeling it as your body in the same way you felt your somatic sense and your body sense earlier.

- When you feel complete, feel this sphere of energy and light turning into mist again, the mist condensing and flowing back into your physical body. When you feel wholly back in your body, wholly physical again, take a moment to relax, feeling your body around you with gratefulness and appreciation. Then stand up and stretch.

Exercise: The House Walk-Through

- Pick one room in your home in which to start and one room somewhere else in your home as your destination or stopping place. If possible, there should be at least one other room through which you will pass between these two. The more rooms you can enter between where you start and where you end, the more variety and depth this experience will hold.

- In your starting room, look around you and take in all that the room contains. Then, standing quietly in the room, feel into its mood, "atmosphere," or energy. What does this room feel like as a presence? What qualities does it hold for you? What does it evoke within you? What is your felt sense in your body standing in this room?

- When you feel complete with sensing this, step out of this room into another.

- Between this room and another room (or a hallway) is a threshold. As you step across this threshold, pay attention to what this feels like. You are crossing from one energy domain to another. The effect may be subtle, but it will be there. Something changes as you pass from one room to another across the threshold (or through the energy membrane the threshold represents). Can you sense this change?

- Entering the new room (or a hallway between rooms), stop for a moment and look around, taking in all that the room (or hallway) contains. Then feel into the energy of this space. What does *this* room (or hallway) feel like as a presence? What qualities does it hold for you? What does it evoke within you? What is the felt sense of this room? How does its energy presence differ from the room from which you just came?

- When you feel complete with sensing this, step out of this room into another.

- Once again, pay attention to the threshold between this room (or hallway) and the next room (or hallway). What does it feel like? How does it differ, if it does, from the sensation of the first threshold you crossed?

- Entering the new room (or the hallway between rooms), stop for a moment and look around, taking in all that the room or hallway contains. Then feel into the energy of this space. What does *this* room (or hallway) feel like as a presence? What qualities does it hold for you? What does it evoke within you? What is its felt sense? How does its energy presence differ from the room from which you just came?

- When you feel complete with sensing this, step out of this room into the next.
- Repeat this process of crossing thresholds and entering and leaving rooms as you make your way to the room that is your final destination. In each place, honor the presence and spirit of the room or hallway in which you enter. How does the energy and presence in the room or hallway connect to your home as a whole? Ask—or try to sense—what it has to offer to you or what role it plays in your life in your home, be it a house or an apartment (or some other kind of dwelling). What is your relationship to it? How does the energy of a hallway differ from the energy of the rooms that it connects? How do the energies change as you move through the home?
- When you reach your final destination, do as you have done in all the other rooms and hallways, paying attention to its unique energy and presence and honoring it as part of your home, part of your life. Then take a moment to reflect back on your entire pilgrimage and all the rooms and hallways you have entered. Give thanks to all the spirit, all the presence, all the energies through which you have passed and which make up your home. Honor the blessings they offer you.
- What is the overall "energy ecology" of your home? That is, how do the rooms and their different energies relate and connect?

Exercise: Inner Sunlight

This is an experimental exercise with which you can have fun. It is based on the subtle perception that the sun itself has different layers of being: it has a physical form which we see every day in the sky above us, but it also has a presence in the subtle realms and, as something we might think of as a "solar soul," it has a presence in the spiritual realms as well. On each of these levels, it generates Light. At the subtle level, the sun's Light translates into a vitalizing force, sometimes called Prana. It may feel as if your subtle body is being energized. On the spiritual level, the sun's Light is often felt as a nurturing, loving force, one that empowers your sense of being and life, giving you a spacious feeling of connectedness to the larger universe. However, what you feel may be unique to you, so pay attention to your unique responses.

If you are able to sense these different levels of sunlight, it will give you practice in discerning the differences between physical, subtle and spiritual energies. These are broad distinctions within which many levels of perception are possible, but being aware of these major categories is a start. And if nothing else, this exercise will give you a chance to relax in the warm rays of the sun. Just don't get sun burnt!

- Sit or lie in sunshine, allowing your body to bask in the rays of the sun (taking precautions, of course, to avoid sunburn).
- Take a few moments just to experience and enjoy the physical feel of sunlight on your body, the brightness of the sunlight, the warmth of its rays, and so on. This is the sun in its physical form acting upon you in your physical form.
- Using one of the methods you've been learning (such as the Threshold Exercise or the Soma to Aura Exercise), shift your attention and awareness into your subtle field.
- From this perspective, see if you can feel the impact of the subtle solar energies upon your subtle body. You will probably remain aware of their warming effect on your physical body as well, but move your attention to a place a few inches away from your body and see what you feel happening there.
- What do you feel when you attune to the effects of the solar Light and energies upon your subtle field? How is this different from the feel of sunlight on your physical body?
- Now shift your attention again, this time to a field of energy that holds your sense of self. In this state, you are neither a physical nor a subtle body but a point of presence, like a point of view, containing your unique individuality and identity.
- What do you feel when you attune to the effects of the solar Light—in this case, literally the sun's soul Light—upon your identity, your sense of self and life? How is this different from the feel of the sun's energies upon your subtle body?
- When you feel ready—or when you feel restless or tired—bring you attention gently and lovingly back to your physical body. Take a moment just to appreciate and enjoy the feel of the sun on your physical body. Then get up, stretch, and go about your daily business.

Here's a picture that illustrates this exercise:

(Spiritual Realms)
Spiritual
Energies

Life-Affirming

Soul   Solar Soul

(Subtle Environment)
Solar
Subtle
Energies

Personal
Energy
Field

Subtle
Body

Energizing

(Physical World)

Sunlight

Physical Body

Warming

FIGURE 12

CHAPTER FIVE
Imagination

Imagination can be a key part of subtle awareness and perception. When I experience a subtle energy, it often gives rise to an image or images in my mind. I'm not "seeing" clairvoyantly, but I am seeing in my mind's eye, the imagination.

Imagination is often misunderstood. We think of it as a faculty for making things up, often with little regard for physical reality. Or we think of it as a creative tool; it's what artists use to write their novels or paint their paintings. In our materialist society which so often prizes objective rationality, we are likely to dismiss imagination as engaging in fantasy and make-believe. If something is "imaginary," it doesn't exist. It is unreal. This way of thinking about imagination is so pervasive in our culture that when my friend Robert Ogilvie Crombie or ROC shared his experiences at Findhorn on clairvoyantly seeing and interacting with nature spirits, he always prefaced his remarks by saying he had no imagination whatsoever.

This is a short-sighted and incomplete way of understanding imagination. Particularly in working with subtle energies, we need to understand imagination as a tool of perception. It's a faculty for creating images. Each of our senses is designed to respond chemically, mechanically, or electrically to impulses from the environment—electromagnetic waves in the case of sight, for instance, or pressure in the case of touch. These responses travel along various nerve tracks to reach the brain where they are interpreted. This interpretation results in pictures being formed in our mind. A certain set of light waves of different frequencies impacts my eye, turns into electrochemical signals that travel through the optic nerve to the brain where it is translated as an image of a colorful coffee cup. This translation happens through the imagination. It doesn't mean the coffee cup isn't real; it simply means that what I "see" in my mind as a coffee cup isn't exactly the same as the bundle of vibrating atoms that's sitting on my desk, which itself is also a bundle of vibrating atoms. I am imaging this pattern of atoms and molecules as a coffee cup.

Imagination turns sensation into form. But the sensations need not be physical. They can be mental, emotional, or subtle. For instance, when I read a novel, I "see" in my mind's eye the world and characters the writer is creating due to the mental and emotional sensations and responses of reading the author's prose. The way I see them, though, may be very different from how you see them.

Before Peter Jackson gave us movie images of Middle Earth in his *Lord of the Rings* trilogy, was the Gandalf I saw in my mind when I first read the books the same as the Gandalf you might have seen in your mind if you had also read the books before the movies came out? Was either your or my Gandalf the same as Ian Mckellan's masterful portrayal of Tolkien's wizard? Did Hobbiton look the same for you as for me, and were the Orcs the same? Each of us imagined this world in our unique way, influenced by the mental impressions and emotional resonances generated by Tolkien's prose.

If I say to you, "I saw a cat yesterday," do we each see the same cat in our respective minds? If I say, "I'm feeling angry today," do you feel and picture my anger the same why I do? Most likely not, but past experience will inform you as to what a generic cat looks like and what anger feels like, enough that we can communicate meaningfully with each other. We can draw on a culturally shared stock of images to clothe the ideas and feelings, the mental and emotional information and sensations, that we pass back and forth. Imagination enables us to do this. You can imagine—i.e. picture in your mind's eye—what I mean when I say I saw a cat. You can imagine what I mean when I say I'm angry or depressed.

In other words, imagination isn't just for artists or for make-believe. It's an integral part of our everyday world, making perception and communication possible, as well as creating worlds that have no direct correspondence in our physical reality. It is a way of bringing reality into being. The Founding Fathers of the United States had to imagine what this nation might be like before they could help bring it into being by writing the Declaration of Independence and the Constitution. Steve Jobs and Steve Wozniak transformed society by imagining—and then creating—the personal computer. In fact, we could say that all human civilization is the concrete product of imagination.

Imagination, then, stands at the interface between mind and world. It turns mental and emotional impulses into images in the mind that can then impact the world and it can take impulses from the world delivered through our senses and turn them into perceptual and meaningful images in our mind. It performs the same function when dealing with information and impulses from the subtle dimensions.

There are books and other sources you can turn to for further information and research concerning the physiological and psychological nature and function of imagination. What I want to focus on here is its role in subtle perception and in working with subtle forces.

Sensations received by the subtle body can give rise to images in our minds just as sensations from the eye or ear can do. The important thing to realize is that while these images are "imaginal" (that is, produced by the imagination's function), they are not "imaginary" (that is, made up or make-believe). On the other hand, we do make up images all the time in our minds. How can you distinguish an imaginal perception from an imaginary one?

One test is to see how easily you can alter the image, shaping it the way you'd like. If the image changes easily, chances are good it's a product of your fancy, something you're making up. If it resists change or it returns to its original form in spite of your efforts to change it, chances are good that it's an imaginal image, one reflecting an objective reality. However, there's a further, and deeper, way of thinking about this.

Something you see in your mind's eye as a result of your subtle awareness may very well be "made up" and imaginary, at least at first. Remember that subtle senses are really not like your special senses; the information they supply is not identical to the impressions of sight and sound, odor and taste that your brain is used to receiving. If you are not used to subtle perceptions, your brain may struggle to interpret the information it is receiving from the subtle worlds. If anything, it may resemble more the kind of information that comes from your somatic senses; yet we prioritize seeing and hearing, so the brain will try to accommodate us and make up an image that approximates what it's sensing. Or it will draw an image out of your storehouse of memory, in effect saying, "Well, I'm not sure what this is, but it's like this other thing with which I'm familiar."

Here's where patience can be a virtue. You may suspect or even be sure that the images arising in your mind are imaginary. You first reaction, then, is to dismiss them by saying, "Oh, this is just something I'm making up." But if you're patient, your brain will have a chance to adjust to the information it's getting from its subtle senses; it will then begin to correct its initial impression. The image will change on its own or it will be replaced by something else, something deeper that takes the form of an intuition or inner knowing.

This works in the other direction, too. You can be too quick to accept an image, finalizing it in your mind, saying to yourself, "Yes, this is definitely what I'm seeing inwardly." Here, too, your brain may still be in a process of analyzing and adjusting to new forms of sensory input; if you accept the first thing it throws out as a possible interpretation, you can short circuit this process as surely as if you'd said, "No, it's just my imagination, and I don't believe any of it."

There's an art involved here, a feel for interpretation that comes with practice and experience. But as a rule of thumb, unless for some reason you know and are confident that what you are sensing and the images arising from it in your mind are accurate and true, give yourself time to allow the experience to gestate. Think of the initial impression as a seed that needs time to grow and blossom into meaning and insight. How much time? Well, that depends on you and on the situation, but for me, if I have any question about what I'm sensing, I usually allow at least twenty-four hours, and I often give myself three days to allow an inner perception to truly mature and unfold within me.

A better question to ask, though, than "is this real or is this imaginary" is this: "What else am I feeling, sensing or experiencing in addition to this visual image?" As I've said, subtle awareness is usually more akin to somatic perception than one of the special senses like sight or sound. Your subtle field as a whole is a single sensory organ. As a consequence, information can come to you in different ways simultaneously—which, when you think of it, is not an unusual phenomenon at all. Your sense of an orange, for example, is more than just what it looks like; it includes its flavor, its texture, its aroma, the sound it makes when you rub your fingers over its skin, and so forth. All of these things make up the perception of "orange."

Likewise, though sensory perception can lead to a visual image arising in your mind, it can also give rise to physical sensations (like chills running down your arm or up your back), to feelings, even to cognitive responses such as sudden intuitions, thoughts, or ideas. If your impression is only in your mind's eye—that is, you only have an image in your mind and no other corroborating or accompanying sensations—this may be a further indication that you are making up the image rather than perceiving an objective subtle phenomenon.

But to repeat, this is not necessarily a bad thing, as the image may simply be the "hook" that draws you into the fuller perception; it's what gets your attention, but it's not the perception or the contact itself. That may need some time to gestate and reveal itself.

The Inner Theater

I think of imagination as an inner theater with an empty stage. If I want to use it as part of my subtle perception, I need to be sure my mind is clear of pre-existing images. Imagine actors trying to perform on a stage that is cluttered with props and scenery left over from some other production. The stage has to be emptied first to create the space in which the actors can do their work.

The same is true for our imagination. We need to empty our minds, empty our feelings, and enter a calm, silent, expectant state, just as if we were in a theater waiting in the darkness as the curtain goes up before anything happens on the stage. Until you are practiced and have some experience, the brain's ability to translate subtle impressions into imaginal representations may be limited. It's like listening to hear a very quiet voice or seeing a figure emerge in the distance out of a foggy night. The more mental or emotional "noise" and activity there is, the harder it can be to discern the impressions from the subtle realms. Inner calm and silence are important components of subtle perception, however you arrive at them. There are many ways to achieve this inner silence, meditation being the most familiar and the most common.

An Imaginal Vocabulary

Over time, if you pay attention, you will likely develop a "vocabulary" of physical and emotional sensations and impressions that will be an adjunct to your imaginal responses to subtle energies. For instance, one kind of subtle energy might consistently feel a certain way in your body, regardless of what images it inspires, while a different subtle force will feel differently.

If your imagination is going to be a useful tool, you need to cultivate it much as you would a garden. Be aware of how you are feeding your imagination, the kinds of images to which you expose yourself through television, movies, and novels. If you have a steady diet of horror stories filled with evil spirits and psychotic people, you have only yourself to blame if an inner contact triggers such images and fills you with fear. Fearful images about the subtle worlds do not help you, and you will want to weed them out. After all, if the only images you have of the subtle worlds are frightening ones, then they will be triggered no matter what kind of subtle energy you encounter. You will constantly be dealing with self-generated fears.

However, the best way to work with your imagination isn't so much by avoiding or excluding things; I enjoy a good ghost story now and then! But I counter all the fearful images that come to us through the news or through stories on television by deliberately incorporating images that are useful and positive. You want to cultivate an "imaginal vocabulary" that rests on your strength, your courage, and your wholeness. One way to do this is to explore just what sensations and images arise when you expose yourself to positive influences or engage with spiritual energies through meditation, prayer, and contemplation. In the first few months of my training with my non-physical mentor, John, he would bring a variety of subtle forces or beings into my presence and wait for me to sense them. He would ask me what a particular energy or presence felt like in my body and what images arose in my mind—or feelings in my emotions—as a result. All of these things contributed to the *felt sense* of the contact. In this way, I developed an imaginal vocabulary or a set of images that would arise when a particular felt sense (and its corresponding subtle phenomenon) was present.

I can't provide this same service for you, but you can do it for yourself by paying attention to how your imagination responds to events in your everyday world. What images arise, for instance, and what felt sense is present when you listen to a particular piece of music? What images arise when you see the beauty of a sunset or a sunrise? By being aware of the role imagination plays in your normal physical perception, you will gain insights into how it may respond to events in the subtle realms.

Imagination and Felt Sense

Your imagination can also provide a "trigger" for a felt sense. Throughout this book, I use terms like "wholeness," "coherency," "integration," and "sovereignty" to describe inner states or the condition of your subtle energy field. But what really do these words mean? What images in your mind do they inspire? What do you think of or imagine when I say, "stand in your wholeness" or "feel the coherency of your energy field"?

When I feel whole or coherent in myself, I feel present, grounded, at peace with my body, free of inner mental or emotional conflict, and spacious. I have an image of myself as a glowing sphere of Light that embraces all parts of my physical body and interpenetrates both the earth and its energies and the soul or spiritual self and its energies. I feel "organized," like all the parts of me of which I'm aware are in the moment in harmony and connection with each other. There is a felt sense of presence that is a blend of body, mind, emotion, and spirit.

In a way, this is an imaginal state. That is, the felt sense of wholeness or coherency, sovereignty or integration conjures up an image in my mind, and if I want to enter into that felt sense, I simply think of this image. It acts like a mnemonic trigger to help me enter a desired state.

I feel part of the practice of engaging the subtle worlds involves learning what a state like "wholeness" feels like to you and what images arise from it. This is all part of developing your unique imaginal vocabulary that can help you sense what you're perceiving and what state you're in when you engage with the subtle realms.

Keeping Perspective

When I first began using a computer to write, what I saw on the computer screen didn't match what the final document would look like when printed. Eventually, though, word processing software developed to where it could accurately reproduce the printed page on the monitor. This became an important feature for the software and was known as WYSIWYG or "Whizzy-Whig," which stood for What You See Is What You Get.

Working with the subtle realms, sometimes what you see inwardly is what you get, that is to say, what is really there, but given the fluid and mutable nature of these non-physical dimensions, this isn't always the case. What appears imaginally in your mind is often an artifact, constructed out of the blending of your energy and consciousness with that of the phenomenon you are engaging. This plays more of a role when dealing with subtle beings who can adjust their appearance in order to make a better connection with you; the object is not to deceive but to co-create something understandable and relatively familiar to our object-based, material ways of thinking and perceiving. The reason this is important is that the form and structure of most subtle beings, existing as they do in more than just the three dimensions we know, is difficult, if not at times impossible, for us to grasp or comprehend, at least in a visual way. So they clothe themselves in familiar images often taken from our own imaginations.

This is less of a problem with subtle energies, but then again, what does "peace" look like, or "love," or "anger," or "joy"? How do we picture electricity, for that matter, or gravity? We often perceive these things indirectly through their effects. A lightning bolt is a discharge of electricity in the atmosphere, but is lightning what electricity actually looks like?

My point is that when working with imaginal images, we need to keep perspective. What we see is often just a working image designed to help us connect and engage. It's not necessarily what's "really there." When working with the subtle realms, it's more often a case of What You See Isn't Necessarily What You Really Get or "Whizzin-Wherg" (WYSINWYRG).

For example, when John first appeared to me, he looked like a man of about forty years of age wearing brown slacks, a light open-colored shirt, and a tweed jacket with leather elbow patches; in short, he looked like a young college professor, an image I was very familiar with having just left the university. He maintained this image for about two weeks, then, as I became better able to blend with his energy field, he let it go. What I saw then was a complex swirl of light and color which was his normal spiritual form. At any time I wished, I could still project out of my imagination the tweedy college professor look upon him, but I knew by then it wasn't what he really looked like.

Likewise, in classes when I've had a group of people attune together upon a particular quality or subtle presence, when we compare notes, people will have seen different things in their mind's eye but the felt sense of what they have experienced is the same, whatever the differences in their imaginations. Through experiences like this, they know they are engaging with something objective and that they're not just making things up, but they also learn that the same subtle phenomenon can elicit a variety of different mental pictures. And it's always exciting when in fact, as often happens as well, a number of people see the exact same thing.

When people have inner visions or see subtle phenomenon, they can get caught in the visual form of the experience—the imaginal form—and lose track of the deeper felt sense of the phenomenon. I've seen people insist that what they see isn't their imagination, and they're right if they mean they're not making it up, but it isn't necessarily what's really there in the subtle realms either. It's important to keep perspective and to use our imaginations and the images they create as tools but not take them too seriously.

EXERCISES FOR CHAPTER FIVE

Exercise: The Inner Theater

When working with subtle energies, you have an important advantage if you can create a mental and emotional space within yourself that is calm and poised and free from pre-existing images. Such an inner space allows new images to arise out of the interaction of your subtle body's perceptions and your imagination. There are different ways that you can enter such a space. Many people use rhythmic breathing and meditation to do so. In my classes, though, I usually suggest the following exercise of entering an inner theater of the heart and mind because it's one that has helped me over the years and it's a common experience to which most people can relate.

- Picture yourself entering a theater where a show is about to being. As you sit, ahead of you, you can see an empty stage. (If you prefer, you can imagine being in a cinema, and in front of you is the screen, now dark and blank.)
- As you sit in the theater, the lights go down. Everything becomes hushed and quiet. The show is soon to begin. Feel the anticipation. Before you is the empty stage or screen. Anything can appear on it; it is a space filled with potential, its very emptiness alive with power and possibility.
- What does your body feel like in this quiet, calm, expectant space, feeling the presence of this empty stage? What does your mind feel like? Your emotions? Who are you in this moment? What is the felt sense of your experience of this empty stage here in the theater of your heart and mind?
- It is this felt sense you want to enter and recover when you are about to imaginally engage with the subtle realms.

Exercise: Imaginal Assets

This is a reflective exercise to give you a sense of the images that commonly fill your imagination, what we might call your "default imagination." For example, do you have the same daydreams over and over? Are there images that reoccur often in your thoughts? The objective here is to become conscious and familiar with how you usually use your imagination and the kind of images that come most readily to mind. This self awareness will be helpful in discerning whether a particular image arising in your mind's eye through an inner contact has its source in that contact itself or is simply one of the images that commonly exists in your imagination, heightening the odds that you are creating it yourself.

- Over the span of three or four days, observe and keep note of the kind of images that most often arise in your imagination. For instance, when your mind is "idling" and you are daydreaming, what kinds of images most commonly fill your daydreams? What is the common emotional "flavor" of your imaginings? For instance, are you prone to fearful images, peaceful images, images of beauty, wishful thinking images, etc.?

Exercise: Imaginal Vocabulary Building

You can be proactive in developing a set of imaginal images based on physical, mental, and emotional sensations, thoughts, and qualities. In other words, you can "stock" your imagination with images you deliberately choose and create. There is no guarantee that an inner contact will trigger these particular images, but if your mind is looking for images to interpret something sensed by your subtle body, it is helpful to have an inner imaginal vocabulary that it can use. In this exercise, you will explore different categories and see what images naturally arise for you or that you can create in each of them. I'm only making suggestions here, so feel free to use different or additional categories and examples that will fit your life and style more gracefully.

- <u>People</u>. Think of categories of people and observe what images arise in your imagination as you think of them. You can shape these images through your intent; at the same time, you are assessing (as in the Exercise above) the kinds of images certain people naturally inspire in you. If you don't like these images, you can certainly change them.
  1. Friends
  2. Enemies
  3. Relatives
  4. Loved Ones

    5. Co-Workers

    6. People of your Nationality, Ethnicity and Religion

    7. People of Different Religions (explore different religions here)

    8. People of Different Ethnicity (explore different ethnicities here)

    9. People of Different Nationalities (explore different nationalities here)

- <u>Elements</u>. What images arise when you think of the following elements?

    1. Fire

    2. Earth

    3. Water

    4. Air

    5. Metal

    6. Wood

- <u>Spiritual Qualities</u>. What images arise when you think of or contemplate the following spiritual qualities?

    1. Joy

    2. Peace

    3. Love

    4. Courage

    5. Compassion

CHAPTER SIX
Swagger

John and I had been working together for a couple of months when he appeared one day and said, "When you engage with the subtle worlds, you want to have a bit of swagger." This was an unexpected bit of advice, and there was a humorous twinkle about him when he said it. But as our training progressed, I realized that there was a serious intent behind his comment.

When we think of swaggering, we usually think of someone who is boastful and overly full of himself. John wasn't advocating narcissism or ego-inflation. But as he clarified later, "you want to be comfortable and proud with who you are as a person and as an incarnate human, for this will strengthen the coherency of your being as you encounter forces and beings who are energetically strong in their identity." John often likened the impact of subtle energies to that of a swiftly flowing river or a strong wind upon an individual; there was always the possibility of being thrown out of balance and "knocked over" energetically. Having confidence in oneself and loving one's identity were the equivalent of having firm and solid footing when the water or the wind struck.

When working with the subtle world, identity has three aspects. There's the psychological aspect, which is our autobiography, our memories, and our sense of who we are, including our body image based on our physical characteristics and condition. There's the spiritual aspect, our soul identity held in what I call our "Interiority," about which I'll have more to say later in the book. And there's our "energy identity."

Just as the cells of our body contain the DNA that establishes our physical identity, so our subtle body contains the *energies of self*. Our physical DNA comes from our parents and ancestors; our energies of self originate with our soul and reflect not only its identity but its purposes and intents in taking incarnation. These energies of self are unique to us, but all subtle energies in one way or another possess a kind of identity.

Imagine a group of people in a field taking turns throwing a baseball. Each baseball will carry the particular energy, spin, direction, and velocity put on it by the person who threw it. One person may throw overhead like a baseball pitcher, one may throw underhanded like a softball pitcher; one may throw it long, hard and fast, another more gently and easily. Another may barely get the ball past his or her feet. The person catching the balls will have to adapt to the nature of the throw. A wild pitch will require more exertion to catch the ball (assuming it's even possible to catch it) than a throw that flies accurately and smoothly into the catcher's waiting glove. A softly thrown ball will have less impact than one thrown hard and fast.

Subtle energies are like this. They carry the particular qualities of energy given to them when they were generated or "tossed." I call these qualities their *vectors*, their equivalent to the direction, velocity, and spin on a baseball as it leaves the pitcher's hand. These vectors may include the strength of will or purpose behind the energy, its intensity and frequency (how "fast" it's moving relative to us), and its qualities, that is, what kind of subtle energy is it? What is its identity? An angry energy will feel very different from one that brings peacefulness. A hateful energy is very different from a loving one.

When they land in our energy fields, they impart that energy to us, as I described in the last Chapter. Temporarily at least, their energetic identity becomes part of us, part of our own field. At that point, we need to do something with that energy so that it doesn't interfere with our own energies of self, potentially creating imbalance or inconsistency in our own subtle field.

Think of a baseball catcher. He squats down, lowering his center of gravity. This gives him more stability in catching the fast balls of a professional pitcher. At the same time, his posture gives him the ability to move quickly in several directions in order to catch a wild pitch or throw out a runner trying to steal second base. Martial artists do something similar when they get into a crouching stance, balanced and poised to respond to whatever comes at them.

The greater the difference between the energy of a subtle energy—i.e. its vectors—and our own energies of self, the more challenging it is to receive this energy in a balanced way and hold it constructively within our own energy field. The incoming vectors can cause our energy field to fluctuate as it attempts to match it and blend with it, and our energy identity can fluctuate with it. We can find ourselves unwittingly taking on and personalizing the identity of these energies in place of our own natural pattern.

For instance, as I described in the previous Chapter, we've all had times of suddenly feeling unaccountably angry or sad, or on the positive side of things, unaccountably happy or confident. Where these feelings come from, we don't know, but we take them on as if they were our own. At such times, we may well be responding to the vectors of subtle energies from outside ourselves that are causing changes in our own subtle field. We are "picking up" someone else's anger or sadness—or their happiness and confidence—and not paying much attention to it, we assume they are our own feelings. Our own subtle field is being shaped by vectors from others rather than from conscious and deliberate choices we have made. These vectors are implanting and imposing an identity upon us. This phenomenon may not last long, but it can happen many times throughout the day, leaving us a bit confused at the end about just what we're really feeling!

Normally our physical body buffers us from the impact of many subtle energies; it's like the glove, the padding, and the face mask that a baseball catcher wears for his protection. What further protects our energy field on its own level, though, isn't padding or a shield but the natural boundaries established by its identity, its own energies of self. How effectively our subtle field can absorb and assimilate subtle energies different from itself is dependent on the strength, clarity, and coherency of its own identity.

When we deliberately open ourselves to engage with subtle energies, we create what I think of as a "sphere of interaction" in which because of our intentionality, our subtle field expands and becomes more susceptible to impressions from the subtle environment. I illustrate this in Figure 13:

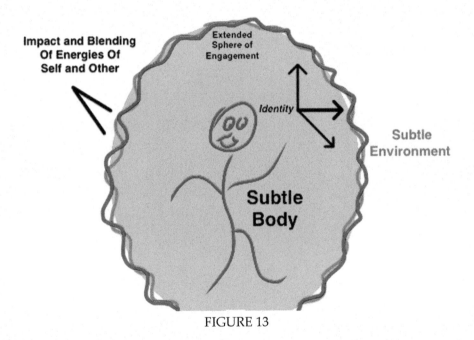

FIGURE 13

By extending our subtle field in this manner, it's as if we were listening very quietly but very intensely to pick up the slightest sound in our environment. We reduce the buffering effects of the physical body. We become energetically more open but also potentially more vulnerable. We are sensitizing the ability of our subtle field to receive impressions, but those impressions can have a stronger effect. Our subtle body can be more easily influenced as it receives and blends with subtle energies whose identity is different from its own.

What John meant by "swaggering" was the act of bringing the felt sense of our whole identity front and center to strengthen this sensitized layer of our subtle body—our "sphere of engagement"—and make sure that it resonated clearly and coherently with our energies of self. In so doing, we would be more open but not more vulnerable.

Working with the subtle worlds is in many ways a matter of working with Identity, ours and that of the forces that we engage. For this reason, I'm going to focus on this matter in the next three Chapters, replicating as much as I can the training John gave me. Even though on the surface he was training me in working with subtle forces, at heart he was training me to be a whole person standing in my Identity.

EXERCISES FOR CHAPTER SIX

Exercise: Identity Assessment

This is a reflective exercise the purpose of which is not to make lists of contents about yourself but to gain a felt sense of who you are as a whole person. Consider this a "quick run over the target," a kind of self-reconnaissance since many other exercises in this book, including the one immediately following on, the "Identity Pouch," will allow you more in-depth reflection.

- Who are you as a physical body? What does your body contribute to your self-image? What features of your body feel particularly empowering to you?
- Who are you as an emotional person? What are the usual emotions you feel during a day, the ones that in your estimation would most characterize you? What part of your emotional life do you feel is particularly empowering to you?
- Who are you as a mental person? What do you feel are the strengths of your intellect? What is your usual mode of thinking: are you more abstract or more concrete in your thoughts? How easily do you learn or change your mind? What part of your mental life do you feel is particularly empowering to you?
- Who are you as a spiritual person? What is the nature of your spiritual life? What role do compassion, forgiveness, love, joy, serenity, calmness, and wisdom play in your life? How would you characterize your spiritual practice or your relationship to transcendental realities, as well as to the material world around you (after all, there's both vertical and horizontal aspects to spirituality)? What part of your spiritual life do you feel is particularly empowering to you?
- Can you sense your "energy identity?" What does it feel like to you?
- If I ask you to "stand in your Identity" — in your felt sense of integrity, coherency and wholeness — what does this mean to you? What does it feel like to you?

Exercise: The Identity Pouch

This is an exercise for exploring some of the positive elements that have gone into making you who you are today. It's a way of touching into your identity—and your subtle energy—using specific, concrete connections with your history. It's also a way of affirming the power of your identity and the "magic" it holds for shaping your world, especially at a subtle level.

Introduction

In many native traditions, pouches that can be worn around the neck or on a belt are used to contain special objects, herbs, talismans, and the like, all serving to give the wearer good "medicine" or spiritual power. This power is deemed as coming from certain objects in the environment that the particular culture and religion regard as being sacred or as possessing "mana" or magical and spiritual energy. Such a "medicine" pouch can become a potent talisman in itself for the individual.

Incarnational spirituality recognizes the sacred energy inherent in all things and the capacity of various objects and plants to hold special and unique energies that can be helpful to a person when properly tapped or used. However, there is also a sacred energy and power inherent in ourselves and in the history and pattern of our lives. Ordinary things that have no cultural or religious significance may be of great significance to us individually as they may mark some event or place that has been special in shaping the energy of our lives. Such items have "incarnational mana" or "medicine;" they can have a magical or spiritual significance and power to us. They help us tap into the spirit and power of our incarnated identity.

In this exercise, you will create an "identity pouch," a leather or cloth container that will hold items that connect to significant and special parts of your life. These items represent elements or experiences in your own life that remind you of or attune you to the power within your own person. This can be sacred, spiritual power, but it can also be mental and emotional and even physical power as well. However you view it, the power is unique to you and manifests through your individuality.

In my own incarnational pouch, for instance, I have little pebbles taken from places that are meaningful to me: from Findhorn in Scotland, for example, where I was a director of a spiritual community, and from the Deerfield River near where I lived in Massachusetts and went to Deerfield Academy. I also have a pebble from my birth state of Ohio and a splinter of wood from my home in Issaquah. I even have some dirt from Morocco, where I spent much of my childhood. Ohio, Morocco, Deerfield, Findhorn, and now my home in Washington State are all places where I experienced significant shifts in consciousness, times of growth, experiences of power, wonderful and joyous memories, all of which are meaningful to me in honoring and tapping into the spirit of my own incarnation. None of these things are "sacred" artifacts in the usual sense of the term, yet they are part of my own incarnational identity and its power, its sacredness.

You can create your pouch to be any size. It may be small so that you can comfortably wear it. Mine is a small leather pouch that I can wear easily around my neck. Or it can be large, something to be kept on a table or an altar, for instance, and able to hold larger things.

In creating and blessing your identity pouch, you are creating a talisman whose power is related to you and your personal life: an incarnational talisman attuned to your unique spirit and sovereignty. However, this pouch is really only a symbol of you and your identity. The important thing to remember is that YOU are that incarnational pouch, a unique sacred space within the world. The incarnational pouch is only a physical representation of what you already are. It should never be seen as the bearer of your magic, energy, and sacredness; YOU are the bearer of your magic, energy, and sacredness. If the incarnational pouch helps you understand and realize this, it has served its main purpose; past that point, it can be a battery of subtle energy which you may or may not wish to have and use. That is entirely up to you.

Here's a picture of my own identity pouch:

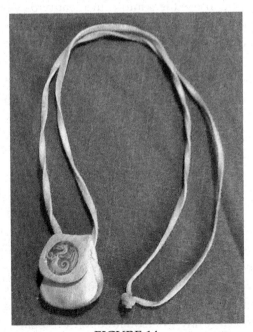

FIGURE 14

You can purchase a pouch to use; this is what I did when I discovered and was drawn to this particular pouch one day in a store. Or you can make your own. If you do so, the act of making it becomes part of the exercise, a chance to attune to the meaning of the pouch and its relationship to your identity. It's a work of building energy between you.

If you do decide to make your own pouch, begin by meditating upon the materials you will use: the thread, the leather, the cloth, the needles, and anything else that may go into the construction of your pouch. As you do, consider the elements that go into making up your own life. Remember that your pouch is intended to be a source of support for you, attuned to the spiritual power of your incarnation. Therefore, pick out special and empowering moments that have brought you strength, joy, and other positive qualities; moments that have defined you as a person and given shape to your life. Don't be afraid to consider negative or hurtful experiences as well; they may have been painful, but they may have contributed to your wisdom and power. Just don't dwell on the pain they have caused you. Look to what you have gained from such challenges in your life.

Imagine that you are your soul crafting your incarnate life. Imagine yourself as you construct your pouch infusing it, as your soul would infuse your life, with courage, strength, joy, compassion, and other virtues. Indeed, if there are particular qualities or virtues you would like to have in your life, attune to them as you work and infuse them into your identity pouch. It doesn't have to reflect only the way your life is; it can hold your vision and desire for what you would like your life to become.

Attuning to the Pouch and the Space It Holds

By virtue of what it is, your identity pouch creates a space that can hold other things. It's a container. However, it's more than just that. In a similar way, you are a space that holds the content of your life: your thoughts, feelings, memories, and so forth. These contents are important, but they do not fully define you. You can transcend them if you need to; you can change and transform because what you are as spirit and soul, as a living identity, is larger than the content of your mind. Like the carpetbag which Mary Poppins carried that could hold anything no matter how large, the space within you, the space of your soul and your imagination, can hold anything you put into it.

Meditate on the space within your pouch, let that image attune you to the capacities within yourself, the space of the soul within your own being which holds all the potentials of your life.

Take some time each day to meditate upon this space. Do this for one week. Don't put anything into the identity pouch yet. The first task is to become familiar with its space and through that, with the sacred space within you. This is the true power which this pouch holds for you. So in your meditation, focus upon the felt sense, the meaning, the experience of this inner space, what it is within you, and how it manifests the sacred for you. If your identity pouch never held anything else but this space, it would be holding the most powerful "medicine" on earth: the presence of your unique, individuated sacredness, the space that can hold and transform your life—and the world around you.

Using Your Pouch

When you feel attuned to the pouch and its space, over time add anything else you wish that you feel represents some part of your personal, incarnational life and its innate spiritual power. When you do, meditate on and appreciate why you have chosen this particular item or element, what it means to you, and how it empowers you. This might be some dirt from the land around your home, something that represents a particularly happy or powerful time in your life, something that represents an accomplishment, etc. Whatever is in your pouch should embody powerful "medicine" for you. It should represent your personal power and energy, reminding and attuning you to the positive, powerful aspects of your life.

Think of your identity pouch as an ally, a friend, a source of support, protection, and good energy. It can be as sacred and magical as you allow it to be and invite it to be, but always remember, it exists to serve your magic, the sacredness that is you.

Remember, this identity pouch is only a physical representation and a metaphor of what you already are. It should never be seen as the bearer of your magic, energy, and sacredness; YOU are the bearer of your magic, energy, and sacredness. If the incarnational pouch helps you understand and realize this, it has served its main purpose. However long you use it, let the content and images it holds attune you to the capacities within yourself, the space of the soul within your own being.

Some Pouch Suggestions

If you're wondering how to start or what you might put into your Pouch first, here's one way to start. Feel free to experiment with them as you wish.

Think of this: you are in incarnation because your soul wished it for some reason, because the world has need of you as part of its own incarnation, and because humanity needs you for its own spiritual evolution. Therefore, you can look for three objects that represent these three elements:

1. Something that represents your soul's purpose—the "Why" or the intent of your incarnation, as best you can understand or envision it.
2. Something that represents your connection to the world as a whole and to the forces and powers of nature.
3. Something that represents your connection to the Soul of Humanity as a whole, the larger evolving collective spirit of which you are a part and to which you contribute.

CHAPTER SEVEN
The Big Three

John's training around the idea of Identity was based on three important concepts: Sovereignty, Self-Light, and Presence. I call them the Big Three. They form the core of my approach to working with subtle energies.

Sovereignty

In Chapter Three, I discussed how the soul injects a current of its own energy into the Incarnate Realms of the Earth in order to generate an embryonic subtle field which then becomes the basis for the incarnate subtle body. In effect, the soul is establishing its sovereignty over the substrate energies of the Earth, imprinting its identity upon them and thus turning them into energies of self.

This current of energy from the soul to the subtle body continues all through the life of the individual and provides a vital link between the soul and the incarnate self. I call this energetic link *Sovereignty*. I do so because it maintains the sovereignty of the soul over that portion of the incarnate energy field of the Earth which it is energizing and also because it gives us our capacity to be self-governing, able to make free choices and to express our unique spiritual nature in the world.

Sovereignty is an expression of our innate freedom to unfold our individuality and give the world the gifts of life only we can give. It is the subtle energy "spine" or "axis" around which our incarnational self forms and integrates as it develops coherency and wholeness. Sovereignty is our personal, internal organizing principle. One of my friends and Lorian colleagues, Jim Hembree, describes it as "the self's innate capacity for integrity and wholeness up and down, over and across, and throughout the various domains of being in which we participate and from which we draw our substance and our form."

Sovereignty is the soul force that promotes energetic identity, coherency and integration within our subtle body. Each of us brings to the world irreplaceable and unique potentials of being and creativity. Sovereignty is the soul force, the life force, that establishes and maintains our energetic boundaries, protecting the individuality that is the womb from which these potentials can unfold and manifest.

In many of the exercises in the remainder of this book, I will ask you either at the beginning or at the end — or both — to "stand in your Sovereignty." The Standing Exercise, which is presented with this Chapter is one way to do this. But however you do it, to stand in Sovereignty is to affirm your identity as an incarnate person and as a sacred being, honoring your individuality and the power of your uniqueness, as well as your ability to make the choices that shape and determine your life.

Sovereignty and Boundaries

Sovereignty creates and maintains our boundaries. Our boundaries shape and form the space within which our Identity may develop its unique capacities and potentials. To "stand in your Sovereignty" is also to "stand in your boundaries".

Boundaries do not need to be walls, all stiff and hard and resistant. Ideally, they are like interfaces or membranes: fluid, dynamic, interactive, and configurable. They exist not only to define and protect an area of sovereignty and identity but to establish the meeting place for interaction, engagement, connection, and co-creativity with the world.

When boundaries are trespassed or breached, sovereignty is diminished. Integrity, coherency, and wholeness may be compromised or lost. Identity is infringed. We become less capable.

Sovereignty as a Universal Principle

Although each of us has his or her unique Sovereignty, Sovereignty itself is a "non-local" and transpersonal phenomenon. It is an incarnational function, the means by which the spiritual realms connect to and interact with the Incarnate Realms through the mediation of the subtle worlds. Rocks have their Sovereignty, trees have their Sovereignty, birds have their Sovereignty, bears and kittens have their Sovereignty, and, of course, all people do. Gaia itself has its planetary Sovereignty. And the paradox is that it's all the same principle of Sovereignty in action. Which means that I can't diminish your Sovereignty without diminishing my own. It's like saying I can't pollute the air you breathe without polluting my air as well.

Nearly forty-six years ago, on March 31, 1968, Dr. Martin Luther King, Jr. gave a talk at the National Cathedral in Washington, D.C. in which he said, among other things,

> "We are tied together in the single garment of destiny, caught in an inescapable network of mutuality. And whatever affects one directly affects all indirectly. For some strange reason I can never be what I ought to be until you are what you ought to be. And you can never be what you ought to be until I am what I ought to be. This is the way God's universe is made; this is the way it is structured."

This is exactly how Sovereignty operates. It's not an "I-can-do-my-own-thing" dominion over others or over the world. It's an inner dominion or organization that grows in strength as others are enabled to know and express their Sovereignty as well.

This may seem strange. What happens if my Sovereignty conflicts with yours? Doesn't this lead to conflict? But to think this way is to misunderstand the nature of Sovereignty and the fields that emerge around it. To be self-governing, I don't have to be other-governing. If I enter into a relationship or connection with another, then a space of "mutuality", to use Dr. King's lovely word, opens between us, and that space has its own Sovereignty, too, a Sovereignty that is not a force of dominion over us but a force of clarity, integration, coherency, and wholeness between us.

We are constantly creating fields of interaction and potential wholeness between ourselves and everything within the world around us. Sovereignty isn't a force of dominion and control through these interactions; it's a force of love, wholeness, and emergence.

To stand in our own Sovereignty and to honor it is to stand in and honor the Sovereignty of all, the Sovereignty of the Whole of which we are a participant.

Self-Light

Self-Light is the second of the Big Three concepts. Recognizing and attuning to my Self-Light was one of the first things that John taught me as part of my training. He defined it as the radiance being generated all the time by the incarnational process of being—and becoming—an incarnate self.

To understand this, we need to look again at Figure 7 which I presented in Chapter Three when I was explaining how the embryonic subtle body was generated by the life-energy of the soul. You'll remember that out of its sacred Identity, its Light and living energy, the soul projects a current of intentionality and love into the subtle field of the Earth. Engaging the subtle energies of the Earth, this current of energy, which I have named *Sovereignty*, galvanizes and attracts to itself what it needs from the subtle substance of the world in order build a subtle body that allows it to participate in the Incarnate Realms. It blends these subtle energies of Earth Light together with its own soul Light to form an alchemical union.

Let's look at this process more closely, as there is more going on than simply the creation of an embryonic subtle body. A new form of soul comes into being also, one belonging not exclusively to the spiritual realms but now part of the Earth as well. I call this the Emergent Soul, as it is an expression of our "soul-ness" that develops and emerges throughout our incarnation. It is the unique soul energy of this particular incarnation.

This alchemical mix of soul energies and earth energies creates a unique blend of soul light and earth light. Metaphorically, it's like a glow stick. When you bend and shake a glow stick, you enable the chemicals within it to mix and react, creating light, the glow of chemical luminescence. In the interaction of soul "chemistry" and earth "chemistry," an analogous reaction occurs, creating the radiance of individualized, incarnate Light. I call this Self-Light. And just as the chemical light of the glow stick is contained within a translucent plastic tube, so our Self-Light is held within the Emergent Soul, the sacred presence in each of us. This Self-Light, like the light of a new-born star, then radiates out into the Incarnate Subtle Realms.

The Emergent Soul is generative; it produces a spiritual energy or Light, fueled by the streaming energies of love and intentionality from the Soul that is continually embracing the formative subtle energies of the Earth and blending with them. This is why incarnation is not an event, like birth, but an ongoing process of creative engagement throughout our lifetime.

The Emergent Soul really is like a star within us, radiating its new frequency of Self-Light. It means that we are each a unique source of Light within the incarnate realm. We are contributing to the overall spiritual energy and Light of the earth.

This radiation of Self-Light creates a "space", a field or matrix of identity and energy around which the subtle body of the newly incarnating individual forms out of the non-physical substrate energies of the incarnate realm. In a way, Self-Light *is* the energetic "DNA" of the new incarnation, setting into motion as I described in Chapter Three the "energies of self."

Self-Light makes the subtle body possible but it is not necessarily part of the subtle body, though it can become such if the life of the individual attunes to his or her Self-Light and draws it out into greater activity. We'll look in a moment at how we might do this as it's an important part of working with subtle energies. We see the role of Self-Light in forming the subtle body in Figure 15.

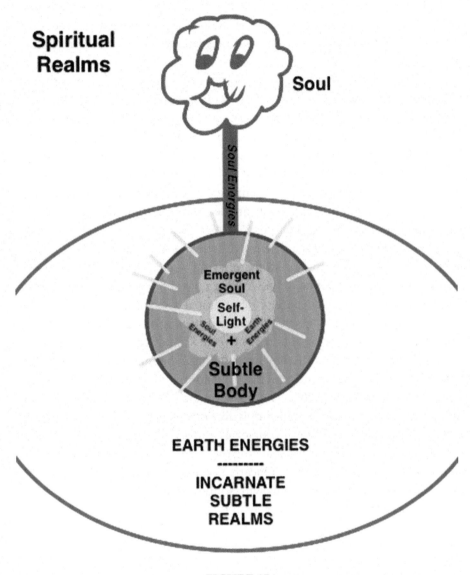

FIGURE 15

We are generating all kinds of subtle energies all the time. Our thoughts generate them, our feelings generate them, even our physical activity and well-being can generate them. But these subtle energies are conditioned by the thinking, the feeling, the activity that gives rise to them. For instance, positive thoughts and feelings, like those of love, joy, and kindness, produce subtle energies that are very different from those generated by negative thoughts and emotions such as fear, anger, or hatred.

Self-Light, though, is different. It is a fundamental quality of spiritual radiance present in every person. It is the radiance of the soul's process of being an incarnate human rather than the emanation of a particular thought or feeling.

It's important to understand that Self-Light is an emergent incarnational phenomenon. It is not soul Light coming from our transpersonal self; it does not have its origin in a transcendental realm, passing into and through us as if we were a length of fiber optic cable. Self-Light emerges from the blending of the Light of the soul with the Light of the Earth. This is a true alchemical blending, a collaboration, not a domination of one kind of energy over another, such as the transpersonal over the personal or the earthly over the soul. Understanding this means that we honor, appreciate and love both sides of this blending, not privileging one over the other.

In other words, you are a generative source of Light simply by virtue of being a soul taking incarnation in the physical realm. The presence of your Self-Light is an important factor in working with subtle energies. It is like an inner "heating coil" that, like the electric kettle that boils my water, can set subtle energies into motion in ways that thinking or feeling alone cannot, ways that can affect the world around you in positive and uplifting ways.

The importance of this idea lies in countering a common assumption that all Light comes from a transcendental place outside of us and that the best we can do is to receive it and reflect it. The fact of our Self-Light means that we, also, are sources of Light. We are not simply like planets that only reflect the light of a distant star. We are like stars ourselves, radiant, generative sources of our own Light. Understanding and realizing this is an important and empowering shift of attitude, an integral part of Incarnational Spirituality. It allows us to be more effective in our engagements with subtle energies.

I illustrate this shift in perspective in Figure 16.

SELF-LIGHT

FIGURE 16

Self-Light is always present. It's a condition of our incarnation much as heat in our body is a by-product of physical exercise. Everyone has Self-Light. However, not everyone expresses it in the same way or to the same extent. We may be stars, but we can be bright or dim depending on the overall state of our being and consciousness.

The main factor influencing the extent to which our Self-Light influences the world around us is the overall condition of our subtle body and in particular of our psyche, which is to say of our mental and emotional activities and their influence on our subtle energetic field. When we are in inner turmoil and our psyche is "turbulent" or our thinking and feeling is caught up in negativity, our Self-Light is obscured. When our psyche is clear and calm and our thinking and feeling are positive, then our Self-Light has an unobstructed energetic pathway into the world. This is represented in Figure 17.

PSYCHE AND SELF-LIGHT

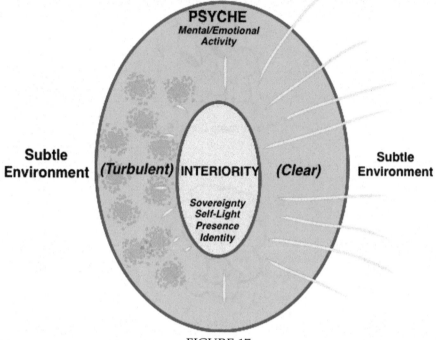

FIGURE 17

Why Self-Light?

Light—whatever its source—is enlivening and *holopoietic*, which is to say it promotes wholeness. It heightens the manifestation of wholeness and life. Self-Light does so as much as does the Light of the Soul or the Light of the Sacred. Why, then, distinguish between forms of Light? The simplest reason has to do with appropriateness. Here's a physical metaphor. The light from the sun is identical to the light from the lamp on my desktop. Both are electromagnetic phenomena; both are photons in motion. But if you placed a piece of the sun on my desktop, not only would it blind me but it would incinerate me as well (not to mention the desktop and probably most of my house and neighborhood to boot). The energy of the sun is far too intense and powerful to use as a light source on my desk. A desk lamp is more appropriate and does the job that's needed.

Self-Light, arising as it does out of the incarnational process and being generated by an incarnate person, radiates in a manner that does not overwhelm the subtle environment (or the Incarnate Realms) around us. It is incarnationally appropriate.

Imagine that you meet a man on the street who needs some money. There's money in a nearby bank, lots of it, but you also happen to have some cash in your pocket. Which makes more sense: for you to dip into what you have on you to offer the man or for you to run to the bank and ask a bank teller to please take some money to the man down the street? Self-Light is available as part of the immediate environment; it is "Light dollars" in our pocket.

There are times when we want to invoke the more intense energy of the Soul or of another transcendental source, or call upon the Sacred, just as there are times when we really do need to go to a bank to get the amount of funds we need as we don't carry that much cash on us. The fact that we possess Self-Light, a personalized radiance of sacredness, doesn't mean that we cannot also draw upon the Light of our soul or the Light of the Sacred. Self-Light doesn't limit us in any way.

But because Self-Light originates out of an incarnational process, it has an innate affinity for the vibrations of the incarnate realm. It can connect with and energize—or bless—other forms of incarnate life and energy very easily and appropriately. To continue with the money metaphor, it's the difference between cash in my pocket that is readily available to spend and a $1000 bill from the bank that I may have difficulty spending because the denomination is too large for the local stores to accept.

Metaphors aside, whatever source you turn to in order to bring Light into a situation, that Light will find a way to become available and to do its work. But when it's appropriate, if you can learn to recognize and draw upon your Self-Light, you will gain a powerful asset in working with subtle energies. And learning to use Self-Light also means learning to develop your loving nature which is a valuable outcome in its own right.

Self-Light can be enhanced, that is, we can increase the amount of "cash" we have in our pocket. The least we can do is open the way for it by clearing, balancing, and attuning our thoughts and feelings and their impact on our subtle body so that they're not obstructing the radiance of our Self-Light. Many things can help here: meditation, breath work, body work, exercise, as well as anything that uplifts us and gives us a sense of joy and love. Beyond this, there are three specific ways of increasing our Self-Light: honoring and loving ourselves, engaging with the world in loving ways (horizontal spirituality), and attuning to our soul or transpersonal self (vertical spirituality).

Enhancing Self-Light

The simplest way to engage and enhance your Self-Light is to honor and love who you are. We touched on this at the very beginning of this book when you did the "Inner Land" exercise. To truly love yourself is not narcissistic; it's not a matter of becoming consumed with self-adulation to the exclusion of others.

It's recognizing your sacredness, your unique identity, your irreplaceable value. No one else can bring to the world what you are bringing.

There are so many voices in our world that want to tell us what's wrong with us, how we're failing, how little difference we can make, what a mess we are. It's no wonder we begin to internalize these messages, energizing a self-critical, self-demeaning voice of judgment within ourselves. But this inner critic is not part of our Identity. It is simply a mental activity within our psyche, one of many but one that can create turbulence within our subtle body. It's not a matter of denying our faults. We can certainly be discerning and aware of how we can improve in our lives, but we can be so out of a spirit of honor and love.

Loving yourself is one way to enhance your Self-Light. Another way is what I think of as "horizontal spirituality." This is a practice of intentionally expressing honor and love to the people and the things around you. After all, they all, too, contain sacredness.

This loving connection is two-fold. It honors the form of things, the physical structure and function that an object provides, or the form of a person or other living creature. Our forms and structures are our points of initial connection with the world around us. Within and behind these forms, though, is a living spirit. It may be an individualized spirit, as in the case of other people, or it may be part of a larger collective spirit or a field of being. Whatever it is, though, it is a part of the Life of the Sacred, the Life that permeates all creation.

By opening your heart to the world around you, you create channels and connections through which your Self-Light can flow out into the world. Such channels of lovingness evoke our Self-Light, enhancing it through giving it means to express.

The third way of enhancing Self-Light is to attune to and evoke the presence of the soul. After all, Self-Light ultimately emerges as a result of the soul's living energy engaging with the energies of the world. If you mindfully attune to the soul and draw its transpersonal energies to you, you are adding fuel to this engagement. You are "stoking the fire," so to speak.

It's important to remember that your soul is in loving collaboration and partnership with your incarnate self or personality. Indeed, your Emergent Soul is an integral part of your incarnate self. You're not invoking the soul to "take over," or to dominate, though the love and wisdom of your soul can certainly add to your everyday human life. The soul and the personality are not at war with each other; rather they are two parts of a larger incarnational wholeness. The object of the exercise is wholeness, not conquest or domination. To love yourself, your personal self, and to align with and evoke the presence of your soul, your transpersonal self, are ways of enhancing this partnership and collaboration.

Aligning with the love that flows from your soul—or from any other transpersonal source to which you feel attuned—is a powerful way to raise the intensity and radiance of your Self-Light.

The "dimmer switch" that raises or lowers the intensity and radiance of your Self-Light is love: love of self, love of the world and the other, love of soul, and through these three, love of the Sacred that is the Ground of Being within them all. When we love, our Self-Light brightens; when we hate or surround ourselves with negativity, our Self-Light dims (though it never goes out).

Presence

If Sovereignty is the organizational "spine" of your incarnation and Self-Light is its specific, individualize radiance, Presence is the expression of your unfolding and dynamic incarnate Identity out into the world. It connects with subtle energies from both spirit and the world and attunes them to your individuality, assimilating those energies into your subtle body. It uses your Self-Light to create coherency and wholeness within your subtle field.

Presence is the expression of the wholeness-creating or *holopoietic* nature of your Emergent Soul. I think of it as something akin to spiritual or metaphysical "mass." Just as in physics the mass of an object bends the fabric of the universe, creating the phenomenon of gravity in the process, so I think of Presence as bending, shaping, and influencing the subtle space around us, as well as drawing to us what we need in order to be incarnated.

When we incarnate, we form many connections that make possible our engagement with the earth. In Incarnational Spirituality, I represent this process by simplifying it to four major connections. I use these four connections to symbolize all the many individual connections and processes that are engaged, integrated, assimilated, and transformed to create our individual incarnations. These four generalized connections are:

- The connection to our transpersonal self, i.e. our Soul
- The connection to Nature and the Earth
- The connection to Humanity and the collective energy of our species
- The connection to our own Personal self, the individualizing energies and processes in our body, our cells, our genetic lineage, and generally within the subtle realms that enable us to be unique, physical entities.

These connections supply information, energy, qualities, and experiences that our Emergent Soul and its Presence assimilate into our subtle energy field and attune to our individual vibrational frequency, making them part of who we are. In effect, Presence transforms world "stuff" into self "stuff." In so doing, it establishes through connection, integration, synergy, and coherency a whole self at the heart of our incarnation.

I use these four symbolic connections as the basis for the Presence Exercise which you will find at the end of this Chapter. It provides an opportunity to explore the felt sense of holopoiesis and integration at work within you as a part of who you are.

I illustrate this in Figure 18.

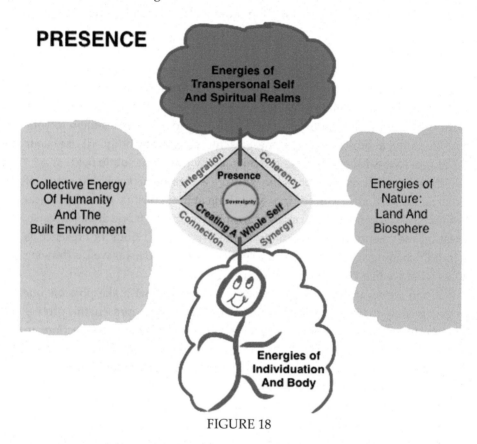

PRESENCE

Energies of
Transpersonal Self
And Spiritual Realms

Collective Energy
Of Humanity
And The
Built Environment

Integration   *Coherency*
Presence
Sovereignty
Creating A Whole Self
Connection   *Synergy*

Energies of
Nature:
Land And
Biosphere

Energies of
Individuation
And Body

FIGURE 18

It is quite possible—and many traditions teach this—to manipulate subtle forces through the projection of mental energies, i.e. through our thoughts and through our will-power. But not all subtle forces will respond to such projections, and the success of such endeavor depends a great deal on how powerful and concentrated our mental projections may be.

Presence, though, is more than just a mental process. It is a state of blending our body, psyche, subtle field, and soul together, enabling them to work in partnership and wholeness

In the martial arts, a fighter seeks to stand in a balanced way and anchors himself or herself in the center of gravity of his or her body. Presence is like the center of gravity of our incarnational bodies, both physical and subtle. When I'm experiencing my Presence, I feel like I'm in the center of a sphere, one that holds and expresses my wholeness, the coherency of body, mind, heart, and spirit, embracing as well my humanity and my participation in the natural world.

But if I'm only centered in my mind and thinking, however coherent and powerful they may be, then I feel like I'm operating out of my head alone, and it feels ungrounded to me. This is one reason I don't use "affirmations" and positive thinking all by themselves as techniques for manipulating or affecting subtle energies as they are too "mind-heavy" for me. They can be expressions of my psyche but not of my Presence.

To stand in your Presence, then, is to stand in the wholeness of your identity, in the unique energetic characteristics and coherency of your individuality. Like a boulder in a stream, this creates an energetic "shape" that affects and influences the flow of subtle energies around you. Further, when you are standing in your Presence, the positive and coherent force of your wholeness and identity mitigates or prevents the impact and effects of unwanted or unpleasant subtle energies. This is why it's important to good energy hygiene, a matter we'll take up later in the book.

Also, the more attentive you are to your environment and the life within it and the more intentional you are about being present where you are and at home in your body, the more easily and powerfully your Presence manifests itself. Although your Presence is independent of the environment, when you connect to where you are in a loving way, it creates a joint field that allows your Presence to expand; in a sense, it takes on "energetic mass" from the loving connections.

What is important is knowing that love, attention, intention, and the forming of connections is entirely under your conscious control. These are deliberate acts which you can choose to do. Doing so is your first line of engagement with subtle forces for ultimately, it is your Presence that both protects your integrity and energy and shapes the subtle environment around you.

Interiority

The combination of our Emergent Soul, Sovereignty, Self-Light, and Presence make up what I call our *Interiority*. This is the part of us that is most expressive of our core Identity and possesses the deepest connection to our soul and the transpersonal aspects of our being.

It is also the part of us that is the channel for the *holopoietic* impulse within us. Holopoiesis is my word for a universal force that seeks to create connectedness, integration, and coherency—or, in a word, wholeness. One of its most familiar expressions is that of love.

Science recognizes a force of complexification in the world, that is to say, a drive towards ever more complex systems, for instance, from atoms to molecules to compounds or from cells to tissues to organs to multicellular bodies. This evolutionary impulse towards greater complexity and connectedness is a physical expression of the deeper holopoietic force.

In our lives, holopoiesis works to create wholeness within us—in our bodies, in our psyches, in our subtle fields, and in our entire incarnational system of soul, energy, psyche, and body—and also wholeness in our connections and relationships with the world around us. And the wellspring of this force lies in our Interiority.

I use the term Interiority not simply to introduce more jargon but really as a convenience or shorthand. Rather than say, "now attune to your Sovereignty, Self-Light, and Presence," or "attune to the holopoietic power within you," I can simply say, "attune to your Interiority." In so doing, you will know the intent is to recognize and align with your Sovereignty, enhance your Self-Light, unfold your Presence, and be a force for holopoiesis—for love and for wholeness—in the world.

EXERCISES FOR CHAPTER SEVEN

Exercise: Standing in Sovereignty

One of the key practices in Incarnational Spirituality is what I call "Standing in Sovereignty." The Standing Exercise can be done independently of the previous "Land" exercise, but when you blend the two, the result can be very powerful as both of these exercises affirm the strength, power, and blessing of your unique individuality and identity. In effect, once you acknowledge and establish your inner land, you then draw its power into your body and self through standing upon it.

As you do this exercise and move up the different levels from the physical to the spiritual, be aware of an axis of power, energy and identity rising up within you, connecting all these levels together. Like an inner spine, this is your Sovereignty. What you are looking for is the felt sense of this energy and identity within you.

- **Physical:**

    The physical action of this exercise is simple. From a sitting position, you simply stand up. Be aware of the physical sensation and felt sense of standing. Feel the work of your body, the power of balance that keeps you upright. If you are already standing, become aware that you are standing and be mindful of the felt sense of standing. In standing you are asserting your physical power to rise up against the power of gravity that would pull you down. You are celebrating your strength. If you are physically unable to stand, you can still assume an inner attitude of standing, perhaps simply by straightening your spine as much as possible.

- **Emotional:**

    Feel the power of being upright. Feel how standing singles you out and expresses your individuality and sovereignty. You stand for what you believe, you stand up to be counted. Standing proclaims that you are here. Standing says you are ready to make choices and decisions. Feel the strength and presence of your identity and sovereignty.

- **Mental:**

    Celebrate your humanness. You are an upright being. You emerge from the mass of nature, from the vegetative and animal states into a realm of thinking and imagining. In standing, your hands are released from providing locomotion. Feel the freedom of your hands that don't have to support you but can now be used to create, manipulate, touch, and express your thoughts, your imagination, and your sovereignty.

- **Magical (Energetic):**

  When you stand, your spine becomes a magical staff, the axis mundi and center of your personal world, generating the field that embraces you. The spine is the traditional wizard's staff along which spiritual power flows and the centers of energy sing in resonance with the cosmos. Feel your energy field coming into alignment with the stars above, the earth below, and the environment around you. Feel your energy aligning with the sovereignty of all beings above, below, and around.

- **Spiritual:**

  Standing, you are the incarnate link between heaven and earth. Your energy rises into the sky and descends into the earth. Light descends and ascends, swirling along your spine in a marriage of matter and spirit. This energy is both personal and transpersonal, giving birth to something new, something human, individual and unique. Feel the magic and energy of your sovereignty that connects soul to person, the higher-order consciousness with the consciousness of the incarnate realms. Feel the will that emerges from this connection, the spiritual presence that blends heaven and earth, aligning with the Sovereignty of creation as it manifests through you.

In doing this exercise of Standing, physically stand if you are able. If you are not able to do so, then be as upright as you can be in your physical situation and in your imagination, "stand" mentally and emotionally. The important thing is to have the felt sense of standing and being upright even if you are physically unable to do so. As you do so, work through these levels of sensation, feeling, thought, energy, and spirit, appreciating the power, the freedom, and the presence emerging within you from the simple act of standing. All of these manifest your unique Sovereignty, connecting and aligning you with all levels of your being, providing an axis around which integration and coherency can occur, creating wholeness and establishing your capacity for agency and self-governance.

Stand in your Sovereignty!

Exercise: Self-Light—Where Stars Meet

- Imagine a spiritual star at the center of the earth. It's a green star radiant with the power of planetary life. Imagine the light from this star rising up through the earth, surrounding you, bathing and nurturing the cells of your body and forming a chalice around you.

- Imagine a spiritual star within the sun in the sky. It's a golden star radiant with the power of cosmic life. Imagine the light from this star descending from the heavens and pouring into the chalice of earthlight that surrounds you and fills your cells.

- Where the green and golden lights of these two stars meet in you, a new star emerges, a radiant star of Self-Light, born of the blending of the individual and the universal, the planetary and the cosmic, the physical and the spiritual. This Self-Light surrounds you and fills you, radiating back down deep into the earth and out into space, connecting with the star below you and the star above you. You are a Chalice of Self-Light within a pillar of spiritual energy rising from the earth and descending from the cosmos.

- Take a moment to feel the star of this Self-Light within and around you. What is the felt sense of this Self-Light within you and radiating from you? It is your connection to the earth, your connection to the cosmos, your connection to your own unique and radiant Self. Take a deep breath, drawing this Light into and throughout your body; breathe out, sending this Light out into your world. Filled with this Light of Self, attuned to heaven and earth, go about your day as a star of blessing.

Exercise: The Presence Exercise

This is one of the earliest exercises I developed for Incarnational Spirituality. Its purpose is to create a felt sense of that part of you that draws all your various inner "selves" into a wholeness. Presence is the expression of that state of wholeness, incorporating both personal and transpersonal, worldly and human elements. It is an expression of your Sovereignty that can, through love, create and maintain wholeness.

<u>Important note:</u> In part of this exercise, you are asked to attune to your everyday personal self. This is not an exercise in judgment or self-criticism. There may be things you don't like about yourself, are ashamed of, and wish to change or improve. That is fine, but that perception is not part of this particular exercise. You may certainly make an honest appraisal of yourself; indeed, this is essential. But do not get into self-blame or criticism or begin listing ways in which you can change and do better. That is another kind of work, one you can engage in at another time.

1. Find yourself a comfortable place to stand. This is a moving exercise, one in which you will be turning to face the four directions. In each direction you will face and attune to a representative type of connection and subtle energy coming into your life to be alchemized into the individuality and hopefully the wholeness of your being.

2. Imagine yourself in a sacred or magical circle, a protected and honored space—an emergence space—that is dedicated to this exercise. Begin by standing in Sovereignty and experiencing the felt sense of your individuality.

3. TRANSPERSONAL SELF:

Choose any direction and face it. In this direction is a vision of your Soul, your Transpersonal Self, the part of you that is connected to the subtle worlds and to transcendent states of communion and unity, spirit and creativity. Take a moment to reflect on being part of Spirit, part of a vast ecology of life and consciousness not limited to physical reality. What does this mean to you? What energy does it carry for you? What do you feel in its presence? What is your felt sense of your transpersonal nature? Be honest in your appraisal.

Take a moment to honor your Transpersonal Self. Appreciate it, give it thanks for its contribution to the wholeness of who you are. It is a channel through which Sacredness—your sacredness—can flow and act. Embrace it with your love.

4. NATURE (OR WORLD) SELF:

Turn ninety degrees and face a new direction. In this direction is a vision of your Nature Self, your World Self, your Earthiness, the part of you that is connected to the physical world and to nature as a whole. Take a moment to reflect on being part of this world, part of the biosphere, part of the realm of physical matter, part of the Earth. This part of you connects you to the World Soul. It connects you to ecology, to nature, to plants and animals everywhere. It connects you to the land, to seas and mountains, plains and valleys, swamps and deserts. What does this mean to you? What energy does it carry for you? What do you feel in its presence?

Take a moment to honor your Nature self. Appreciate it, give it thanks for its contribution to the wholeness of who you are. It is a channel through which Sacredness—your sacredness—can flow and act. Embrace it with your love.

5. PERSONAL SELF:

Turn ninety degrees and face a new direction. In this direction is a vision of your Personal Self. Take a moment to reflect on your uniqueness as a person. Reflect on what defines you, what makes you different from others. This is your ordinary, everyday self. What does this mean to you? What energy does it carry for you? What do you feel in its presence? What is your felt sense of your personal self? Be honest in your appraisal, but do not engage in self-criticism.

Take a moment to honor your personal, everyday self. Appreciate it, give it thanks for its contribution to the wholeness of who you are. It is a channel through which Sacredness—your sacredness—can flow and act. Embrace it with your love.

6. HUMANITY (OR SPECIES) SELF:

Turn ninety degrees and face a new direction. In this direction is a vision of your Humanness, the part of you that connects you to the human species and to human culture, creativity, and civilization. Take a moment to reflect on being human. Your humanity gives you various attributes and potentials not shared by other creatures on this earth. Your humanness makes you part of a planetary community of other human beings, part of the spiritual idea or archetype of Humanity. What does this mean to you? What energy does it carry for you? What do you feel in its presence? What is your felt sense of your humanness? Be honest in your appraisal, but do not engage in self-criticism. Humanity may have its faults and it may behave badly in the world, but that is not the focus here.

Take a moment to honor your human self through which you connect to and participate in the human species. Appreciate it, give it thanks for its contribution to the wholeness of who you are. Being human is a channel through which

Sacredness—your sacredness—can flow and act. Embrace it with your love.

7. PRESENCE:

Turn ninety degrees back to the direction you were facing when you started. At this time, turn your attention to yourself at the center of these four "Selves," your personal self, your human self, your world self, your transpersonal self. You are the point of synthesis where they all meet, come together, blend, partner, cooperate, merge, and co-create wholeness.

Feel the energies of these four selves, these four directions, flowing into and through you, blending, merging, and creating an open, evocative, creative space within you. Feel what emerges from this space. Feel the holistic Presence of your unique incarnation and sovereignty rising around you and within you, enfolding you, supporting you, becoming you. Feel the Presence that can connect with, embrace, and integrate these four aspects of the world within you, blending and synthesizing them into your wholeness.

Who are you as this incarnational Presence? What is the felt sense of your Presence?

8. Stay in the circle feeling the reality and energy of your Presence for as long as feels comfortable to you. When you begin to feel restless, tired, or distracted, just give thanks. Give thanks to your wholeness, to your Presence, and to the Sacredness from which it emerges and which it represents within the ecology of your incarnate life. Absorb, integrate, and ground as much of the felt sense and energy of this Presence as you can or wish into your body, into your mind and feelings, into yourself. Take a moment to once more stand in your Sovereignty. Then step forward out of your circle, thus ending this exercise.

CHAPTER EIGHT
The Soul Connection

When we engage with subtle energies, we do so primarily through the instrumentality of our subtle body. It is the part of us evolved to function within the subtle worlds and in particular, within the subtle environments close in vibration to the physical dimension. Whatever we do to strengthen the coherency, integrity, and radiance of the energies of self that make up the subtle body will aid us in this engagement. This is what I've been focusing upon up to this point in this book.

Certainly, the physical body plays an important role in supporting and influencing the condition of the subtle body, and, as we have seen, it can be the launching platform for extending our awareness and perception into the subtle vibrations of life. Likewise, our everyday, normal activity of thought and feeling, our psyche, can directly affect our subtle body and the energies that emanate from it. There is a fourth partner, however, which is equally important. This is our soul.

Conventionally, the soul is pictured either as something inside us or, because it normally operates at a higher dimensional frequency, as something existing "above us" on a higher plane. For instance, I could draw the relationship between soul, subtle body, psyche, and physical body something like this, a simpler version of Figure 1:

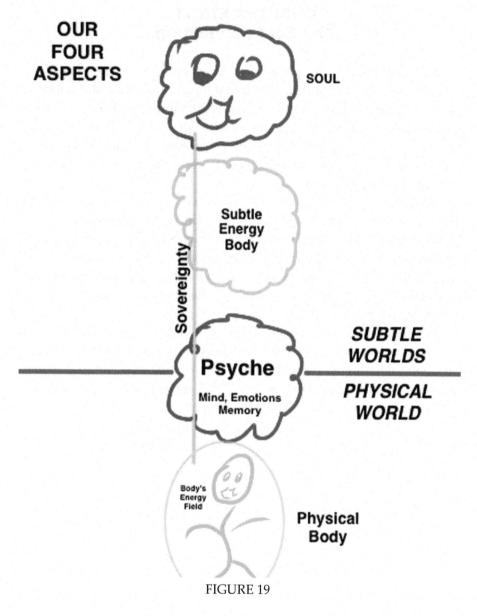

OUR FOUR ASPECTS

SOUL

Subtle Energy Body

Sovereignty

Psyche

Mind, Emotions Memory

SUBTLE WORLDS

PHYSICAL WORLD

Body's Energy Field

Physical Body

FIGURE 19

This would be a simple and familiar way of looking at the soul as existing at the top of a vertical, hierarchical structure and the physical body with its energy field at the bottom and what I call Sovereignty as an energy link connecting all four levels. (Note that, as we have seen in earlier chapters, the psyche is that part of us that can operate equally on either side of the "veil" between the subtle and physical worlds and thus provides a connecting function in its own right.) From one perspective, this is a perfectly useful and accurate way of looking at things. But it's not the only way, nor is it the most accurate.

We need to remember that these four aspects of ourselves and all they represent actually share the same space; they are interpenetrating frequencies; they are not stacked on top of each other like layers on a cake, however useful it may be to see them in this way. The soul is not simply "inside us" but is a field of energy and presence that is both within our bodies, infusing our bodies, and surrounding our bodies.

A different—and in my experience, more accurate way of looking at the soul and its relationship to incarnation—is seen in Figure 20 below.

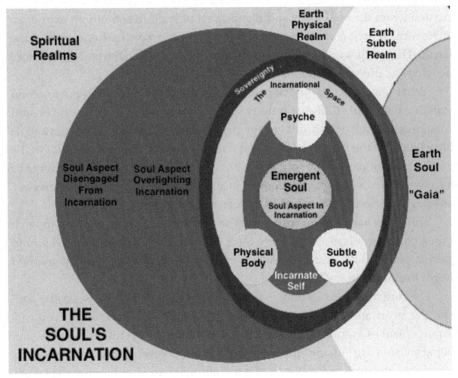

FIGURE 20

Here we see the soul as a single sphere with differentiated aspects. The soul does not so much "enter" incarnation the way a driver enters a car as it dedicates part of its energy, life and consciousness to engage with the soul, the subtle energies, and the physical substance of the Earth, i.e. with "Gaia." This is not all that different from how you might dedicate part of your life and attention to your work, your workplace, and the colleagues with whom you do your job. There is still a part of you left over that engages with other aspects of your life, with family, hobbies, and so on.

The effect of this is to create what might be called a "spectrum of soul's attention and engagement," ranging from deeply and fully attentive and engaged to rarely or not at all attentive and usually disengaged. We see this in Figure 20 with the three soul "aspects" from the part that is "in incarnation," the part that overlights and monitors the incarnational process, and the part that is busy and engaged on its own level of life and consciousness.

In this picture, I try to show how the part of the soul that is focused on the incarnation—on its "new job"—creates an "incarnational space" through the function I call Sovereignty. Here Sovereignty is portrayed not as a vertical line but as a circle or boundary that encloses and forms that space. It is a boundary created when the soul fuses and blends part of itself in something akin to an alchemical reaction with the physical, subtle, and spiritual energies of the Earth. The result is an incarnational "space" within which the embodying soul develops its physical body, psyche, and subtle body.

What also develops is what I call the "Emergent Soul." This is not a second soul or a new soul. Rather it is that aspect of the soul that learns, evolves, and changes as a result of its direct engagement with the Incarnational Realm and its blending with the subtle energies and with the soul or spiritual energies of the Earth. It is the part of the soul in which new qualities or capacities emerge as a consequence of being an embodied, incarnate self. One effect of this process, as I have previously described, is the generation of Self-Light.

This is not a mysterious process. It's very much like what would happen if I took on a new job as a carpenter. Over the months of doing this job, I would gain carpentry skills, and the knowledge and spirit of a Master Carpenter would begin to emerge in my life.

Looking at Figure 20 allows us to see the relationship between the soul and the incarnate self from a new perspective which the traditional "vertical" arrangement of Figure 19 does not allow. We can see that rather than the soul being somewhere "inside" the incarnate self, the reverse is true. In mysterious ways, our physical and subtle bodies are enfolded and held within the larger, more complex energy field of the soul. The soul doesn't "come down to earth"; the soul doesn't really go anywhere. Instead, it creates a dedicated "space" or field within itself, bounded by an act of Sovereignty, intentionality, and love, within which soul and planetary energies can meet, meld, and manifest an incarnate life.

In this context, death isn't so much the liberation of the soul from the body as it is the expansion of the Emergent Soul—which holds the basic identity that we think of as our personal self and the autobiography that has developed throughout the embodied life—into the larger, more spacious sphere of the soul in its wholeness and totality. This is like saying that if I lose my job as a carpenter and become an architect instead, I don't lose all my carpentry skills and knowledge; I take them with me to apply to the larger responsibilities and craft of architecture. These skills and knowledge are expanded in a new context.

Are we, then, not really in the physical world or the subtle environment at all? Are we actually in some domain of consciousness created and maintained by the soul within its own energy field, like a virtual reality simulation? As I've said before, trying to understand the relationships of physical and subtle realities and realms in a spacial way is doomed to failure. I can use words like "above" and "below," "within" or "without," "inside" or "outside," but none of them quite capture the permeable and interpenetrating nature of the situation. Is the television broadcast of my NBC channel "inside" or "outside" the broadcast of the ABC or CBS channels? Are they inside my living room? Is my living room inside them? These ways of describing these electromagnetic frequencies don't make sense. The same is true with trying to describe the relationship of the soul to the personality, body, and world in spacial terms. In the end, it doesn't work.

In my experience, the perspective presented in Figure 20 of the soul enfolding our life rather than being above it or inside it works better than a purely vertical perspective when it comes to engaging with the soul as part of my working with subtle energies. It lets me know that I don't have to "go" anywhere to contact my soul; I don't have to discover some occult means to attune to some higher heavenly realm. I am already held in the energy field and consciousness of my soul. What I need to do is to expand my consciousness into its larger embrace and the perspectives of connectedness and wholeness that come with it. So I look to those experiences or elements that will help me feel and think in a more spacious and expanded way. Joy does this. Beauty does this. Most of all in my experience, love does this. Entering into a loving state is the royal road into the soul.

If we look more closely at Figure 20, we can see that the energetic space circumscribed by the boundaries created by our Sovereignty is like a bowl. In it the spiritual and subtle energies of soul and planet are mixed and blended, creating for each of us the patterns and configurations that make up our unique incarnate self. I think of this space as our personal "Grail" space, using the metaphor of the cup that holds sacredness. In many ways, this is exactly what the incarnational space created by our Sovereignty is. It holds the sacredness of our soul in combination with the sacredness of the earth, allowing the alchemical emergence of a new expression of individuated sacredness: our incarnate self. I show this in Figure 21. It's as if we're looking down into the bowl of a chalice, seeing the elements that comprise the alchemical mixture of Self.

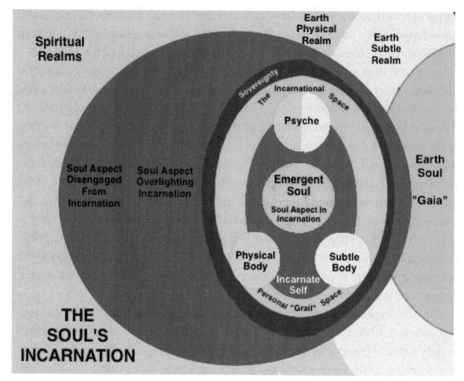

FIGURE 21

Although our subtle body is the immediate instrumentality for engaging with the subtle energies found in the subtle environments of the Earth, in fact our whole self is implicit in this engagement. I wrote of this earlier in Chapter 1. When we attune to our soul, we heighten the energy within the totality of this incarnational space, blessing body, mind, emotions, and our subtle field. We fill the Grail of our incarnational self with the spiritual energy and presence of the soul. This has a holopoietic effect, enhancing the wholeness and coherency of all parts of us, drawing them into greater integration and collaboration, which in turn strengthens what we bring to the encounter with subtle energies. Our identity is enhanced.

As I discussed in Chapter 2 and showed in Figure 5, my experience of the non-physical dimensions divides them roughly into two, the spiritual realms and the subtle worlds (there is a "mixed" zone between them that in my book *Subtle Worlds* I call the "Transitional Realms," but we need not concern ourselves with this in this context). The spiritual realms may simply be considered as realms of qualities, the qualities that generate and support the energies of life. Although we often identify these qualities with specific emotions and feelings, such as joy, love, peace, courage, serenity, and the like, they are much more than the emotional sensations we associate with them. Like the vitamins and minerals that sustain our bodies, these qualities are really building blocks of life, essential to the health and wholeness, coherency and integrity, of living systems.

These qualities are complex and powerful configurations of living energy and spirit. One of the functions of the soul is to receive these qualities from the spiritual realms around it and, acting like a transformer, "step them down" into forms more easily accessible to the subtle environments and the Incarnate Realm. The incarnate self with its personal Grail space is an essential part of this transformational process. When we attune to the soul and invoke its presence, we are also opening a channel through which the living qualities of the spiritual realms may pour into us, filling our incarnational Grail, and from us, pouring out into the surrounding world as subtle energies arising from our own subtle body, as Self-Light, and as blessings.

To some extent this transformational flow happens whether we are aware of it or not and whether we do anything about it or not, although in a person whose incarnational space is clogged with negative and disconnected, unintegrated energies and thus suffering from energetic incoherency, this flow is much, much less or can even be obstructed and blocked. When we make a conscious effort to attune to our soul and to the transpersonal levels of life, however, this flow increases as our openness and alignment widens the channels through which it flows into us and through us, into the world. I illustrate this relationship in Figure 22.

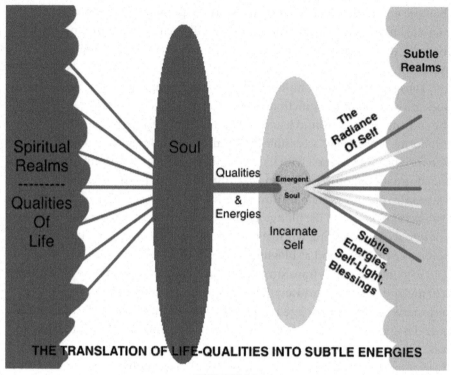

THE TRANSLATION OF LIFE-QUALITIES INTO SUBTLE ENERGIES

FIGURE 22

As I've said, when dealing with subtle energies, as much as we can, we want to do so as whole persons, engaging our physical, subtle, and spiritual aspects. Not only does this strengthen our identity and the integrity of our subtle energy field, but it gives us a more holistic engagement with the subtle energies themselves. After all, these energies are alive and sentient and have their own connections with the physical and spiritual realms as well as with the subtle environment. Even when they are defined by their specific vectors, they are still part of a living, whole universe. The more we can encounter them from our own wholeness, the more we engage with them in this universal context. Incorporating attunement to our own spiritual, transpersonal nature, our own soul, and through it to the transpersonal realms is an important step in this direction.

This can be important when dealing with subtle energies that have been damaged in some manner, cut off from their wholeness or given destructive and potentially harmful vectors. Sometimes our own Self-Light and the integrity and power of our own subtle body are enough to transform these negative and dysfunctional energies, but there are times when they are not. We may not be able to solve the problem at the level at which it is manifesting. Something more fundamental, more all-encompassing and life-affirming may be needed, which is exactly what the spiritual realms can offer. At such times, being able to draw such transpersonal assistance into the encounter through the mediation of our soul is exactly what is needed, both for our own safety and for the proper transformation and healing of the disconnected or damaged energies themselves. Spiritual qualities and transpersonal energies are holopoietic in nature and for this reason can restore wholeness to a situation when subtle energies with their particular vectors cannot.

Taking time to build a relationship with your soul through meditation, contemplation, prayer, ritual, or whatever methods appeal to you or are familiar and useful to you is time well-spent in gaining skills in working with subtle realms. What is important to realize, though, is that the transpersonal is not there to dominate the incarnate self and its personal energies but rather to forge a collaborative partnership in which each aspect of our being adds its particular gifts and talents to the wholeness we bring to the world.

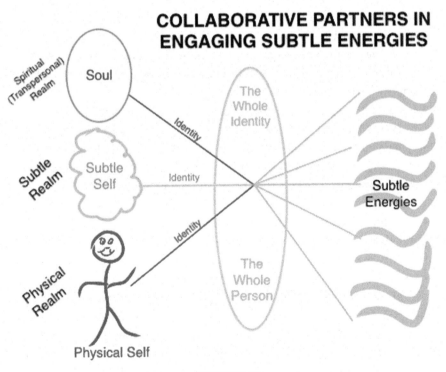

FIGURE 23

EXERCISES FOR CHAPTER EIGHT

Exercise: Attuning to the Soul

Attunement to the soul is an intimate relationship unique to each person in its character since in effect it's an act of internal unity and integration within a particular individual. The religions and spiritual philosophies of the world have given us many techniques and insights to facilitate such attunement. It is incumbent upon each of us to discover what works best for us. The following exercise is simply a suggestion based on Figure 21 in the preceding Chapter and the accompanying text.

- Imagine yourself held in a bowl-like space created by the presence of your soul.
- Imagine this bowl filling up with a loving energy of life coming from your soul. As it fills, it surrounds you the way the waters of a warm, comforting bath surround you.
- Allow this loving, life-affirming energy to penetrate all parts of you, bringing you vitality.
- Imagine a particular quality you would like to receive, something like joy or peace, love or compassion, courage or strength. Whatever it is, imagine this quality dissolving like bath salts into the fluid soul-energy surrounding you.
- Just let all parts of you absorb this quality as you soak in the energy of your soul.
- When you feel complete, imagine yourself absorbing this bowl and all its energy into your body and subtle field. Stand in your Sovereignty and Self-Light. Then go about your everyday business.

Exercise: Attuning to the Transpersonal

Overview

We attune to a transpersonal energy (whether from the soul or another source) by coming into resonance with its identity and function; in effect, we become an embodied "fractal" of the transpersonal source. Two ways we may do this are through the use of qualities and through the use of imagery. In both cases, we are expressing within ourselves something that corresponds to that which we are invoking, using a principle of like attracting like.

One important thing to note is that contacting a transpersonal level shouldn't feel like a strain. These levels are inclusive, rich with love, and are seeking connection with us as part of the larger wholeness of which they are aware as much as we may be seeking a connection with them. We may feel ourselves separate from our own transpersonal nature, but that higher wavelength of ourselves doesn't experience this separation.

So any clear intent to establish connection through resonance with the transpersonal level will almost certainly be met with a response. The trick is to not to tighten up or become over-anxious about "feeling something;" just be open and allow the connection to unfold in its own way.

Also, always remember that the transpersonal comes as a partner to the personal, not as an overlord or a dictator.

Part I—Qualities

One of the simplest and most effective ways of invoking a Transpersonal wavelength is to use a quality that corresponds to that which you wish to invoke. So, for instance, you could use a quality of peace or calm, one of courage or strength, or one of love. (Love, I find, is especially strong in this regard.)

- Determine the quality, Identity, or nature of that transpersonal force which you wish to draw into relationship with you.
- Identify a quality or set of qualities that to you correspond with this transpersonal force and its characteristics.
- Hold this quality or set of qualities in your mind and heart and allow the felt sense of it to fill you and your body. Draw it into your Presence.
- Imagine this felt sense expanding out around you with your Self-Light into your subtle energy field (as in the "Soma to Aura" exercise from Class Three).
- Mentally voice a clear invitation for a transpersonal partner who resonates to this quality or set of qualities to join with you in infusing, expanding, and enriching your Presence and the Self-Light and blessing you are jointly bringing to the world. Feel yourself opening to and welcoming this expanded wavelength.
- When you are complete with the subtle energy work you wished to accomplish, ground yourself. Give thanks to your transpersonal partner and ally and release the connection. Stand in your Sovereignty and then go about your normal daily business.

Part II—Imagery

The use of imagery is similar to the use of qualities but using more of a focus and shape to help engage with the transpersonal forces. It may be that finding the quality you want seems too abstract or you're not sure of the quality. Instead, imagine what kind of Transpersonal source or being would be most helpful as a partner in collaborating with your Presence and Self-Light. In this regard, we have been gifted in all the great religious traditions with a wide variety of images of gods, goddesses, sacred figures, saints, Masters, and the like that we can draw upon to get our imaginal juices flowing into a resonant connection. So, if the Christian tradition holds the most meaning for you, you could turn to the image and figure of Jesus or Mary or even one of the saints. What's important, though, is that whatever image you use brings you into contact and resonance with the realm of qualities (and it doesn't have to be the image of a person—it could be a landscape or a place, for instance, as long as it puts you in touch with a sense of a larger wholeness and the "feel" of the transpersonal). So if you used Jesus, let's say, this image should connect you with love, or the image of Buddha might connect you with compassion. In this way, the "path of imagery" blends into the "path of qualities" described above.

- Determine the quality, Identity, or nature of that transpersonal force which you wish to draw into relationship with you and your Presence.
- Imagine a figure, a place, or a condition that to you corresponds with this transpersonal force and its characteristics.
- Hold this image in your mind and heart. Feel yourself coming into relationship with this image and the qualities it represents. Allow the felt sense of this to fill you and your body.
- Imagine this felt sense expanding out around you into your subtle energy field (as in the "Soma to Aura" exercise).
- Mentally voice a clear invitation to a transpersonal partner who resonates to this quality or set of qualities embodied in the image you are holding in your imagination. Invite this partner to join with you in infusing, expanding, and enriching your inner Presence and the Light it radiates to the world. Feel yourself opening to and welcoming this expanded wavelength.
- When you are complete with the subtle energy work you wished to accomplish, take a moment to stand in your Sovereignty. Give thanks to your transpersonal partner and ally and release the connection. Stand in your Sovereignty and then go about your normal daily business.

CHAPTER NINE
The Spectrum of Love

Throughout this book, I've been describing subtle energies as alive and sentient and that the more we can engage with them through a loving and respectful relationship, the more successful we shall be. This is easy to say, but over the years, I've discovered in the many classes I've done that individuals don't always understand how to love. Or rather, they have an image of what loving means, and if they cannot match their feelings or actions to that image, they feel they are not loving or cannot love. This is particularly so if we believe that, in order to be spiritual, we need to love unconditionally, something that many people feel is beyond their capabilities.

Love is an act of connectedness, but there are many ways of forming connections. It is also an act of creating wholeness—i.e. of holopoiesis—but there are also different ways of bringing wholeness into being. Some of these ways are simple and may not seem like what we think of as "loving."

To put this in a sports metaphor, I don't have to be an Olympic runner to enjoy or benefit from a simple walk. The important thing is to get my body moving. This doesn't mean I have to run a mile in under four minutes.

In my work with the subtle worlds, while love is valued and always held up as an important part of engaging with subtle energies, there is an understanding that there's more than just one way to love. We could say that there is a spectrum of love.

There is nothing new to the idea that love exists as a spectrum of feelings and activities or that it can manifest in more than one way. The ancient Greeks identified four forms of love: *eros* or intimate and possibly sexual love; *storge* or familial love, such as parents for children and vice versa; *philia* or the bonds of friendship and the love that creates community; and *agape* or selfless, unconditional love, sometimes thought of as "spiritual" love, the love of the Sacred for all creation and of creation for the Sacred.

My own sense of a spectrum of love grew out of the work I did with my non-physical mentor, John. As I describe in my book about my training with John, *Apprenticed to Spirit*, he once gave me an assignment to love a man whom I had seen on TV. A predatory pedophile, he had committed a particularly heinous crime against a young boy. Seeing him on the news, I felt he looked more like a large, thin, ugly rat than a human being. I was filled with loathing and disgust not only for what he did but for him as an individual. Even thinking about loving him, much less actually doing it, was as far from my mind as it could be. I felt it simply wasn't possible for me. But John insisted, so I took up the challenge. It literally took me months to accomplish this, but eventually I was able to move to a place of truly opening my heart to this person and caring for his wellbeing. I discovered I really was able to love him, and in so doing, I discovered a vitally important capacity within myself.

There was no way at the time that I could leap from loathing directly to loving, but I could begin by simply being willing to acknowledge and accept his presence in the world. This was the lowest setting for me on my "dimmer light-switch of love." He became the focus of a daily meditation in which I would hold him in my mind and heart and try to turn that switch to a higher setting. In so doing, I experienced different ways in which loving could manifest, and from this, I began to develop the following ideas about the spectrum of love.

The first act of love is **perception**. At one level this is as basic as seeing that another exists at all. By perceiving, I am drawing that person into the field of my consciousness and awareness. I am saying inwardly, "I'm not shutting my eyes on you." I may not like the person or what he or she is doing or stands for, but as an act of love, I'm not blanking them out and saying he or she doesn't exist.

This act of seeing goes beyond a simple perception that someone or something is there. It is an act of deliberate, mindful awareness of the unique characteristics of the person who is seen. You are drawing them out of the background haze of perception, out of the abstraction of "humanity," and seeing them as a specific person. You may not like them. You don't have to like them. You may wish them to go away or for you to go away so that you have nothing to do with each other. At this stage of love, that's ok. But if you do move away from each other, you do so having seen the other.

To see the other is the opposite of ignoring the other. You are not treating the other as if he or she were not there at all, as if, like Mr. Cellophane in the musical Chicago, this person had no existence worth noting. You may not like that existence, but you are seeing it. If love is a way of valuing someone or something, you have to see that person or that thing is there before any value can be assigned.

When someone says to me, "I just can't love this person," my response is to say, "Well, don't try to be loving. Be perceptive." Taking the time and making the effort to see another may be the step that begins to open the heart and thus turn up the dimmer switch on your lovingness. Likewise, just feeling seen can lead another to open his or her heart, taking a step towards a better relationship.

The second stage is **acknowledgement**. This is very similar to perceiving, and the two can blend into each other, but I find it helpful to distinguish between them. To perceive is to say, "You exist." To acknowledge is to say, "You have the right to exist. I see that you are here in the world with me and you have a right to be here in the world with me."

We all see things in the world that we don't feel have a right to be here. When we see someone behaving in violent, abusive, and hurtful ways, we are right to say we don't want that kind of behavior to exist. But this is different from saying we don't wish the person to exist. If someone exists, he or she has the possibility of changing and transforming. If we take that existence away, no change is possible. Love in the form of simple acknowledgement opens up the possibility of change, redemption, growth, and blessing.

The third stage I call **honoring**. Honoring values the dignity of the other, a dignity rooted in their uniqueness as a soul and as a person. Honoring is saying, "You have a right to exist and to be different from me. I respect this difference and the potentiality it holds." This is where love as we usually think of it begins to show itself, for when we can honor differences, we can value the individuality of the other person, which is the basis of a healthy loving relationship. Love is all about valuing and nourishing a person's uniqueness, enabling his or her individuality to thrive and discover itself and to find appropriate ways of connecting to the rest of the world. If I deny you the ways in which you are different from me and I try to change you to be more like me, then I am not loving you in an honoring manner. I am denying you your individuality.

There is nothing about honoring that prohibits anyone from changing in order to better connect with another; it simply says that this is not necessary in order to be loved.

From honor grows **appreciation**. This is closer to the kind of affection and acceptance we often think of as love, though I can certainly appreciate someone without particularly liking him or her. I think of appreciation as being open to knowing you and through that knowing, valuing you. As I do come to know you, ways can emerge in which our differences can work together and become co-creative.

Appreciation is a recognition of the place another person (or an object) occupies in an interconnected cosmos. It's an acknowledgement of its participation in a larger ecology of being. Appreciation is an act of being aware of someone's or something's qualities and the connections they form with the world. Appreciation gives a sense of the part someone or something plays in the emerging wholeness of the world. In a way, to appreciate is to apprehend in the sense of being open to getting to know someone or something better and seeing them more clearly. Out of this can also grow a feeling of gratefulness that this person or thing exists in the world.

Appreciation leads to a sense of **caring**. Now I not only appreciate that which I love, I also feel a sense of participation in its well-being and perhaps even its destiny. I feel invested to some degree in what happens to the object of my love. I want to do what I can to help it find its own unique wholeness, identity, and fulfillment. As caring deepens, it becomes **affection**, a resonance of the heart and a sense of kinship that brings with it a desire for the highest good of that which I love.

As I deepen and broaden in my capacity for love, I begin to experience new depths of **connectedness** with the world around me. Out of this grows a sense of **identification** with the other, a realization that I and the other are an interdependent, interconnected part of an emerging, evolving oneness. At this end of the spectrum, love becomes what I call **holopoiesis**, the impulse or force that creates wholeness.

What about unconditional love? I feel there are times when this concept is misunderstood. There may be no conditions or reservations on love itself, but there can be conditions on how we use it to engage with another. We exist in a conditional world, and we need to honor this. There is nothing to prevent me from loving, but we need to understand how to express it in ways that don't damage another's boundaries or that are inappropriate.

Even in ordinary circumstances, I would like to fit my loving to what an individual actually needs or can receive. My love may prompt me to buy my wife a box of chocolates, but it will be more appreciated if I understand the specific kinds of chocolates she likes. We are each particular beings, not generic ones, and if we're going to love unconditionally and without reservation, we can still be aware and responsive to the particularities that determine the conditions of our lives.

Realizing that love is a spectrum that runs from perception and acknowledgement to affection and beyond has been very helpful for me. If I can't manage the "high end" of this spectrum in a particular circumstance, I don't have to give up and say, "I just can't love in this circumstance." I can find a place on this spectrum where I can start out and then I can work up from there.

We can be loving in a variety of ways that don't always look like the stereotypical images of "spiritual love" or "unconditional love" but which still embody the essence of the Sacred's primal gift. Of course we may strive for that kind of unconditional and compassionate love that we imagine is the province of saints, adepts and spiritual masters of one kind or another. But if love is a spectrum, then we don't have to have the dimmer switch set to "brightest" in order to express love, and that means we don't have to beat ourselves up, consider ourselves unworthy, or sit in judgment on our spiritual nature if the best we can muster is "well, ok, I see you and acknowledge you exist and have a right to do so." It is unloving to ourselves to beat ourselves up for our failure to be saintly!

What I have experienced over the years is that if I accept that "dim love" is better than no love at all, it doesn't leave me satisfied with that dimness but it doesn't leave me critical of my performance either. I accept what I can offer in a particular situation to a particular person in the moment, and that acceptance becomes a seed in my heart from which a fuller expression of love can grow.

The fact is that even mustering the effort and energy to perceive, to acknowledge, to honor, and to appreciate can be challenging and can exercise our "love-muscles" and contribute to opening our hearts more fully. We all start somewhere. Even winners of multiple Olympic gold medals started by crawling.

In short, as we turn the "dimmer switch of love" up towards increasing "brightness," we shorten the psychological and spiritual distance between ourselves and the person (or object) we are considering. We begin with "I see you but I don't necessarily want to know you or have anything to do with you," and move towards, "I appreciate you and am open to knowing you and having something to do with you." We are moving increasingly towards a love that is inclusive, accepting, and holopoietic.

Affirming your ability to love opens your heart to that inner presence that is so important to successfully working with subtle energies in ways that create and nourish wholeness.

EXERCISE FOR CHAPTER NINE

Exercise: The Touch of Love

- Fill yourself with a felt sense of lovingness, drawing on your Self-Light. You might imagine, for instance, your heart overflowing with love or your spine glowing with love.
- Feel this love flowing out from the core of your being, down your arms and into your hands. Feel this love pooling in your fingertips.
- Reach out and touch something. As you do so, feel the love in your fingertips overflowing. In this Touch of Love, you do not take anything into yourself. You do not really project it into anything, either. You simply let it pool in your fingertips and overflow, allowing that which you touch to absorb it in its own way.
- As love flows through your touch, it also stirs and flows and circulates through your own being, bringing love to all parts of yourself just as you are bringing it to the things you touch.
- Touch as many things as you wish. When you feel finished, just remove your fingers and allow the love to be absorbed into all parts of your body.

We touch each other's incarnations all the time. The energies we project to each other, the way we think of each other, the feelings we surround others with, the looks we give, the tones of voice, the words we use: all these are touches. But are they touches that help us to incarnate and help the incarnation of another, or do they hinder and obstruct? That is what only we can determine.

CHAPTER TEN
Joy

When I attune to the subtle environment around me, I can sense a layer of energetic activity that reflects the objects in the environment itself. For instance, the energy around my bookcase or the books upon it is relatively subdued, as I might expect from inorganic objects. By contrast, there's a lot of activity around the plants in the room, and I can feel the energies flowing between the various plants and trees in the yard outside. But if I attune more deeply to what's happening underneath all this surface activity, I become aware of a subtle force—a presence, really—that is bursting with vitality. It's as if I touch into a celebration of life itself, an uplifting vibrancy. I imagine that it may be what mystics experience when they speak of experiencing celestial choirs of angels singing. I call it *joy*.

I feel this joy emanating as much from my computer and my computer desk as I do from the maple tree in my backyard. It sings from the surrounding mountains as well as from the nearby lake. It vibrates with intensity from the rug beneath my feet as well as from the every other part of my house and the land on which it is situated. There is no place where this joy is not.

Joy is a particular frequency of subtle energy, and if I attune to it, I can easily fall into ecstasy. The interesting thing about it, though, is that it transcends what we think of as happiness and sadness. I can feel this energy of joy even when I'm emotionally down, feeling sad or afraid. And I can feel it when I am happy. In fact, the emotion of happiness, because it's pleasant in itself, can actually get between me and the deeper experience of joy itself.

We so often equate joy with happiness. Happiness, though, is associated with events, particularly those that bring us pleasure. Joy is an emanation of beingness itself. It is present whatever events are happening, no matter how wonderful or tragic. In the subtle worlds, joy is a quality of living energy. It is not an emotion, even though we may experience it in our emotional nature. In a manner of speaking, it's like sunshine, an empowering source of energetic vitality and nourishment.

In all the years of my association with non-physical reality, I have found joy to be ubiquitous. Healthy, flowing subtle energies are inherently joyous. On a surface layer, other qualities and energies may be experienced; there are definitely depressed, dark and angry—even hostile—subtle environments, often reflecting the thoughts and emotions of the humans who populate the physical counterparts of such environments. But what's on the surface doesn't negate what's underneath; in a very real way, the quality of joy is what permits subtle energies to exist even if they are expressing in damaged or negative ways. When a person brings the quality of joy to their work with subtle energies, it greatly increases the degree of attunement and response that one can experience.

Cultivating joy is an important practice in the life of anyone who wishes to work seriously and consistently with subtle energies.

When in my classes I have discussed the importance of joy, it's not unusual for someone to say, "How can I be joyful? My life is a mess!" or they protest that being joyful is naïve or even selfish in a world so filled with pain and suffering. Feeling joy, however, doesn't blind us to the sufferings of others. It enlarges and expands us beyond our own personal concerns. Joy gives wings to the heart. Depression and anger are stones that weigh it down.

Joy is inclusive and expansive; it empowers; it energizes. I'm more open to others when I'm joyous than when I'm fixated on sorrow. Joy opens the heart; it doesn't close it! I can be selfishly happy but not selfishly joyful. But fear, depression, despair can certainly make me insensitive. They can lead me to escape into my own pleasure, distraction, addiction to avoid the pain, to blunt the suffering, to take the edge from despair.

There is so much suffering in the world. It definitely demands a response from us, whatever we can do, however we can do it, to lessen that suffering. But denying joy is not an adequate or helpful response, from my point of view. It certainly does not help us in dealing with toxic or stuck subtle energies.

From a subtle energy standpoint, joy is a curative energy. It vitalizes and animates subtle energies that have become stuck, making it more likely that transformation and healing can take place. The more joy I can add to the world, the more there is to uplift and heal negative situations. Joy uplifts and transmutes; it totally alters the "chemistry" of a subtle environment, enhancing a vitalizing and healing flow of subtle energies that can in turn benefit any healing work being done on the physical and psychological levels.

Joy gives us a passion for the well-being of all and the courage to shape the world on behalf of that well-being. If we are serious about doing inner work, we need to give ourselves permission to be joyful.

This means paying attention when life brings joy to us. It is a cliché but still true that little things like sunsets and children's smiles can bring joy. For such a powerful force, joy can enter our lives in very small and trivial ways. Keep alert! Joy can ambush you at any moment. Be open to its arrival and its presence.

EXERCISES FOR CHAPTER TEN

EXERCISE: Joy Mining

In the subtle worlds, joy is more than just a feeling of happiness. It is a heightening, animating, vitalizing force. When we can hold joy in our hearts and minds, letting it permeate our energy fields, it acts like heat, getting things moving and flowing. But can we summon joy into our energy fields when we want to? For many people, joy is a result of something good happening. Absent that good event, where does the joy come from?

This is a simple practice that I call "joy mining." Think of yourself as deliberately looking for "nuggets" of joy in your daily affairs and drawing them into your field, depositing them in an inner "bank account". To do this, you need to realize that joy doesn't have to be a dramatic experience of ecstasy and pleasure. It can be very simple. What you are looking for are moments that hold the potential of heightening you and your energy. The trick is to make a habit of noticing and acknowledging them so that we begin to realize that truly joy abounds and is all around us and within us for us to draw upon.

What might constitute of "nugget" of joy? It could be anything that in the moment gives you a happy feeling. It could be the pleasure of a good cup of coffee on a cold morning. It could be a smile from a friend. It could be seeing the blue of a clear sky or hearing the soothing sound of rain on the roof. It could be a song you hear, a funny remark, a bite of something delicious. It may not be the joy of winning a lottery of thousands of dollars or the joy of getting married, but it's a nugget of joy nonetheless. The more we acknowledge and collect them, the "warmer" our subtle energy becomes, a warmth we can then send out into the world around us.

This exercise is simplicity itself. The moment you feel pleased by something or have a sense of happiness about something you experience, pause for a moment and "collect" it. You do this by acknowledging the moment and honoring its felt sense. Say to yourself something like, "This is a nugget of joy. In this moment, I am touching joy. Let it become part of me that I may radiate it onward and outward in my life." Then give a silent thanks for the moment. Gratitude and joy go hand in hand.

Do this throughout a day and see what develops for you.

Exercise: Joy Refining

In this exercise, you're taking the bits of joy you've been mining and refining them into a shining presence within you that you can offer back to the world for both energy hygiene and for protection. Central to this idea is the realization that you, like every other being and object on earth, are immersed and embedded in the living energy field of the Soul of the World. What becomes part of your personal energy field by induction flows out to become part of the field of the World. We all radiate energy into a common pool which we all share. A powerful act of service, then, is to bring joy into this common field, no matter how small that "nugget" of joy may seem to be. We really do not know and cannot measure the effect our gift of joy may have in creating a channel for the joy of the Sacred to pour through into the world.

In this exercise, you are taking all the nuggets of joy you've been collecting and "melting" them together in your imagination, refining them into a felt sense—a presence—of joy within yourself. Feel this joy in your body, in your heart, in your mind. Feel yourself filled with it and surrounded by it.

Once you have this sense of being in joy—of being joy—from the bottom of your feet to the top of your head, feel and imagine the quality of this joy radiating out from you into the world around you. For instance, I sometimes imagine this joy as a sphere around me shining its Light into the energy field of the surrounding environment. Then I imagine a spiral starting at my feet and spinning around me like a rising whirlwind of joyous energy, spiraling up above my head and sending joy into the Soul of the World to become part of the field of life from which we all draw.

Do this for as long as you feel comfortable. When you feel restless or tired, just bring your mind and heart back to your own body, your own joy, and allow the energy to settle within you. Stand in your Sovereignty and give thanks for the joy you receive and the joy you can share.

Remember, you *are* a generative source of joy when you choose to be.

PART 2
ENGAGEMENT

CHAPTER ELEVEN
Beginning and Ending

Like fish swimming though water, we are always in touch with the subtle energies that fill our environment, even if we are not always aware of this. Working with subtle energies, however, is a matter of paying conscious attention to this contact. It's an intentional act. As such it has a beginning and an ending and is shaped by both your environment and what you bring to the act out of your own wholeness. In this Chapter, I want to present the generic characteristics of this act of engagement with subtle forces. How do you start? How do you end? As for what happens in-between, well, that is unique to each such act and is for you to discover in the moment.

What does it mean to "work with subtle energies?" What exactly is this work? What is the "act of engagement" I'm talking about here?

Well, working with subtle energies can take the form of heightening and blessing the subtle energy environment around us, empowering the healthy flow of spiritual and subtle forces around us. It can be an act of "energy hygiene," of protection, cleansing, and healing. It can be an act of "subtle activism," bringing needed and helpful subtle forces to bear upon areas of the world that are in turmoil and in pain. It can be working with the incarnational and life forces of Gaia. In short, working with subtle energies can take many different forms, and I'll be exploring some of them with you in this Part 2 of this book. However, every act of engaging with subtle forces has certain common characteristics and has a beginning and an ending; it is bounded in both time and space.

Being Present

An experience of subtle energies can come to us unexpectedly in a moment of receptivity, when we are not entirely sure what is happening (or even that we want it to happen!). We may only be partly present to the experience. It may be exciting and stimulating, or we may shut it out or file it away as quickly as we can as an unwanted intrusion from some unknown dimension into our familiar world. If we are serious about working with subtle energies, however, then we must approach the experience as mindfully as possible, being present to ourselves and to our surroundings.

When I'm going to deliberately work with subtle energies, no matter what the objective of this work may be, I being by taking in what is there in my immediate environment: what it looks like, what it feels like, what is happening around me, and so forth. To be incarnate is to be in a specific place at any given time, not floating about, not spaced out. Although I'm going to alter my conscious awareness somewhat to connect with the subtle environment, I'm not leaving where I am. I'm still in a particular place, whether it's a room in a building or a space outdoors in nature.

Working with subtle energies requires awareness and attention, yet much of the time we go about our lives only half-present, lost in our thoughts and imaginations, planning what we're going to do next, thinking about our past, and generally only paying enough attention to avoid walking into things or being run over. More often than not, the environment—where we are—is treated like a backdrop or stage setting where we can perform our actions and have our relationships. And why not, for we generally believe that the environment is nothing more than dead matter or unconscious nature.

As I've been saying, though, this is not true of the subtle worlds and of subtle energies. As I said in Chapter 1, we exist in a living, sentient universe, something that becomes more and more apparent the more one attunes to and works with the subtle worlds. So to attune to that universe, the place to start is to acknowledge the life and spirit in the physical world around us.

My way of doing this is to find the wonder in where I am. It's easy to lose sight of the energy within things when we see them every day and our vision is clouded over with familiarity and a sense of "ordinariness." To feel the wonderment inherent in the things around me awakens me to the life within them. My own energy is heightened in the process.

What do I mean by "wonder" here? Well, I suppose it's akin to what I felt when I first went to Disneyland and felt the magic of the place. Of course, as an amusement park, it's designed to elicit such feelings. But any place can, when looked at properly and with fresh vision, present us with wonder at the magic and mystery of what exists within it. The main point is to appreciate the living energy in the environment and to stop seeing it as "dead" or "ordinary." When you can do this, you are already halfway to an appreciation and awareness of the subtle realms.

This appreciation of the wonder of where I am when I'm about to do a piece of inner work with subtle forces helps me to be more present. This is important. I want my energy to be coherent and integrated, both within myself but also with my immediate environment. If, for some reason, I don't like where I am, then I should change my environment if I can. If I can't, then I look for ways of inviting the environment to be an ally and of seeing it as a partner. I look for what I can appreciate and allow that to open my heart in a loving way to where I am. Otherwise, I have to work against that part of me that wants to be elsewhere or that is energetically trying to cope with or pushing back against the environment. I'm not fully present

Many people accomplish this by doing their inner work in a special place they've dedicated to it, or by performing a ritual to alter or shape the energies of the local environment. Both of these are excellent techniques, but my approach is more free-wheeling. I want to be able to engage with the subtle forces anywhere I am as a natural and organic part of my life. I may be in circumstances where doing a ritual is not feasible or in a place that is certainly not dedicated to inner attunement and spiritual work. I don't want the environment or circumstances to limit what I can draw upon from within myself, and if possible, I want to make the environment my ally by approaching it with appreciation, respect, and love. In short, I want to be as present as possible to where I am and who I am before opening myself to the currents of the subtle worlds.

Boundaries

It's important in working with subtle energies to establish boundaries for your work. These are boundaries of space, time, and intent. You want to be clear about what you're trying to do and the specific objective of your inner work. You want to be clear about where you're doing it and how large a space or how many people or objects you're attempting to affect in an energetic way. And you want to be clear about beginnings and endings and how long the effect you're intending should last. So, for example, if my purpose is to cleanse a room of negative energies, I'm not trying to deal with all negative energies throughout the world that have existed since humanity began acting as self-conscious beings with free will. I'm not working with generic "negative energies" as a category. I'm working specifically with a defined place—a particular room—which has within its walls, which are its boundaries, a particular kind of negative atmosphere—it's filled with angry energies, for instance—and I'm dealing with these energies as they manifest right now.

Of course, in the subtle worlds, boundaries are very permeable, and what affects one area will definitely have an effect in connected areas. But for your purposes, you need to focus on the specifics of what you are trying to accomplish, keeping it within a scale that you can manage. You want to honor and pay attention to the local conditions.

If you are working in a room in a building, the walls, floor and ceiling of the room provide a natural boundary to define your work. If you only want to affect a specific part of a room for some reason, then you need to hold in your mind very clearly where you are drawing the boundary and thus where you wish the effect to happen and where you don't. If you are outside where there are no walls, you need to use the configuration and elements of the natural environment and landscape to determine your boundaries, again holding them in your mind like imaginary walls within which your work will take place. For instance, if I want to do some energy work in my backyard, I don't want to deal with all the energies flowing through or rising from my whole neighborhood.

So I visualize a curtain of energy around my backyard and specifically state my intention of only working within the bounds of this curtain.

This does not mean that the effect of such energy work may not or cannot flow outside the space within the indicated boundaries, but if it does, it will do so naturally and organically through the connections that space has with the larger environment. The point is that *I'm* not trying to influence that whole larger environment; my focus and intent is within a specific set of parameters.

If I fail to pay attention to boundaries, then my efforts can become diffused over too large a volume of space and time or I can be overwhelmed by trying to take on too much all at once. Establishing intentional boundaries is important in almost all instances of working with the subtle worlds.

The Stance

When a martial artist is getting ready to engage in combat, she adopts whatever stance is basic to her technique. Being in the right physical position, as well as being poised, balanced, and alert, allows her to respond quickly and appropriately to the moves her opponent makes. Whatever subtle work you wish to do, whether it's blessing, cleansing, protecting, subtle activism, or something else, you also want to do so from a poised place of generativity and strength, inner balance and presence, alignment and connectedness. This creates a heightened field around you that you can focus through your intentionality, imagination, and will. I think of this inner posture of coherency and connectedness as the "Stance."

THE
STANCE

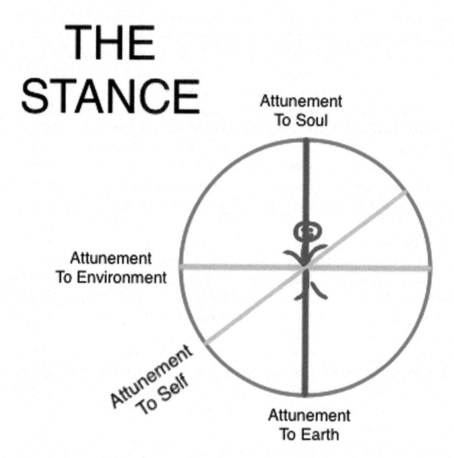

The Whole Person

FIGURE 24

This is important because when working with subtle energies, the state and quality of your own personal subtle field helps shape the subtle energy environment around you. There are exceptions to this; sometimes, the energies inherent in a particular place will have been "stuck" and stagnant for so long that they will possess an inertia that resists change. But most of the time, the rule of thumb is this: shape yourself energetically, and you begin to shape what is around you.

In entering the "Stance," you gather your own subtle energies and inner resources, heightening your own energy field. This is the time when you want to stand in your Interiority, in your Sovereignty and Self-Light, honoring your personhood and identity. You attune to your body and you bring your thoughts and emotions into a clear and poised space. You attune to your soul and its links to the transpersonal, spiritual realms. You attune to the Earth, and you attune to the environment around you. You do this in your own unique way, creating your own individual way of being in the "Stance."

The "Stance" reminds us that we don't exist in isolation. We are each connected to the planet on which we stand, to the lives around us, and to our own soul and its transpersonal realms, as well as to the depths of our own minds and hearts. We are a unity that embraces and integrates all these connections, and it is from the coherency of this integration that we want to engage with the subtle realms. This coherency is our inner center of gravity, our energetic equivalent to the center of gravity of our body which plays so much a part in the practice of martial arts, dance, and other movement-oriented activities. It is the center of our identity as a whole person.

The object of the "Stance" is to begin your inner work from a place of inner coherency, integration, and balance, standing in your identity and heightening your energy with love and appreciation as you begin to expand into your subtle awareness and energy field.

Guy Wires

One way of engaging with the local environment that I have found very helpful when working with subtle energies is the use of what I call "guy wires." This is simply a way of connecting in specific, energetic ways through love and appreciation with my immediate physical environment. I discovered this principle in working with my non-physical mentor, John. He would come to me from a higher dimension, and he always carried a great deal of energy and Light with him. I found that if I took time to mentally and lovingly reach out to the life in the things around me—like the chair I was sitting in or a nearby table or lamp, or to the floor and walls of the room I was in—then this broadened out the field of my own energy and made it much easier to take on John's presence. In effect, I created a collaborative field with the environment around me by connecting to specific things in that environment. Then I could distribute his energy within this field. This was hugely helpful in enabling me to keep my own inner balance.

The principle is not that strange. We do it all the time when we use guy wires to support a tall pole or tower which otherwise might be top-heavy or liable to sway or topple over. Or to use a different image, it's the difference between catching a falling man yourself or using a net held up by several people. In the first instance, you have to deal with the kinetic energy of the man, which may be overwhelming, but in the second instance, this energy is spread out through the net so that no one person has to bear the full load.

As with being present, it's a matter of making the local environment—or specific things within the environment—your ally as you work with subtle energies. When I do this, I take a moment to pay attention to each of my chosen anchors and find the felt sense of a line of energy extending from me to that object, linking us in a loving and appreciative bond that is mutually supporting. When I do so, I can feel my own subtle energy field expanding, becoming what I call a "collaborative field" held between me and the "anchor objects" for my energetic guy wires. I illustrate this in Figure 25.

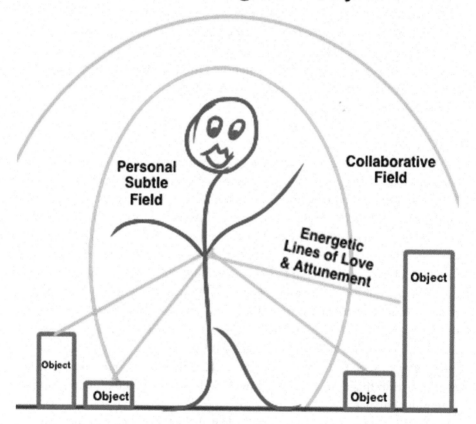

"Tower" with Energetic "Guy Wires"

Personal Subtle Field

Collaborative Field

Energetic Lines of Love & Attunement

Object

Object

Object

Object

EARTH

Attunement to Environment Creates Collaborative Field & Grounding

FIGURE 25

Opening Out

I described this process in Chapter 4. It's a matter of extending and expanding your awareness into your subtle field. For me, the process is this: you attune to your body and gain an awareness of yourself as a physical being. Then, you stand in Sovereignty and in the strength of your identity, aware of yourself as a unique, generative, strong, integrated individual. (You've already done this in your "Gathering.") Then you expand this into your proprioceptive awareness, the sense of your body in space, enlarging this "space" with your imagination, expanding it into the subtle energy field around you. You make the shift from physical to subtle awareness as you did with the threshold and candle exercise in Chapter 4. At this point, you have moved your awareness from "soma" to "aura." This is illustrated in Figure 26. Once you have the felt sense of being in touch with your subtle energy field and with the subtle environment around you, you can begin your intended inner work.

Remember that this subtle awareness may not manifest itself through sight or sound. The subtle body has its own way of sensing its environment and, as I have written earlier, this sensing may not take familiar forms. You may experience this subtle sense throughout your body as a field sense or somatic experience rather than as a special sense like sight or hearing. It may seem more like touch or pressure, or it may be a sensation all of its own which your brain will need to learn through practice to recognize and interpret. The important thing, though, is that you are projecting and establishing your presence as a radiant energy source within the local subtle environment, and this will begin to have an effect on the subtle energies around you. At this point, you can begin to do your work, whatever it may be.

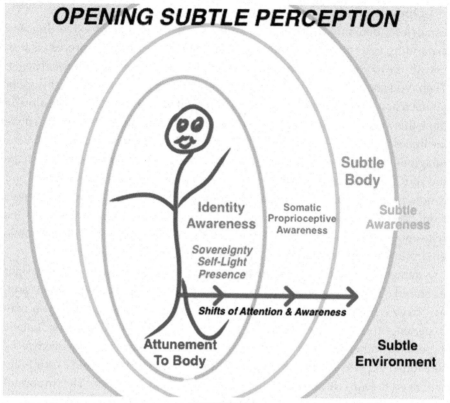

OPENING SUBTLE PERCEPTION

FIGURE 26

Shaping Subtle Energies

Many esoteric, metaphysical and spiritual teachings refer to the power of the mind to influence and shape subtle forces. "Energy follows thought" is an often used maxim. In other words, your thoughts about what you wish to accomplish or what you wish subtle energies to do provide the power to make it so. This technique is much applied in popular practices of manifestation which depend on "the power of positive thinking" and on affirmations. (For a different approach, see my book *Everyday Miracles* or the *Manifestation Card Deck*.)

There is no doubt that our thoughts do influence and shape subtle energies. However, there are two qualifications to this. The first is that what we commonly call "thought" is often not much more than carrying on an internal conversation with ourselves; it's a stream of consciousness largely defined by words. This kind of thought doesn't generate much mental energy, and when it comes to influencing subtle energies, in most cases it's the felt sense of the meaning behind the words that carries the power, rather than the word itself. This is one reason a clearly held image may have much more ability to shape subtle forces than a sentence made up wholly of words. In short, when it comes to generating energy that our subtle body can use in engaging with its subtle environment, words and what often passes for "thinking" fall short.

The second qualification follows on from this. We are more than just thinking or mental beings. Ever since the Age of Reason, we're privileged thought as the defining characteristic of what makes a human being. But thinking is only part of who we are. We possess a physical body, emotions, and a soul as well. Our feelings, sensations, intuitions, and inspirations are part of us as well. What we want to bring to our engagement with the subtle worlds is our whole being. We want to stand in our wholeness, which is really what the "Stance" is all about. From this inner posture, we generate Presence, and it's this Presence, shaped by our intentionality, our imagination and thought, and our will, that has the greatest impact and influence upon the subtle environment and the energies within it.

Here's a way to picture this. Imagine you see someone doing something wrong. You can yell, "Stop!" and he may or may not listen to you. Your words by themselves may not be enough to change his behavior. Or, in addition to saying "stop," you go over and physically engage with him, perhaps holding him so that he cannot continue his actions. Now you are acting with your "full body presence," which gives you much more impact and influence than your words alone.

Working with subtle energies is not any different. A mental or emotional command will have some effect but often not enough to accomplish your intent. What is needed is your full presence. I suggest this process in Figure 27.

As you can see, thought, intentionality, imagination and will are all important. But they provide a lens that actually focuses and channels the real power which is that generated by your expression of your Presence. Instead of "energy following thought," it is more accurate to say that "energy follows beingness." The state of being you adopt and manifest when working with subtle energies is what will influence and shape those energies to accomplish your purpose.

ENGAGING SUBTLE ENERGIES

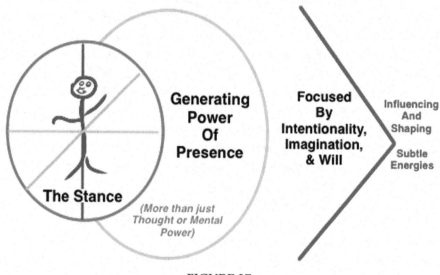

Generating Power Of Presence

The Stance

(More than just Thought or Mental Power)

Focused By Intentionality, Imagination, & Will

Influencing And Shaping

Subtle Energies

FIGURE 27

So What Does Subtle Work Feel Like?

Since subtle work takes place in dimensions beyond normal sight and hearing, from the outside it can look as if a person doing such work isn't doing anything. He or she may simply be standing or sitting in a calm way or perhaps moving about, but there's no outer indication of what is happening.

What, though, does it feel like to you when you are doing the inner work? How do you know when you're actually doing something and having an effect?

This is something you will need to discover for yourself. It's like asking what it will feel like when you fall in love. No one can exactly describe what this experience will be like for you, other than to say that you'll probably recognize it when it happens. You are a unique individual and your relationship would be with another unique individual. No two people exactly like you have ever fallen in love before, so no one can say just what the experience will be like for you.

But millions of people *have* fallen in love, so there are common experiences that can be looked to for some guidelines. Likewise, many people have experienced the subtle realms and know what it's like to work with subtle energies. You can certainly do some research to see what others have felt, though if you do, remember that your experience may be and probably will be different for you. So don't expect or try to mimic what another has experienced.

Here is what I experience when I work with subtle energies. As I shift my attention from "soma" to "aura," that is from my physical body to my subtle body, I have a felt sense of expanding. I feel a sense of spaciousness. I have a sense of becoming "rounder," as if I'm now embodying a sphere rather than a vertical body. As I pay attention to the boundaries of this sphere, I begin to feel sensations there; I'm aware of a play of energies on the surface of this sphere. At the same time, as I feel this, images and information begins to appear in my mind. This is my brain interpreting what these sensations feel like and what they mean. I've had practice at this. If you were doing this for the first time, you might not know what these sensations are like or what they mean, only that they are present. However, it's been my experience that in some way my physical body will respond to what is happening to and around its subtle counterpart, giving rise to physical sensations as well.

This is where imagination plays an important role, just as it does in normal perception. It offers a way of interpreting or representing these sensations and impressions. As I described in Chapter 5, we commonly think of imagination as a faculty for "making things up," but it's so much more than that. Think of it instead as a faculty for thinking in images or as a faculty for translating the subtle impressions coming from the subtle field into comprehensible information, often in the form of spontaneously arising images (especially if we've taken the time to develop a "vocabulary" of images to draw on).

Thus, the feelings and sensations arising from the engagement with subtle energies begin to shape images in my mind which help to convey information to me. More importantly, it's not just mental pictures that develop but an accompanying felt sense. Subtle contact for me is a whole person experience, not just a mental, emotional, physical or imaginal one, though one of these modes may predominate.

Closing

Closing a session of subtle work is as important as the opening. After doing inner work, you want to return to your daily life in a whole and integrated fashion. You don't want to have stray, unintegrated threads of connection remaining between you and whatever subtle forces you were working with. You opened a door into a specific level of working subtle awareness, and when you're done, you want to close that door. It's part of establishing the boundaries within which you are working.

Doing so is a matter of reversing the process shown in Figure 25. I begin by thanking the energies with which I've been working and stating that I am now disconnecting from them. I visualize any "threads" or lines of connection between my energy field and the energies with which I've been engaged now separating and dissolving. I hold a clear intention about closing down any connections between myself and the subtle work I've been doing. I then focus my attention back on my own identity and my own body, in effect moving my consciousness in the opposite direction from that shown in Figure 25 until I feel fully present in my own body. I then thank my environment and the objects that have served as anchors for my energetic "guy wires." I complete the process by standing in my Sovereignty.

Highs and Lows

It is not uncommon for subtle energy work to give us a feeling of being energized and even "high," especially while it's in process, and then leaving us feeling "low" afterward. If we personalize this, it can affect us emotionally as it can seem like being on a roller coaster rising into exuberance and then crashing into depression. How much we experience this—or how we experience this—depends on our overall emotional makeup and our experience.

The fact is that we are energizing ourselves to start with, and our contact with various subtle energies, particularly if they are coming from a highly energetic source, can further energize us. We can feel great in the moment, like riding an emotional or mental high. However, subtle work is just that: work. It takes energy the same as physical labor does, and it will leave us tired, even on a physical level. After being and working with my non-physical mentor, John, I always felt hungry and usually had a snack. Further, when we "come back" into our body, so to speak, and shut down our expanded connections to the subtle world, we return to our natural energy state, which by contrast can feel less energetic. We go from the "high" to a "low."

If we understand what is happening, we can easily shrug this off. Some rest, some physical exercise like a walk, something to eat or drink can all restore us very quickly. The point is to be aware that this can happen and not be alarmed if you suddenly feel like crashing emotionally and physically after doing some inner work. With experience, this effect is greatly minimized, but I've found after more than fifty years of inner work, it never goes away entirely. There is a natural energy differential between the physical world and its subtle counterparts. Go back and forth across that threshold can be like walking up and down a hill. You build up your muscles with practice so it bothers you less and less, but you never forget that there's a hill.

Grounding

One important way to deal with this phenomenon of energy differential is through grounding. Many inner states create a different energy condition or mode of consciousness than what we are used to; "coming back" means crossing that energetic differential which can pose some challenges of its own. Some consequences are that we can feel disassociated, drifting, light-headed, or out-of-touch with ourselves, as if we're not "all here." We may have information that we don't know what to do with, images we can't interpret. We can feel restless, filled with energy, or in the opposite direction, we might feel depressed, enervated, and sleepy.

If you find after working with subtle energies that there are forces or sensations that linger that make you feel ungrounded, you can take further steps that can help you be more integrated into your body. Remember, your body is your ally here. It is an organ of grounding in itself. Imagine an Intelligence within you, like the intelligence of your physical immune system, that fully knows how to receive, distribute, assimilate, integrate, and release subtle energies. Ask this Intelligence to be your ally in integrating the results of any inner work and in appropriately releasing or transmuting anything you cannot integrate. Trust in this Intelligence and let it do its work.

Self-awareness is a large factor in grounding and integration. When you ground and integrate subtle energies, they become part of you. The sensations seem to disappear, just as the taste of the food you eat disappears as the food is digested and assimilated. You need to be willing for this to happen. Sometimes when people have a powerful spiritual or energetic experience and feel exalted or ecstatic as a result, they want to hang on to that experience and not let it go. This is literally like holding your food in your mouth so you can continue to taste it but not letting yourself swallow it so that it can actually nourish you. Feelings of specialness, of glamour, of not liking your everyday self or the physical world around you—in short, feelings and thoughts of separation rather than of integration make grounding more difficult. Self-awareness and trust are keys to resolving this.

There are many ways of grounding yourself. You need to experiment with what works best for you. The important thing is recognizing when you need it. I offer some suggestions in the Exercise section of this chapter.

EXERCISES FOR CHAPTER ELEVEN

Exercise: The Stance

The "Stance" is simply a reminder that when you work with subtle forces, you want to stand in a particular state of being, one of alignment, presence, and connectedness: the stance of being a whole person generating presence. This exercise draws on the felt senses that you have been practicing in previous exercises.

- Standing in Sovereignty, fill yourself with the felt sense of your generative identity, your coherency, and your Self-Light. You are poised and ready to act from the strength and power of your wholeness and Presence

- Align with the felt sense of your soul within you and your openness and attunement to transpersonal levels of Life. Fill your energy field with the love and joy that are the essential qualities of the soul. You are poised and ready to act to support and nurture the healing and empowering energies of Life.

- Connect to the Earth beneath you and to the surrounding environment and the life around you with appreciation and honor. You are poised and ready to act with the power of love and joy to engage the subtle environment around you in whatever way is appropriate and needed.

- Attune to this connectedness with self, soul, and other (Earth and environment). Feel its coherency and wholeness, its strength and balance. Feel the flow of subtle energy circulating through your being and around you as a result of this connectedness. Feel the confidence and poise that comes from this state of being.

- Pay attention to the felt sense in your body, your mind, and your feelings of being filled with this poised, coherent, balanced inner Presence. This is the felt sense of your "Stance." Remember it so that you can step into it anytime, anywhere, under any conditions

Exercise: Guy Wires

In this exercise, you are creating energetic "guy wires" or lines of attunement with your immediate environment using various objects in that environment to do so. I now do this automatically whenever I'm working with any kind of non-physical phenomena. It helps to ground and anchor me in the specific place where my body is, and it creates a collaborative field of energy that supports the subtle work.

- Begin by standing in your Sovereignty, feeling the strength and integrity of your identity and personhood. See this as a "spine" of Light within you. Let this Light expand out into your subtle field.
- Take a moment to attune to the felt sense of being in your energy field (moving from "soma to aura").
- Looking around you, pick four or five objects in your immediate surroundings to be anchor points. You can use pieces of furniture, the floor, the walls, plants, anything that's stationary and won't move out of the environment while you're working (in other words, don't use animals or people). You can certainly use the earth itself as one of the points of connection.
- In whatever way feels comfortable to you, from your energy field extend a felt sense of appreciation, love and attunement to each of these objects, imagining a line of energy running from you to the objects. Ask their help in creating a collaborative field of energy within the environment that will be your ally and help you with both grounding and with working with any subtle forces. Invite the sacred life within these objects to partner with you.
- Do you have a felt sense of a larger field of energy coming into being in the environment around you as you make these connections and invite this partnership? If so, expand your sense of your own field into this larger field, this collaborative field.
- How does it feel to stand in this larger field as compared to being in your personal field alone?
- When you are finished with whatever inner work you are doing, give thanks to the space around you and to each of the objects that you used to anchor your energetic "guy wires". Then withdraw your energy back into your own field, ground yourself, and finish by standing in your Sovereignty.

NOTE: The object of most of these exercise/experiments is to gain a felt sense of a particular mental, emotional, and physical state. Thus, the idea of the "guy wires" is really to gain a felt sense of being in tune with, anchored in, and energetically supported by the living presence of your local physical environment when you are engaging with non-physical phenomena. Once you have this felt sense of attunement to where you are, the image of "guy wires" is unnecessary. It's the attunement and the resulting sense of a collaborative field of energy that is the objective, however you arrive at that inner state.

Exercise: Grounding

Here are some suggestions for ways of grounding yourself after an inner experience.

1. Just sit, taking a moment to recollect yourself. Remember what you may have just experienced. Be aware of any energies, sensations, images, feelings, and thoughts you may be experiencing. Be mindful of how they are affecting you, if at all.

2. Stretch while sitting. Be mindful of any places in your body that may be feeling tense. Breathe into those parts and stretch or rub them. Feel the strength and vitality of your body. Feel the miracle of your physical nature. Feel gladness at being in your body. This helps ground you physically. Stand in your Sovereignty.

3. Look around you at where you are. Pick out at least one thing in your environment that you love or that pleases you. If it is within reach without getting up or moving about, touch it and feel the pleasure of that touch. Be glad to be back with it again. Remember and feel at least one thing that gives you enthusiasm and pleases you about your life and who you are. Be glad to be yourself. Be glad to be part of the physical world. This helps ground you emotionally.

4. Think about what you have experienced and any information, understanding or insight that you now have as a result of the inner work, meditation or journey just completed. Have a notepad or journal nearby and immediately write down anything you want to record. This helps ground you mentally.

5. Give thanks for your blessings. Appreciate all that is around you. Be aware without invoking any particular energies that you are part of spirit, you are part of the sacred. Feel the presence of spirit in the world and in your life. Connect to your sense of spiritual sovereignty and the gift and power inherent in your unique individuality. Embrace yourself in a loving feeling. Remember with gratitude someone or something that you love and care for and embrace them in a loving feeling. This helps ground you spiritually.

CHAPTER TWELVE
Sensing

Once you have shifted your awareness and sensitivity into your subtle field, the first step in any subtle energy work is simply to sense as fully and as best you can just what the energy environment is like and what forces are active within it. After all, if there were a situation at your home or work that required you to take some action to address it, your first step would be to determine just what was going on. You would want to assess the situation in order to understand what appropriate steps you should take to make things better and not make them worse. Working with subtle energies in the non-physical environment requires this kind of assessment as well.

In Chapter 2, I offered a basic definition of subtle energies as I understand and have experienced them. I said that there were basically four types: energies of self, pattern, and configuration; energies of connection and communication; energies of blessing, and a substrate of basically neutral energies waiting to be shaped or patterned in some fashion. These four categories are very generic and do not take into account subtle energies that have been damaged, disconnected, or given a negative, hurtful spin in some way. For a more complete picture, we need to look more specifically at some of the different forms subtle energies can take and what you might encounter as you work with them.

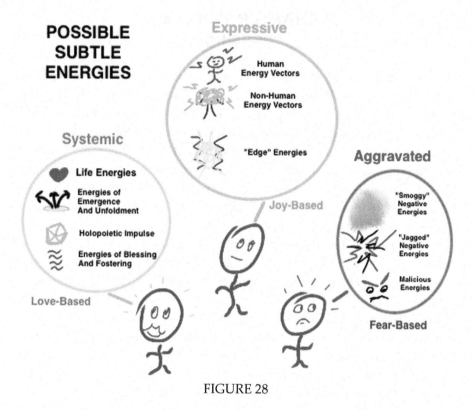

FIGURE 28

Figure 28 shows some of the kinds of subtle energies I have experienced over the years and the reactions they can produce; it's a "visual field note." Given the vast range of possible manifestations of subtle energies and forces, it is by no means complete. But it can get us started in learning to sense and identify what is present in the non-physical environment.

I discern subtle energies primarily by the effect they have on my own subtle field. In a way, it's like knowing what direction a wind is blowing or how fast its going by feeling its impact on my skin, or knowing it's raining by feeling the raindrops falling on me. As I said in Chapter 4, the perception of subtle energies does not necessarily correspond to sight or hearing.

Imagine you've walked into a cocktail party. There's a general buzz of conversation, some of it intense, some casual, some argumentative, but none of it necessarily demands your attention. There are some conversations, though, that are stimulating and inspiring, leaving you feeling better. On the other hand, there are some corners of the room where people are actually cursing one another in violent disagreement and being decidedly unpleasant and unfriendly. As much as possible, you'd like to avoid getting involved with that group, while on the other hand, you seek out the more inspiring group. All the other activities and conversations are just background noise, important to those involved in them but not requiring your attention.

Broadly speaking, subtle energies impact me in ways analogous to these three states in a cocktail party. They can be vitalizing and enriching, making me feel better than before; they can feel relatively neutral or at worst a bit turbulent, though no one is getting hurt. Or they can feel damaging and irritating, aggravating my subtle field in some manner. They may even feel malicious and dangerous.

I show this in Figure 28 in the three separate circles, one labeled *systemic*, one *expressive*, and one *aggravating*. Each circle shows the kind of subtle energies that they embrace (understanding that these "circles" can overlap).

The subtle energies that I call "systemic" are everywhere. They are made up of fundamental life energies, energies of emergence and unfoldment, the holopoietic impulse, and energies of blessing and fostering.

Life energies are the fundamental animating forces within anything, not just within those organic entities we call "living." They are found within atoms as readily and fully as within antelopes. Although it could be said that really there is only one life energy, which emanates from the ultimate source of creation, it is modulated or modified by various levels and types of consciousness. The analogy is with water: all water has the same chemical composition, but it can have a variety of different things dissolved in it, giving it a different taste and effect. Thus you can have fresh water, your basic, universal H_2O, but you can also have sparkling water, lime-flavored water, lemon-flavored water, salty water, caffeine-water, and so on. Thus, even if there is a fundamental, universal life energy, most things on the earth also manifest a variation of it that is "flavored" by a variety of sources which in our case would be by Gaia, by our own souls, by our personal, incarnate natures, by our bodies, and so on.

Although understandably they might be considered a natural part of the expression of life energies, what I'm calling the *energies of emergence and unfoldment* have a quality of their own. They possess directionality, a sense of yearning and power moving towards a desired state. There is a sense of potential seeking expression. If life energies feel like a "field" to me, then these energies of emergence feel more like a current flowing in a particular direction—the difference, say, between a still pond or lake and a river.

Most everything is in a process of learning and unfoldment, moving and emerging from one state to another. This may be a very slow process, one lasting years, dozens of years, thousands of years, or even millions of years, or it may be very fast, depending on what it is. However slow or quick the process of this emergence may be, I have often felt the energetic presence of this impulse towards unfoldment in the things around me. I have felt it, for instance, in the substances that make up my house, the furniture, the carpet on the floor, and so on. It may seem strange to think of my coffee cup as evolving, and in fact it's not evolving as a coffee cup. But the life within the atoms of the different materials that make my coffee cup has potentials that are seeking to unfold. The energy that makes up the coffee cup can be heightened and can become more "awake" or "aware," energetically more responsive. There is a sentiency in the energies and materials that form my coffee cup, and it's a sentiency that can evolve.

I sense this energy of emergence either as an active force—that is, evolution or unfoldment is happening as I sense it—or as a potential, a kind of yearning. This is not an emotional state. It's more like a tropism in a plant, an instinctive bending towards the light or towards a source of water or food. Whatever potentials for unfoldment exist within a particular expression of life and consciousness, the energy of these potentials will move along a gradient towards any source of energetic nourishment that can foster the realization of these potentials. The more the object is "heightened" or "awakened," the more powerfully it will move along that gradient and absorb what it needs from the energy currents about it. This forms the rationale behind a particularly powerful kind of subtle energy work that I'll discuss in Chapter 16.

Interestingly, I sense this impulse towards unfoldment within collective fields as well. For instance, when a group of people get together, the field they create has its own potentials, and within it, there will be an impulse of varying strength, depending on the group, its intentions, and how long it stays together, to realize those potentials. This can be happening whether the individuals are conscious of it or not.

The third kind of energy I can sense in the subtle realms is one I call the *holopoietic impulse*, or the impulse to connect and create coherency and wholeness. I've discussed this earlier in the book. Subtle energies seem to want to be connected and to have interaction; they seem to want to cohere in ways that create larger, more complex patterns of flow and exchange. I have sensed this holopoietic energy in things, in people, and in places and situations. There's always a boundary of some nature that defines the nature and limits of the coherency and integration, but then these boundaries become themselves participants in creating still larger systems of wholeness. So atoms seek to be whole internally but also to connect with other atoms to create a new wholeness called an element or a molecule; cells are holopoietic within themselves but also in relationship to other cells, creating multicellular organisms. The same urge towards greater states of connection and complexity exists in the subtle realms as much as in the physical.

These three subtle energies—life, emergence, and holopoiesis—are fundamental. I sense them operating everywhere and in everything. Indeed, they are the same basic forces at work in what I call our Interiority. There are principles that guide their interaction, just as there are principles of physics and chemistry that guide the interactions of atoms and molecules. There's a fourth category of subtle energies that basically support, foster, and maintain these basic three. I think of them as energies of blessing and fostering.

For example, I live near a lake in the foothills of the Cascade Mountains, not far from Mt. Rainer. I'm often aware of particular streams of subtle energies that radiate out from the spirit of the lake as well as from the spirit of the mountains, infusing the surrounding countryside with vital forces that act in the subtle environment in ways analogous to sunlight in the physical world. Such energies enhance the life force, the emergence of potentials, and the forces of connectedness and wholeness in the environment around me.

These four types of subtle energies represent basic, positive, life-affirming functions that are systemic and organic. In one form or another, they are everywhere present. Life would not exist on the Earth without them. Also, in a broad way, I would say that such energies are all love-based and in some fashion manifest love in action.

Such energies can definitely be allies in any kind of subtle energy work as we shall see as we proceed through the upcoming chapters. When I sense them, they always make me feel more alive; I find them stimulating and inspiring in a deep way. They enhance my own feelings of wholeness and connectedness and often make me feel larger and more spacious in my own being. Interestingly, although I may sense them within a particular environment, such as in the rooms of my home or outside in the neighborhood, they don't feel local. Instead they give me a sense of participating in the universe as a whole, a living universe as I have said.

However, these four are not the only kinds of subtle energies that I sense in the subtle environment. There are a multitude of subtle forces that are generated by our activity, thought, and feeling, and these all have their own "human" flavor or characteristics. I think of them as human energy vectors. These can range from the individual Self-Light that all people radiate to some degree to the influences and effects of all the subtle bodies and psyches that make up humanity and their emanations, not to mention physical energies. Such human subtle forces are particular concentrated as one might expect in cities, town, villages, and wherever human beings congregate in significant numbers, but in one way or another, often thanks to our technologies, human energies circulate throughout the globe for better or worse.

In a similar way, there are *non-human energy vectors*, all the subtle energies and forces given off by all the flora and fauna—and the minerals—that make up the biosphere and nature as a whole. These forces can be felt in their greatest concentration in wilderness, which people can find both refreshing and energizing, and overwhelming and disconcerting. For example, the maple tree in my back yard gives off its own distinctive vibrations, which join with the energies from other neighboring trees, the grass, the bushes, the flowers, the squirrels, the birds, and so on, not to mention the trillions of microscopic bacteria and microbes that have their own subtle energy fields as well.

For the most part, all these subtle forces blend together in an ecology of inner life, but here and there are places where *edgy energies* can arise much as can happen when two streams merge, creating turbulence as they blend and begin to flow together. These can be places where human and non-human energies meet and fail to blend, or areas where a force at a higher energy meets one at a lower energy, creating an energy differential that produces energetic "storms."

For example, there is a resort hotel that's in a semi-wild area not far from where I live. It's a beautiful building, but the subtle energy around it is not pleasant. The reason is that the hotel was built straddling and thus obstructing a line of subtle energy running through the earth. Think of a dam placed across a river. Energies begin to back up and to seek other channels around the obstruction, which in turn affects the balance in the local energy ecology. This is not at all an uncommon situation given that human beings, particularly in the modern Western world, don't pay attention to subtle energy flows when constructing our buildings, unlike the practice of *feng shui* in the East.

These areas of turbulence and edgy energies can feel "negative" when we encounter them, but they are not necessarily negative in nature. They are simply stirred up in ways that create uncomfortable energetic conditions.

These three types of subtle energy—human, non-human, and those "eddies" or "vortices" arising from the coming together of different energy streams—make up what I think of as *expressive* energies. That is, they arise from the normal, everyday expressions of countless forms of life and energy on our planet. For instance, I may feel the energy states of the people around me or the energy states of the trees in our backyard. My subtle body's own energy field may temporarily vibrate in resonance with these other, expressive energy states as a way of perceiving them and then, in most cases, let them go, like the surface of a lake ripples under the impact of a breeze and then calms again.

I think of these expressive energies as being joy-based. I'm not referring to joy as an emotion here but rather as the exuberant energy of expressing one's own nature. These are energies that manifest the joy of being and becoming, the joy of self-in-action, even if the actual manifestation that we feel does not seem what we would call "joyous."

Finally, there are energy states that are truly negative, even harmful and toxic. Such energies are negative because they are badly obstructed or disconnected, not merely turbulent, or they have been deliberately given a hurtful and malicious vector. I think of these as *aggravating* (or one might also say *aggrieved*) energies. They can create unpleasant, discordant, distressing, and even hurtful responses in our personal energy fields.

While it's possible such energies could arise in nature, I've personally never encountered them apart from human activity. In my experience, all such negative energies arise from human intents and actions, particularly from those actions that are violent and meant to harm others or to benefit oneself to the detriment of others. Anger, hatred, lust, a desire for dominance over another can all produce these aggravating and malicious subtle energies to one degree or another. They are, in effect, *anti-holopoietic*, disrupting and destroying wholeness, integration, and coherency.

The most common of these form what I think of as "psychic smog" arising from disturbed human emotions such as anger, fear, and the like. Such "smoggy" subtle energies can arise from instances of human mental and emotional turmoil and confusion, or in a more pronounced way, from suffering, whether caused by a natural disaster such as an earthquake or flood or by human activity. Such psychic smog generally doesn't seek to perpetuate itself, but it can linger in an area unless it is cleared away by dedicated subtle energy work.

A more problematic manifestation is when the negativity arises due to human intent, as on a battlefield or where one person is deliberately abusing or hurting another. The presence of intent can make the subtle energies more jagged and hurtful and more likely to spread out like a virus to infect others because their vector embodies this intent to damage and to hurt. Fear is particularly subversive this way. When the Trade Towers came down in New York City on 9/11, it sent a wave of negative, fearful energy cascading through the collective energy field of the United States, like a tsunami of terror. People in places that would never see a terrorist attack of any kind nonetheless became seized with fear as their subtle bodies reacted to and absorbed this wave of subtle energy rippling out from New York City.

Finally, the worst and most toxic and predatory negative subtle forces are the product of a focused intent to inflict suffering and to create damage. The intentional violence and abuse are not only intended to create physical pain but to destroy the spirit as well. The Nazi concentration camps of World War II provide an example of the kind of activity that can produce such energies, but any form of torture and abuse will do so. Here are subtle energies being deliberately shaped through hatred to act in harmful ways. When released into the subtle realms, they can persist as long as they can find like-minded hosts to supply them with energy and new momentum. If unsupported, these energies will eventually dissipate and dissolve, but unfortunately in our world with its numerous conflicts and divisions between people, they can often find sources to keep them in a malicious existence.

Thankfully, though I have certainly known angry and disturbed people, I have only very rarely encountered subtle forces I would call truly evil energies, filled with hatred and an alloyed intent to harm. There are inner beings whose primary work is to diminish and transmute such aggravated energies. Likewise, I have known friends whose inner work has also been to deliberately engage such forces and transmute them, restoring them to a reconnected and more holopoietic state. This has never been my work or my calling, but I'm grateful to those who undertake such tasks. It's something that requires courage, love, and a great deal of skill in working with subtle energies, as well as strong allies in the spiritual realms. I will, however, discuss how to deal with such energies should you encounter them in Chapter 14, *Protection*.

Sensing systemic energies is a bit like sensing sunlight or gravity; these energies represent universal principles at work, principles of life, wholeness, connectedness, and nourishment. But though I know sunlight and gravity are there and part of my life, I may not pay much attention to them as I focus on my daily work and interactions with people, think about my plans for the day, solve problems, and so forth. What usually occupies my awareness are all the ordinary human activities around me that make up my daily environment.

Similarly, we may overlook the systemic subtle energies and be more aware of the everyday expressive energies—the emanations of thought, feeling and physical activity—going on all around us. We may get intuitive "hits" about what another is thinking or feeling or about some event that is about to occur; it may be less usual to sense the ubiquitousness of life around us or to feel the presence of fostering and blessing energies, even though they are everywhere present.

I find that I can enhance my awareness of systemic energies simply by projecting love into my subtle energy field. When I look at the world around me with love and honor, the presence of these fundamental systemic energies responds, and they become more evident to me.

At the other end of the spectrum, I have found it doesn't take much to sense aggravating energies. Just as a sour or nauseating odor can cause us to immediately react with distaste and revulsion, the presence of intense fear, hatred, or maliciousness in the subtle environment can cause a reaction in our energy field. We want to get away from what we're sensing. Something in us feels repelled, unless through our own hatred, anger, and negativity we've inured ourselves to such energies. Aggravating energies *hurt* on a subtle level;

they hurt even those who are producing them or resonating with their toxic frequency.

Here's an important point: in the expressive category, we can certainly meet people who are experiencing emotional or mental distress of one kind or another; it's practically a characteristic of the human condition. Running into an angry friend or hearing someone express their hatred for another — or their fear — is not that unusual. The "expressive" category can contain some unpleasant energies, too, as well as some very pleasant ones, as when we feel the joy or love emanating from another. Likewise, we can encounter turbulent "edge" energies that are uncomfortable and that can feel "negative" to us; depending on what kind of energies they are and how they impact us, they can hurt as well.

When I was a director of the Findhorn Foundation community in Scotland back in the early Seventies, we had a rash of complaints about illnesses and disturbing emotions that were all centered on a particular trailer in one corner of the community. I and another man, Robert Ogilvie Crombie, or ROC as he was affectionately known by his initials, were asked to investigate because of our sensitivities to subtle energies. As we walked the land around the trailer, we could certainly feel something was amiss, and the epicenter of the energetic disturbance appeared to be an iron rod that had been thrust into the ground. ROC bent down to pull it out, and as he did so, there was a discharge of subtle energy so strong that it knocked both of us down. For me, there was a flash of light and then the next I knew, I was picking myself up off the ground some two or three feet from where I'd been standing, and saw ROC doing the same. At the same time, the vortex of edgy, turbulent energies was gone. Apparently, there was a buried stream that run under the property, and the iron rod had inadvertently acted to block the flow of subtle energies along that stream, causing them to back up and become a source of obstructed energies that were literally making people sick when they encountered it. There was nothing inherently "negative" about the energies, and once they'd been released, all went back to normal.

Aggravating energies, on the other hand, express fear, anger, hatred, and other emotions in a corrosive way, a way that doesn't just disturb the energy of one's subtle body but actually begins to break it down, creating incoherency, disintegration, and a loss of wholeness. Think of a parasitic life form taking over the vitality of your body and siphoning it away from you to sustain itself in existence, and you have a good analogy of how these aggravated and toxic energies can affect us. They go beyond instilling a temporary emotion of anger or fear in us, as angry or fearful expressive energies might do, and instead affect our identity, turning us into angry and fearful persons.

As a simple rule of thumb, systemic energies feel good, drawing us to them; expressive energies feel like what they are, whatever that might be, and for the most part we can take them or leave them, though some may feel turbulent and disturbing; aggravating energies feel hurtful and nasty, repelling us. These are broad strokes, and within each category, we can with patience and attention, tease out more detailed information about the different energies we may be facing and their characteristics.

The important thing is that as a prelude to any kind of subtle energy work, you take time to sense into the environment or the situation with which you'll be working. Are vital energies of life and blessing readily present? If so, they can become invaluable allies. Are there hurtful and malicious energies around? Then you will need to pay more attention to protecting yourself. Do things feel turbulent or unsettled? Then perhaps adding any extra energy to the environment would not be a good idea. What you want is to do something to calm things down and even things out; in such a case, doing nothing at all may be the best approach, at least at first. What you are able to sense will help determine how you approach and deal with the energies of the subtle environment.

Perception through Being

In Chapter 3, I discussed the "Zone of Engagement," the outer layer of your subtle body. This is generally where subtle perception takes place; your entire subtle body is an organ of perception, at least at its surface. I showed this in Figures 8 and 9. I want to refresh your memory on this point. Your subtle body basically perceives its world by energetically configuring to what it encounters, like soft mud taking on the impression of what presses against it. In effect, your subtle body perceives by becoming that which it perceives.

So, for example, when I see my coffee cup on my desk with my eyes or touch it with my fingers, I'm aware that it exists separate from myself. My physical senses and the way the brain interprets their information tells me this cup is different from myself. It's on my desk over there and I'm in a chair over here. However, when I reach out with my subtle field to perceive the subtle energies around and within this coffee cup, it's as if those energies are within me. My subtle body perceives by becoming through resonance or reflection the energies it is sensing. It blends with the cup's energies to some degree.

Through experience, I've learned how to distinguish this subtle perception in order to say, "These energies are not me; they belong to the coffee cup." But sometimes, the distinction isn't so clear, especially when there's no corresponding physical object to help my brain and mind objectify the experience. Subtle energies that have no apparent immediate physical source can be harder to discern as being "other" and belonging to the environment rather than a manifestation of something happening inside myself.

It's important to understand this principle of "perception by becoming"; otherwise, it's easy to mistake a subtle perception for a feeling or thought arising from your own psyche. It's then easier to take on and personalize or identify with what is being perceived, seeing it as part of you. As we shall see in the chapter on Protection, this can create problems if the subtle energy being encountered is an aggravated one.

Silence and Attention

How do you sense subtle energies, whatever their nature may be? Do you need to be psychic or have special powers? The answer is no. But you do need to pay attention to subtle information coming to you from the environment, information of which a part of you is always aware. This information may come in different ways: through your body in the form of physical sensation, through your emotions in the form of feelings, through your mind in the form of images and thoughts that suddenly arise, or through other means, such as an intuitive knowing whose origin you cannot explain in the moment. You then have to ask, what are these sensations, feelings, images, or intuitions telling you? What is the gestalt of the information they are presenting? What is the overall *felt sense*?

Ultimately, how you do this sensing is up to you. You need to discover through practice what is natural to your way of being and working. My own way, the one I present in this book, is through an awareness of the felt sense, largely in my body, of the reaction of my own subtle field as it interacts with the energies in the subtle environment. Your way might be different. If you're interested in further research in this area, I highly recommend the book *Second Sight* by my friend Dr. Judith Orloff, a psychiatrist who uses her psychic awareness of subtle energies in a number of therapeutic ways.

However you go about it, though, you need to pay attention to what you're sensing about the subtle dimension of an environment—or of a person. And often this means that you need to cultivate an inner silence in order to more easily apprehend this information. If I'm chattering away to myself mentally or I'm distracted emotionally or physically, I simply may not "hear" what the subtle environment is telling me. I find it important to cultivate an ability to enter a state of inner silence so my attention is not diffused or distracted.

There's another reason why inner silence is important, and it relates to what I just wrote about perception through becoming. If my mind is filled with my own thoughts and emotions, it's harder to discern whether or not a particular feeling or image is coming from me or is arising from something my subtle field has perceived. If I'm in a room filled with people, it's harder to tell if someone new has entered the room from outside, but if the room is empty, then I can see when the door opens and someone comes in. If my mind is quiet, then it's easier to recognize that a thought or emotion is coming from the stimulation of or impression upon my subtle field.

This state of inner silence can be developed through meditation, but actually, it's not really that difficult to achieve by ordinary means. Think of it simply as listening attentively. Imagine if someone is whispering to you so that you have to be quiet and focused to hear what they are saying. Or imagine you are in a darkened room and you know someone else is in the room with you but without any light, you can't see them. So you are very quiet in order to hear any sound they make that can help you locate them. We all know how to be quiet in this way when we need to be.

The kind of silence that assists subtle awareness is one in which our minds and emotions are temporarily calmed down. I think of it as a state of inner poise. Deep or regular breathing can help. But being very attentive in the moment can bring us to this state as well.

Information from subtle sensing comes to us often in unfamiliar ways; we need to pay attention to recognize that in fact we really are sensing something. Our brains are not used to consciously deciphering information that doesn't arrive through the usual channels of sight, sound, smell, taste, or touch. So the mind struggles to interpret what it's sensing, creating images, feelings, and sensations that are not necessarily accurate in themselves but that point towards a correct interpretation. It may take time and practice to discern just what kind of subtle energies are present. But the more we accept and open to the possibility of subtle awareness, and the more we practice and come to recognize our own individual ways of "tuning in," the easier it will become. The vague feelings of an energy that "feels good" or one that "feels repulsive and frightening" will begin to resolve itself into more precise and accurate observations, ones that will be increasingly helpful in working with the phenomena of the subtle realms.

Frequencies

Before leaving this chapter on sensing subtle energies, I want to remind you of the distinction I made between subtle and spiritual energies in Chapter 2. There I used the metaphor of a hotel with two swimming pools, one filled with salt water and one with fresh water. The former represents the energies found in the subtle environment and the latter the energies found in the spiritual worlds. This is a broad distinction; in fact, there can be many degrees of salinity in the one "pool," from a salt content so low as to be practically indistinguishable to one so high that you can't sink into the water. Likewise, fresh water can possess different degrees of "freshness." It could have a high mineral content or hardly any dissolved minerals at all, and still in either case be potable.

The point is that subtle energies exist at many frequencies, and all of these can co-exist in the same volume of space. Two questions then arise when it comes to sensing what energies are present in that space: which frequency predominates and is "loudest," and to which frequencies are you naturally attuned and thus are the ones you are most likely to pick up.

Aggravated energies by their very nature do not exist in the higher or spiritual frequencies. A given space may be filled with aggravated, negative subtle energies but also possess spiritual energies at a different frequency. As we will see, being able to attune to and draw on those higher frequencies can be an important element of dealing with subtle energies that have been damaged or aggravated in some manner. Being able to sense a wide range of frequencies—that is to say, being able to wade in both pools—is a vital skill.

For this reason when it comes to developing your capacities to sense subtle energies in the non-physical environment around you, it's important to include some form of regular attunement to the higher frequencies, which usually means some form of spiritual practice. If you rarely take time to experience and instill in your subtle field "higher" spiritual qualities such as love, compassion, joy, serenity, and courage, you lessen your ability to detect such frequencies when sensing into the subtle environment. The subtle frequencies—that is, the "salt water energies"—are vibrationally closer to the "particulate dimensions" that constitute the Incarnate Realms and thus easier to detect.

If, for instance, a person is giving off waves of subtle energies shaped by and expressive of depression or anger, you may feel these energies more readily and intensely than the Self-Light or spiritual radiance such a person may also possess. You may quickly react to the anger rather than connecting to the soul presence within that individual. I'm not saying you shouldn't be aware of the anger or depression, or whatever the emanation might be, only that if you can also be aware of the higher frequencies that are present, it gives you a wider range with which to work. You can deal with the anger while at the same time honoring, embracing, and drawing forth the soul presence that is also there.

Having a practice of deliberately attuning to the higher frequencies of the spiritual dimensions, both within yourself and within the world around you, enables you to better sense these frequencies in your environment. This is the objective of many spiritual practices that ask you to meditate upon or attune to qualities such as love, forgiveness, compassion, wisdom, and the like, perhaps through focus upon a revered spiritual figure who embodies and is an exemplar of these qualities for you.

I feel it's important to remember that the subtle side of the universe is vast and largely mysterious. Even at our best, we only sense a tiny fraction of the many kinds and frequencies of subtle forces that fill the cosmos, just as we see only a small slice of the electromagnetic spectrum with our physical eyes. This book really just barely slices the surface—or the depths, if you wish—of the subtle domains of life. It focuses on those energies that I have experienced most commonly in the environment around us and that are the most relevant to our daily lives. But as you open to your subtle self and begin to be increasingly aware of the non-physical dimensions around you, you may well sense phenomena and energies beyond anything I've described here. Most of all, I hope you will realize just how complex, interweaving, and multi-faceted the subtle realms are. Trying to describe them in words or pictures is in many ways a futile task; they must be experienced as living realities, not simply as mental concepts.

So pay attention and keep notes about what you experience so you can grow in understanding just how you uniquely sense the subtle worlds and the energies they contain. Learn from the experiences of others, but at the same time, don't compare yourself or judge yourself by them. Discover your individual way of perceiving the many frequencies of life with which you are surrounded.

EXERCISES FOR CHAPTER TWELVE

Now that you have some experience with other exercises in this book, I'd like you for this chapter to go back to the beginning and try the Room Sensing exercise of Chapter 2. For your convenience, I repeat it again here.

This time, I'd like you to see if you can feel the systemic energies in the room, the energies of life, emergence, and holopoiesis or connectedness and wholeness. One way to open to these energies is to project your own love and presence out into the room, appreciating it and honoring everything in it. Can you feel the life, the "will-to-be" in the inorganic objects in the room? Can you feel a deep, unconscious striving for greater life and awareness?

Can you feel any energies of blessing in the room? One way to explore this is to acknowledge an overlighting presence, the "house angel" whose function is to energetically bless and nurture all within the energy field of the home. What does this presence feel like? Can you sense a flow of blessingful energy from it to the room you're in?

As it says in the original exercise, do this in a fun, easy way. Don't strive for a particular experience, but be open to the subtleties of the energetic environment around you.

Are there any areas in the room where the energy might feel stuck or turbulent? Don't try to do anything about them at this point, but if they are there, just notice them and see if you can discern what may be causing the obstruction or turbulence. Don't, however, try to take it on or heal it at this time, though if you are able to contact the house angel, you can ask it to send cleansing, balancing, holopoietic energies to those stuck areas.

Exercise: Room Sensing Revisited

I'd like you to do this exercise in a fun, easy way. You're not trying to have a psychic experience or engage with subtle energies. Don't strive or strain for any particular effect or experience. Just be aware of whatever you feel in the room as you do the exercise, which in fact may be nothing at all!

Pick a room in your house or apartment where you live. Be aware of your body in this room. Now close your eyes and extend yourself into the space formed by this room, just sensing and feeling it in silence. What is that like? What do you feel? Do you feel any kind of energy in the room? A particular "atmosphere" or "mood?" If so, what is it like? Pay attention in a calm, easy way for as long as it feels comfortable, then open your eyes, ending the exercise.

Now repeat this exercise in another room. How does what you feel and experience in this second room, if anything, differ from the first room? Is one room energetically more powerful or more distinctive than the other?

If you wish, try this again in a third room, again comparing that experience with the ones you had in the other rooms.

CHAPTER THIRTEEN
Heightening

The simplest and many times the most effective way of working with the subtle energies in an environment is to expose them to the fundamental "systemic" energies of love and joy. Love and joy enhance life, emergence, connections, holopoiesis, and wholeness. You can think of their action as akin to turning up the heat on a pot of water. The more energy there is due to the heat, the more the water molecules become active, moving and dancing about. Heightening through love and joy is a form of energetically "turning up the heat." This can enable energies that have become a bit static or sluggish to move fluidly again, and it calls forth through resonance the corresponding systemic forces within that environment.

Often this is all that is needed to help in a particular environment, or if more needs to be done, it is the first step to affecting these subtle energies in other ways, whether it's blessing, cleansing, healing, protecting, or something else. The healthy state of subtle energies is one of flow and connectedness. When they're not in this state—and there are many reasons why this might happen—they can become stuck and obstructive and less able to respond to your intentions.

The first steps in heightening are to stand in your Interiority—that is, in your Sovereignty, your Self-Light, and your Presence—and from that generative place, fill your own energy field with loving and joyful energies. Think of it like warming up before undertaking strenuous exercise, getting your own "juices" flowing, so to speak. Then you enter your "Stance," aligned with the transpersonal, spiritual forces of your own soul, the energies of the earth around you, and connected to your immediate environment in an honoring and loving manner.

Heightening the subtle energies in a particular space doesn't always have to be done using subtle means, assuming your own personal field is in a positive state. Subtle forces in the subtle environment tend to reflect what is happening physically in that environment. This means there are some surprisingly simple and easy physical ways of making a difference; for instance, music, movement, and laughter (assuming the laughter isn't mean, hurtful or at someone's expense). Anything that helps you to bring love and joy into your surroundings will be helpful and will make a difference to the subtle environment.

If you then wish to work more directly to heighten the surrounding subtle energies, you want to assess what the situation is and what is needed—or what you think will work best. You approach each situation according to its unique characteristics. However, here are some basic principles for both heightening and for all kinds of subtle energy work

1. **Love and joy are the foundation for all working with subtle energies.** Even if dealing with negative energies, you want to stand in love the same way a doctor has compassion and love for a patient without having to love the illness. Love opens pathways and connections that otherwise might be closed.

2. **Heighten the energy in your own subtle energy field.** Often just thinking about heightening your energy field will stimulate it, but it's not all a process of thought alone. Standing in Sovereignty can help. Think of yourself in a situation that gives you energy. Gather your "joy nuggets" (as in the "Joy Mining" exercise I presented in Chapter 9) and stand in a felt sense of joy. Depending on the circumstances, doing something like singing or moving may help. Based on your self-knowledge, be creative about choosing how to heighten your own energies in your own energy field.

3. **Have a normal attitude and approach about what you're doing.** Working with subtle energies is a normal thing to do; it's part of who we are. We do it all the time, albeit unconsciously. You can feel joyful and powerful in forming a good relationship with the subtle energies around you, but it's best not to adopt a "Warrior of Light" stance, imagining yourself as wielding powerful inner forces to shape the environment to your will. This may only build resistance and end up working against your intentions. Peaceful, calm, loving intent based on a sense of ordinariness, honor and appreciation for where you are, and collaboration works best, I find.

4. **Respect the conditions in which you find yourself.** It's one thing to heighten the energies in an empty room and quite something else to try to do so in a crowded subway! The more complex the situation, the more people there are involved, the more competing currents of energy will be present or can arise. Heightening may just add energy to an already complex and charged environment, perhaps making a volatile situation worse. Be mindful and aware and use your intuition and your good common sense about whether or not to attempt to heighten the local energy field, and if so, how best to go about it. But always, always, always, act with respect to what is already present. If you were an electrical worker trying to ground a loose live electrical wire, you would respect the energy that's flowing through that wire, which could be enough to shock and injure you if you don't work carefully. Have the same respect for subtle forces.

5. **Work outward using imagery and intent.** Imagine and feel your own heightened energy field expanding out from you into the environment around you and sharing its qualities and heightened state with the surrounding subtle energies. You can use your mind and intentionality to give this movement outward clarity, focus, and power; you can use your imagination to "see" your energy expanding outward. In this instance, energy really does follow imagery and intent.

6. **Start Small/Work Gradually.** Let your energy field expand in small stages, not trying to encompass the whole space at once. I usually find it best to focus my effort on an area immediately around me, using a kind of induction much like a radiator. As the air around a radiator warms up, it expands and moves out and warms up more air in the room. Subtle energies can respond in a similar way. If I want to work with the energies in a room, I rarely try to tackle the room as a whole at first (or even at all). Instead, I focus on what I can physically touch, like the floor or maybe a chair I'm sitting in or a table nearby. I let it be my ally and let my energy flow into and around it. Since the floor or the chair or the table are themselves connected to the room, I trust the energy I put into them will find those connections and radiate outward.

7. **Respect energy differentials.** If you're trying to heighten energies that are seriously depressed, they may not immediately respond, or they may respond with inertia and resistance, throwing your energy back at you. Imagine trying to jolly up someone who is very despondent and depressed; your efforts may roll off their back or may make them angry and resentful. The energy difference between you and them is too great; they can't make the leap from their depression to your cheeriness. So you want to go easy and, as I said, start small, establishing a respectful and loving relationship. This holds for subtle energies, too. Again, it's a case of being mindful.

8. **Know when not to act.** Sometimes, it's best to do nothing. You want to be aware of your own limits and the extent of your knowledge and skill. If you're not sure what to do or how to do it, then pause. Maybe you're not the one to take action in the situation. As with giving aid physically, you don't want to inflict harm or make a situation worse. Especially if the subtle energies feel volatile to you, adding more energy may be like putting fuel on a fire. Just being a calm and neutral presence may be the best action to take.

9. **Don't look for miracles.** You want to be realistic and mindful of

the state of the subtle energies you're engaging. If they are in a place where negative energies have become deeply embedded in the surrounding matter, you're most likely not going to change it overnight. It will take time and persistence. Heighten what you can as much as you can, and give thanks for even small changes.

Grail Space

There is a particular technique of heightening the energy level in a given area; I call it creating a *Grail Space*. It can work both indoors and outdoors, but it's mainly for use in environments built by humans, such as a room in a building where the space is physically defined by obvious boundaries such as walls, floor and ceiling. This gives a specific area with which to work which helps keep everything focused. If this technique is used outside, care must be taken to mentally define the area in which the energy work is to done and to make note of those elements in the landscape that will serve as boundary markers. You can't heighten the energies for all of nature! It's also true that there are forces at work in the natural world that accomplish much the same thing that Grail Space seeks to accomplish; such forces, though, don't have the same influence within human-made environments whose structures are as likely to cut off a flow of energy as to augment it. It's precisely because the energy environments within our rooms and buildings can become depleted of vital, flowing currents that Grail Space becomes important.

Rooms generally have an average base energy state, much like the ambient temperature; this energy state often is "lower" or less vital than what you would find outside. One reason this is so is that to the spirits inhabiting the natural world and working with the currents of vital energy, everything in nature is alive. There is no division between the inorganic and organic. A rock, a tree, or a bush are all perceived as vibrant living entities within the subtle environment and are related to as such. There is a continual flow of "conversation" going on across many levels of life, energy, and interaction.

But this is not the perspective that most human beings have of their world, particularly not in the technologically developed and materialistic societies that occupy so much of the planet. In an average room, the normal perception is that, aside from any plants or animals that might be present, everything in the room—the walls, the floor, the ceiling, the furniture—is all dead matter. They don't represent potential partners but rather backdrop components, like stage settings, within and around which we lead our lives. They are things to be used, not entities to be recognized and engaged.

Imagine if you were totally ignored by everyone around you and treated not like a human being, or even a living being, but simply as a thing. Your energy would probably drop as you gave up on any kind of interaction, making you feel listless and lifeless; you would shrink within yourself, leading an inner life perhaps in your own thoughts and feelings but giving up on any outer engagement. Metaphorically, this is what can happen to the things around us. Without loving, appreciative, vitalizing interaction, their energy may withdraw and drop in radiance and intensity as well. I think of the life within the matter, the substances, that make up our environments as "going to sleep." The ability of the things within the room to hold life energies—in effect the "energetic carrying capacity" of the room—drops.

Grail Space is a way of collaboratively engaging with one's surroundings to wake this energy up, enhancing the carrying capacity of that space.

One aspect of the practice of Grail Space is simply to acknowledge and appreciate the energetic life within a room (or within whatever the space is with which you are working). But the practice goes more deeply than this. It's more than just recognizing the subtle environment that fills that space. It is a way of bringing to the forefront the presence of what I think of as the "Whole Space"—which includes its sacredness.

To explain this, let's look for a moment at our own lives. We can describe ourselves as having different parts operating on different levels of our life. The description I've been using most often in this book is a three-fold one. We have a physical self, an energy or subtle self, and a spiritual self or soul. These three interact in various ways, and they are interpenetrating and interconnected. Our consciousness can reside in any of the three. But from another perspective, we are one self, of which body, energy field, and soul are components. All three arise from the "Ground of Being" that is our sacredness. When we fully realize this, we can experience our whole self, our Whole Person. When we do, we feel more spacious; the felt sense of presence expands beyond being just a body, or just an energy field, or just a soul.

When we have this Whole Person experience, I could say we are experiencing our inner Grail Space, so called because like the mystical Grail, it is a state in which, because we are feeling whole, we are holding and experiencing our sacredness. I suggest this experience in Figure 29.

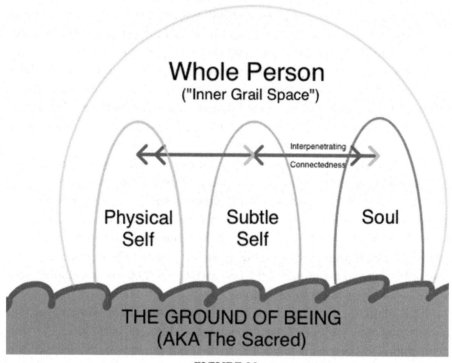

FIGURE 29

The practice of Grail Space does something similar in our environment. It emphasizes and brings into the forefront the "Whole System" nature of the space—which for me includes its sacredness. This is contrasted with seeing and engaging the space within the room either only as a physical space, as a subtle environment, or as a spiritual space. In fact, the physical environment and the subtle environment of a room are part of a wholeness; they are aspects of a whole space that is neither wholly physical, wholly subtle, or wholly spiritual. It's "Sacred," which transcends yet includes these categories. I suggest this in Figure 30.

So in Grail Space, you're linking with all aspects of the environment around you to heighten or awaken the space to its whole nature, its sacred nature. The function of Grail Space is to promote and express Wholeness. One way to do this is described in the Exercise section of this Chapter.

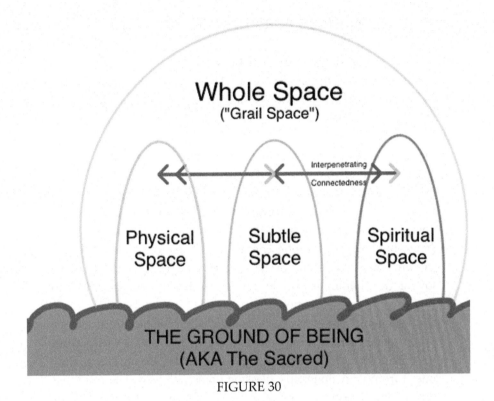

FIGURE 30

EXERCISES FOR CHAPTER THIRTEEN

Exercise: A (Spacey) Touch Of Love

This exercise is a variation on the Touch of Love exercise I presented in Chapter 8. It's a simple way to begin heightening the subtle energies in the environment around you.

- Do the Touch of Love exercise, feeling love flowing outward from your center into your arms and fingers.
- This time, let this love flow from your fingertips into your subtle energy field. Imagine your own surrounding field becoming heightened and energized with the love flowing out from your fingertips.
- Now, imagine your subtle energy field expanding and touching the surrounding energies in the space in which you are. Allow this loving, heightening energy to flow out from your energy field into the surrounding subtle field.
- Do this as long as feels comfortable; then, when you feel tired, restless, or complete, imagine your personal energy field drawing back around you. Stand or sit for a moment, allowing the love to continue to flow into it from your fingertips, blessing your own field. Then call that flow of love back from your hands, up your arms, and back into your center, allowing it to diffuse throughout your body.
- Take a moment to stand in and reaffirm your Sovereignty.

Exercise: Grail Space

This is an exercise you do with an entire space, like a room, and with all the objects in it. I call it "Grail Space" because it forms an energetic state—the "Whole Space"—that can hold a presence of sacredness, thereby helping to heighten the subtle energies in the space. It uses the principle that where two or more are gathered in acknowledgement of their mutual sacredness, a field comes into being that holds a greater presence of life and Light than any one of the participants could have held on his, her, or its own. It is a collaborative engagement with the life energies of the things around you. It is one of the main practices of Incarnational Spirituality.

- Stand in your Sovereignty, Self-Light, and Presence.
- Imagine yourself as a radiant star, generating a field of love that fills the room around you.
- All the objects in the room have their own interior connection with the sacred, their own evolving life-force. They all have their physical side, their energetic nature, and their spiritual connections. Honor each of these aspects and the evolving life that unites them.
- Invite all these objects to join their evolving life-force with your own, their fields touching and blending with yours. The result is a shared field of presence and energy, co-created by you and by the objects around you, a field of Gaian connection.
- Feel this jointly held field, this Grail Space, manifesting the wholeness of the space around you. You and the room about you are collaboratively, jointly, heightening to express the Whole Space that is physical, subtle, and spiritual but more than these three as well. Feel the wholeness of the room filling with a presence of the Sacred that blesses and fosters the evolution and life of all of you within this field.
- Hold this field for as long as feels comfortable. When you feel complete, or feel tired or restless, give thanks to your partners and to the Presence that filled the Grail Field. Then withdraw your energy back into your body, knowing that all the objects in the room that participated in the Grail Space are doing this as well.
- Stand in your Sovereignty and Self-Light, grounding yourself however you feel you need to, absorbing the blessings that came from the Grail Space.
- Go about your normal business.

CHAPTER FOURTEEN
Blessing

Heightening and blessing are very close to one another, and in some circumstances, it may not be possible to tell the difference. The act of heightening could be a consequence of blessing, and vice versa. But they are not exactly identical, so I deal with them separately.

Heightening is a way of waking things up and getting subtle energies stirring and moving in an area where they might otherwise be stagnant or "sleepy". Think of walking into a musty old room that hasn't seen much change for a long time and imagine what the energy may feel like, the mood and atmosphere of the place. It most likely feels stale and stuck. This is where heightening comes into play. It's simply a way of adding more energy, more movement into a stagnant situation so things can begin to circulate and flow again. In the picture of this musty, old room, it's like opening a window to sunlight and fresh air, allowing the staleness to blow out and fresh air and light to come in.

Such a change can certainly seem like a blessing—and it is a blessing if it makes for a livelier, healthier environment, one that is better able to connect with the larger world around it. However, what I mean by the action of blessing as a specific way of working with subtle energies is something different. Where heightening works with subtle energies and thus with our subtle body, blessing works with the life and spirit within things. It is a manifestation of our Self-Light—and of Light in general.

I have found that many people think of blessings as coming from God or from some transcendental, transpersonal source. But in Incarnational Spirituality, we are also sources of blessing, not simply in the good deeds we may perform for others but energetically as sources of the spiritual energy contained within our Self-Light.

I think of blessing as a way of working with subtle energies that enhances the holopoietic impulse within them, the impulse to connect and to create wholeness. All things strive to be in wholeness both in themselves and in relationship with the world around them because where there is wholeness, subtle energies flow more freely, coherently, and co-creatively, leading to enhanced life and vitality. Blessing works with this impulse

In the broadest sense, a blessing is anything we do that enhances the life of another in positive ways, making his or her way in the world easier. So there are many physical ways we can offer blessings, such as contributing our time, money, energy, and skills to others to help them out. From a subtle energy perspective, though, I think of blessings as coming in three "flavors". I call them the "transfusion," the "zap," and the "hug". Each comes from a different place within us and has a different effect.

The Transfusion

This is essentially a process of using your own energy field to heighten the energy field of another. In effect, you are giving the other person a subtle energy transfusion. In this process, you are providing vitality and a heightening, empowering subtle energy to another. Touching the other person can be very helpful but is not essential. Doing the "Touch of Love" exercise with another is an example of one form of a transfusion, passing a loving energy into the body and subtle field of another. This kind of transfer, more often than not, is directed by your thoughts and intent. That is, you mentally project the energy you wish to share into the field of another.

But this can also happen spontaneously, perhaps in a healing session where body work is being done, or just in a physical touch or embrace; such a spontaneous transfusion can happen if one person has more vitality than another and the one with less vitality is open to being energized. In such an instance, it's possible that energy can "leap the gap" so to speak and flow from the person with greater energy to the person with lesser. As a rule of thumb, if the energy transference is going to be significant, it's better not to supply it from your own vitality or energy field as you can be easily and quickly drained (though you would certainly recover once you have a chance to be on your own). In such instances, you want to connect yourself with a transpersonal source of vitality and life energy and act as a conduit, connecting the other person to that greater source. But if what's needed is just a small, quick jolt of energy, then you can project this from your own vitality, as long as you know when to stop. Intuition, discernment, skill, and experience all come into play here.

The Zap

The Zap is similar to the Transfusion with two major differences. First, you're using Self-Light rather than your own subtle energies, and you're drawing on this Self-Light from your own Interiority which by its nature is connected to your innate sacredness. So you begin by standing in Sovereignty, attuning to Presence, and opening to your Self-Light.

The way I do this is to visualize myself as a radiant star, a star that embodies the generative wholeness of my being. I see this star-form extending and radiating out in a spherical way several inches, perhaps as much as a foot, from my body. I then visualize a beam of "starlight" (or "star-self-light") extending out to the person or situation I wish to bless. I do not see this beam as coming from my subtle energy field, nor do I conceptualize it as a "ray" of subtle energy or vitality. Secondly, I do not direct this "zap" of Self-Light into the other's subtle energy field but rather towards their own inner, generative star, that is, to their Interiority and their Emergent Soul. In this way, I'm not trying to heighten their energy field. I'm acting to enhance and stimulate in a loving way their own generative capacity and Self-Light.

With the Zap, you're enhancing with your Self-Light another person's capacity to radiate their own Self-Light.

The Hug

This is the way I usually give a blessing. It's not as direct as the previous two methods, the Transfusion or the Zap, but it's more versatile. This also uses Self-Light. It consists of creating a space around an individual in which that person's Sovereignty and Self-Light have room to express themselves, allowing the innate sacredness of the individual to emerge and shape the situation if it is able to do so.

Here's one way I imagine this process. Imagine that you are in a crowded room, so filled with people that you can hardly hear yourself think, much less move about freely. You might be a celebrity or rock star surrounded with fans all clamoring for your attention, all shouting at you, all reaching out to touch you. Now imagine that a team of bodyguards moves in and pushes people back, creating a clear space around you in which you can move and express yourself more freely. You have a space in which you can be yourself.

In a way, especially when we are feeling down and less-than-radiant, this is the situation in which we can find ourselves psychically: surrounded and bombarded by the thoughts, feelings, subtle energies, and psychic projections of others or of humanity in general. It's hard to touch into our own sacredness, our own Sovereignty and Interiority. What we need is some psychic space in which our own innate Presence and sacredness has a chance to assert itself and unfold.

The Hug as a form of blessing surrounds the individual or a situation with a neutral, supportive Light that invites (never compels) the Presence and wholeness of the individual or the wholeness of the situation to emerge and unfold. In effect, the Hug provides a space for the individual to bless himself or herself, or for a situation to unfold whatever inherent possibilities for blessing exist within it.

The Ethics Of Blessing

In all cases, but especially with the Transfusion and the Zap, you have to be careful not to impose upon another. Anytime you project or insert subtle energy into another's field, it's important to do so with care and with wisdom.

Except in cases of emergency, it should never be done without the individual's knowledge and permission, and even if it's an emergency in which the individual is unable to give permission or acknowledgement, perhaps because he or she is unconscious, care must be taken. A person's energy system operates in a system of balances, just like their physical body; too much energy or energy too swiftly applied can cause imbalance which can lead to both physical and psychological consequences. I have seen people become ill (and in fact, have become ill myself) from receiving too much energy from another, often in a misguided attempt on their part to be helpful. Energy work of any depth or power requires knowledge, wisdom and skill the same as practicing medicine does, and for the same reason: you don't wish to do anyone harm.

This is why I usually think of a blessing not as an exchange of energy (even though it can be, as I've described above) but as the creation of a neutral field that surrounds the individual and acts to shield him or her from external forces and energies that may be complicating their own subtle field. The purpose of the Hug as a blessing methodology is to give a person inner space to find his or her own balance and to allow his or her own inner wisdom to act, free from interference. It is based on a trust in the restorative, healing, balancing wisdom and intelligence that is within each of us. Because it doesn't interact directly with a person's energy field and doesn't represent any kind of infusion of subtle energy into the person, this kind of blessing can be done without the person's knowledge or in situations where outwardly giving a blessing might seem strange or off-putting to people and create resistance. However, as a rule of thumb, whenever possible, even this kind of blessing works best if done with the knowledge, understanding and permission of the person or persons involved.

The Zap and the Hug both use Self-Light as their primary mode of operation. As I understand it, Self-Light (or any kind of Light that we may invoke) can stimulate subtle energies if directed to do so but it can pass through the subtle energy field to act directly and collaboratively with the Self-Light within the other individual. This is what distinguishes a blessing from simply heightening subtle energies. The Transfusion is, as I said, really a form of directed heightening focused upon an individual's subtle energy field, and thus care must be taken not to over-stimulate that field into an unbalanced state. The Zap, however, goes to the "generative star" within the person and seeks to empower it, though even here, care must be taken.

As a rule of thumb, Zaps and Hugs are always powered by love. Transfusions need not be and can be a product simply of intent and will setting subtle energies into motion and directing them towards a person, although obviously if love underlies such an action, it will be less likely to cause problems. There's a place for such Transfusions, but they need to be done with the person's permission whenever possible.

There are also what could be called natural and spontaneous kinds of blessings that occur between people all the time since there is a circulation and flow of energy between us, especially where there is goodwill, friendship and love present. Even with our boundaries, we are always sharing subtle energies with the world around us, if only at a surface layer of our subtle body. The mere fact of holding in one's heart a sincere wish for their well-being and happiness can result in a positive flow of energy and blessing to other people we meet. This is the Touch of Love in action. We may, for instance, be walking down the street and see a stranger smile hello at us and feel a charge of positive energy. The stranger may not have been deliberately projecting a blessing towards us, but his or her friendly and positive demeanor naturally engages our energy field in a blessing-like way.

This kind of natural flow of blessings doesn't have to regulated; it's just part of the innate play and joy of life and is well within the parameters of what most people's healthy energy fields can accept and deal with.

In fact, in most cases, our energy fields are resilient and able to handle a range of influences without difficulty or going out of balance, though how wide this range is depends on a number of factors such as the innate sensitivity of the individual, the state of bodily health and energy, and so on. The kind of blessings I discuss above—the Transfusion, the Zap, and the Hug—are when we deliberately set about to work with subtle energies and direct them in a particular way through our presence and our intent. Natural blessings, spontaneous blessings, on the other hand, occur all the time without our having to necessarily think about them.

In this book, we're not covering the phenomenon of working with subtle beings. That's the subject of the third book in this trilogy, *Collaboration with Subtle Worlds*. But I will say here that if you wish to send someone a blessing but are unsure how to do it, then you can always ask for help from an inner ally to act as your intermediary or as the source of blessing itself. Every person has associated with him or her a group (of variable size) of inner allies, rather like a collective "guardian angel". I call this group the "Pit Crew". You can certainly ask for help from an individual's Pit Crew in blessing that individual and as an alternative, send your energy or your Self-Light to them. Just ask that whatever beings are holding the highest good for that individual and acting as his or her allies receive your expression of goodwill and love and your gift of a blessing energy and direct it through their wisdom to provide the individual whatever help will be of most benefit.

This can also be done with situations and places.

Blessing objects and places is a little different. Here you need to discern what is needed. If you are blessing an object to be a talisman, a kind of psychic battery that can hold a "charge" of blessing, then you will most likely use some form of "Transfusion," though you can certainly reach out to the Light within the object through your own Self-Light to heighten the presence of the sacred within that object. If you are blessing a landscape or a place, then you must take into account not only the inorganic aspects but all the organic beings that are part of this space and their energy fields. Here you must proceed with respect and love, for you are doing something to their environment, and it's best if you can invite their partnership with you in creating a circle for a joint blessing. I presented one example of this in the Grail Space exercise in the preceding chapter.

In any kind of energy work, whether with people, places, or objects, you want to be sensitive to when to stop. Think of pouring liquid from a pitcher into a cup. How much you pour depends on the volume of the cup. Pour too much, and it begins to overflow.

In doing subtle energy work, you can actually feel this overflow if you pay attention. For me, it feels like the energy begins to back up into me. This is a palpable physical sensation of pressure, but I know people for whom the experience is one of their hands or bodies heating up. As a rule of thumb, any time you're doing any kind of work with subtle energies and you begin to feel physically uncomfortable or restless—or tired—stop what you're doing. It's a good sign that energy is backing up into you.

If you would like to explore this matter of blessing at greater length, I recommend my own book on the topic: *Blessing: The Art and Practice*. It's an older take on the topic, but it still reflects my current understanding and is filled with exercises.

EXERCISES FOR CHAPTER FOURTEEN

Exercise: Being a Blessing

We automatically think of blessing as an action, as something we do, but it begins with a state of being. Blessings flow from our capacity to accept and recognize ourselves as being a blessing in our own person, as who we are as an incarnate soul. It's often easier to see blessings as coming from someplace else, from some higher Presence, and ourselves simply as a channel through which the blessings flow. This exercise is simply one of reframing this perception and, while acknowledging that we can indeed be collaborative conduits for the introduction of blessings into our world from spiritual dimensions, we are also ourselves a blessing incarnate.

- Find your "Stance," the place of inner poise, attunement, strength, and coherency, aligned with your Sovereignty, your Self-Light, your Soul, and the environment around you. Step into its felt sense.
- Feel yourself as a dynamic presence of circulating energies: energies of life, wholeness, love, and the sheer joy of being.
- Without feeling a need to take action or to do anything, just appreciate this state of being. As a generative source of positive, life-affirming, holopoietic energies, you are a presence of blessing. You have the capacity to bless and to be a source of blessing that will benefit others. You are an agent of life and wholeness—a presence of blessing—just by being.
- Pay attention to the felt sense of this state in your body, in your mind, and in your emotions. This is your "Blessing Presence." Remember it and know that you can enter into it anytime, anywhere.

Exercise: The Community of Blessing

We are part of a living universe. Everything around us, large and small, organic and inorganic, is a potential radiant source of living energy, contributing its Light to the planetary field we all share. Because of this, we live in a community of blessing in which anything can be a source of blessing for us just as we can be a source of blessing in return. When we acknowledge this and consciously connect with the life around us as partners in blessing, we heighten the presence of a community of blessing that can nurture, foster, and empower all of us. When this awareness is combined with the creation of Grail Space, it can be very powerful indeed.

- Stand in Sovereignty and in your Blessing Presence.
- Be aware of what is around you in your immediate physical environment. Sense into and give honor to the life energies emanating

from all the things and beings that are present.

- Give thanks to the life in the things around you for the blessings they offer, particularly to you, and offer your blessing in return. See yourselves as partners in creating blessings for the world as a whole. From your Blessing Presence, link up in your imagination with the things around you as if you were holding energetic "hands" together.

- Feel the blessings flowing and circulating amongst you and around you. Visualize each thing and being present in this community of blessing, including yourself, being bathed in life-affirming, life-nurturing, life-blessing energy and presence, absorbing its vitality and being empowered with it.

- Give thanks to your blessing partners in this blessing community. See yourself gracefully letting go of the energetic "hands," standing in your own Sovereignty as a whole, complete, coherent individual, and then going about your business, filled with the blessings you have given and received.

Exercise: The Four Blessings

This is a blessing I often use to begin an event such as a class, a workshop, or just from time to time during my day as a way of connecting to my world.

- Bless this place in which I am, with honor and gratitude for its presence and its gift of space.
- Bless myself, with honor and gratitude for the uniqueness of spirit, life, insight, and creativity which I bring to the world.
- Bless others around me, seen and unseen, with honor and gratitude for the gifts we bring to each other, for the creativity and energy that can emerge from our collaboration.
- Bless the activity I undertake, that it may prosper and be a blessing to all my world.

CHAPTER FIFTEEN
Holding

Holding can be seen as another form of blessing, one that's related to the "Hug," but it's an important enough way of working with subtle energies that I wanted to highlight it in its own chapter.

We're all familiar with holding. We hold things all day long. A moment ago I was holding a tea cup which in turn was holding my tea for me to take a sip as I sit here writing. But there's more to holding than just this. Holding is a creative act. Specifically, *Holding is the act of creating a space defined by particular boundaries in which a unique activity can take place.* It is this "space" which is important. What holds the tea in my tea cup is the space that the sides of the cup create. The substance of the cup itself doesn't intermingle with the liquid molecules of the tea (at least I hope not!); one atom of porcelain is not attached to and holding one atom of Earl Grey. But the atoms of porcelain shaped in a particular way form a space that can be filled with the tea.

Holding tea, though, is a passive act. As a way of working with subtle energies, Holding is very active. So let's think of another example. Let's think of the rules of Poker. These rules contain or hold the unique activity of Poker. Within these rules, one isn't playing Blackjack, Old Maids, or some other card game. One is not reading about Poker, either, or using Poker hands in an oracular way to divine the future (though they are being used, one hopes, to gain one's fortune!). When playing Poker, one's activity is constrained and contained by the agreed-upon rules of the game, but within these boundaries, within the unique "space" created by these rules, a dynamic and ever-changing activity can take place in which there will be winners and losers and money will change hands.

The tea cup holds my tea. The rules of Poker hold the game of Poker. Likewise the rules of Baseball hold that game, while the walls of my house hold the unique space in which my home comes into being.

Let me repeat: *Holding is an act that creates a space within which a unique activity or set of activities may unfold.* This activity could be a game, it could be a blessing, it could be a whole life. Holding creates this space by forming and maintaining boundaries. The rules of Poker are boundaries that determine what can and cannot be done with the cards and what the cards mean. The sides of the tea cup forms the ovoid space in which tea can be poured. And the intent and love of the soul creates the boundaries that hold the space within which our incarnations develop and unfold.

Holding is a universal principle active at all level of existence. The Sacred holds the universe in its love, creating the conditions—the space of beingness and potential—that allow the cosmos to exist, flourish, and develop. Gaia, the World Soul, forms the boundaries and holds the space that allows planetary life to evolve. The Soul creates and holds a space that allows a physical incarnation to exist and hopefully develop and flourish as well.

The important realization for us is that Holding is something we as everyday personalities can do. It's not just for Gods or Souls or Planetary Beings. We can hold ourselves and the world around us in our love, deliberately creating a space for blessing and unfoldment.

Holding not only creates a space but it supports it and the activity within it as well. When I say to someone, "I'm holding you in my heart," the idea is that I am actively thinking and feeling in ways that support who they are and what they are doing or experiencing. In effect, I'm creating a space within myself—as well as around them—that allows my image of them, my felt sense of them as a person, to unfold and be held in blessing.

When we bring love into our acts of Holding, we create a special space indeed. When a child is in distress and a mother sits and forms a lap, she is creating a space in which she can hold and comfort the child. As a loving space, it can help the child find peace again. When we hold a loved one, we are creating a space in which mutuality and a loving relationship can emerge. Love creates spaces that nourish and empower. It is exactly such a space that the soul creates through its love that allows our incarnation to unfold.

We are all "space-creators". We fill our lives with acts of Holding. The capacity to create inner "chalices," loving "spaces" or conditions of heart and mind that can hold energy, hold spirit, hold each other, hold ourselves, hold the earth, and hold sacredness is an integral part of our incarnational capacity. Incarnation is about Holding. It is about the holding of spirit in the midst of matter; it is about holding matter in the presence of spirit. It is about being an alchemical chalice in which different elements may come together and combine to form the alloy of a radiant life.

Obviously, we do not always hold ourselves well, or others either. We can create evil spaces of violence, abuse, and bondage; we create spaces for activities that damage ourselves and others and generate suffering. It is the tragedy of humanity. But the fact that we can use this principle for harm does not negate that it can be used for healing, and for empowerment. There is a whole art of blessing and life-enrichment that is based in the idea of Holding, for what is blessing but a particular kind of space that enhances the flow and expression of sacredness within whatever is held within that space?

Holding Others
When holding another energetically, you want to be non-invasive. You're

not giving them subtle energy, you're not even directly blessing them. Instead, you're surrounding them with a subtle field that minimizes outside interference and supports their own subtle body, its well-being and wholeness, enhancing its ability to act effectively and integrally. Metaphorically, it's like giving someone a quiet place to work and standing guard outside the door to see they are not interrupted. Or, to use a more parental image, it's like holding someone on your lap where they can feel safe, protected, and supported while they deal with whatever issues they are confronting.

Healing

One of the most ancient uses of subtle energies is for healing. *The Encyclopedia of Energy Medicine* lists 65 different disciplines of energy healing, drawing on Eastern, Western, and shamanic sources. Depending on the nature of the illness or complaint, healing work with subtle energies can be curative, but in most cases it serves as an adjunct to physical healing efforts. By heightening a person's energy field and bringing it into a greater state of coherency and vibrancy, the natural healing processes of the body can be enhanced, which assists whatever other medical treatment is being applied. Energy work is never a substitute for appropriate physical level medical care, if such is needed; after all, there are limits to what subtle energies can do, just as there are limits to what physical energies can do. As in so many aspects of our lives, a holistic approach that takes into account both our physical and our energetic, subtle sides is best. But if a physical ailment is being caused by an imbalance in the person's energy system, then the use of subtle energies may be exactly what is needed to restore that wholeness.

I have never been trained as a healer, and when it comes to energy healing, I firmly believe proper training is essential. There are people whose subtle energy fields seem to naturally radiate a healing presence, but even they can benefit from knowledge of physiology and anatomy, not to mention an understanding of the proper use of subtle energies. I well remember a time many years ago when I was ill and a friend attempted to do energy healing on me. Normally, I don't let anyone work on my energy field unless I'm sure they know what they're doing. But in this instance, I could feel his sincere desire to help, and I was feeling pretty lousy. So I thought I'd take a chance. I thought, what could it hurt? Ten minutes later, as he was channeling a lot of energy into my subtle field, I found out. I began to feel overwhelmed because I couldn't absorb all the energy he was sending, and I could feel that he was inadvertently "overloading my circuits." I had him stop, but by then I was developing a huge headache, and feeling unpleasantly disassociated with my body. Rather than helping, this energy transfusion made me feel worse. It took me a couple of days to recover from his "treatment." It was a valuable lesson for me and for him in taking care when working with anyone's energy field.

So, lacking the proper training, I don't attempt to do healing work with subtle energies, any more than I would attempt to prescribe drugs or do surgery on a physical level. However, there are things that can be done energetically that are the equivalent of simple first aid, which sometimes is all that is needed, and Holding is one of these.

Holding can be used to energetically support the body's own healing capacities. In many cases, this may be all that is needed, but even when more serious medical attention and procedures are required, supporting a person's energy field (not to mention their morale, thoughts, and feelings) can facilitate the healing process. Again, I would stress that to hold someone is to give them energetic support, expressed through loving and empowering thoughts, feelings, and visualization; it does not infuse or project energy into that person's energy field directly. It's like setting out a buffet of nourishing and delicious foods and then allowing a person to choose what they want to eat, as much as they want when they want it. Holding honors and supports an individual's sovereignty and boundaries. This is especially important when there is an illness or surgery has taken place, and a person's energetic boundaries may be weak or in flux as a consequence.

The Body Elemental

Our bodies are made up of trillions of life forms which we call "cells," "microbes," "bacteria," and so on. If they contain our DNA, they are our somatic cells, but the health of our bodies also depends on many other kinds of microbial life that are genetically different from us but essential to our physiology. Holding the energy of all these lives, each of which has its own subtle nature, its own intelligence and awareness, in connectedness and coherency is the task of a part of us I call our "body elemental." I think of it as the supervising intelligence of the body and thus as one of the sources of the body's innate ability to self-regulate and heal itself. In the incarnational process, this "elemental" is a gift to the incarnating soul from Gaia, the World Soul. It is, in my understanding, a little piece of Gaia within us each, working in blended collaboration and cooperation with the soul. It connects us to the larger planetary world even as it holds the energetic space for the cellular integrity and wholeness of our body.

This elemental is not all-powerful; it can be impacted both positively and negatively by our actions and by the kind of subtle energies we attract and generate. But it is highly resilient and in many ways is one of the most ancient parts of us, embodying a consciousness that has evolved through millions and millions of years. Just as it holds the energy of our anatomy and physiology, so we can hold it. As a form of self-care, whether you feel ill or not, holding your body elemental in love, in Light, in appreciation, and in the healthy flow of subtle energies in and around you can pay dividends. As this entity is strengthened within you, its capacity to generate health within your body is enhanced.

EXERCISES FOR CHAPTER FIFTEEN

Exercise: The Lap

This exercise is very simple: sitting down and forming a lap. A lap is a physical form of holding. When we sit, our bodies form a kind of bowl or cup. Imagine kids climbing into a lap: it is a place of love, comfort, healing, and transformation. Imagine when you climbed into a lap and how good and safe it felt.

In this exercise, simply sit down and form a lap. Go through the following elements as you do so, exploring the felt sense of each. Inherent in the lap is your power of holding.

- **Physical:**

    The physical action of this exercise is simplicity itself. From a standing position, you simply sit down, allowing your legs to form a lap. Be aware of the physical sensation and felt sense of being a lap. Feel the relaxation of sitting but at the same time the power and receptivity of forming a lap. Explore the felt sense of the space that is created in front of you, around you, and within you when you sit and form a lap.

- **Emotional:**

    Feel the power of being a space of holding. In your lap, you are forming a space of comfort, a space of healing, a space of encouragement and upliftment. In this space, negativity can be received and transformed as you hold a presence of peace, of love, and of strength.

- **Mental:**

    Your mind is also a lap. It is a cup that holds your thoughts. As you sit, let your mind go beyond the contents of any thoughts you may be holding. Let it simply appreciate the power of holding thoughts. Appreciate your mental space, the spaciousness of your mind. If thoughts come within this space, simply welcome them and let them sit in your mind-lap for a time, then move on. Remember, you are holding them, they are not holding you. You create and own the space they occupy. Sit in that space, be at peace, and feel the power of your mind to be a lap.

- **"Magical":**

    The cup is the oldest of magical images. It is the grail of the sacred, the cauldron of magic and wisdom, the cooking pot that creates nourishment, the womb of life, the cup that holds the cosmos. Your lap is this space, this grail, this cauldron, this womb, and this cup. When you sit and a lap is formed, you are in resonance with this primal container and its spaciousness—the womb of God from which new life is born.

- **Spiritual:**
  Sitting, your lap is the presence of the sacred. It is a place of love, a place to receive and comfort pain and suffering, a place of healing, a place of rebirth and regeneration. In the space of your lap you are in resonance with the sacred space that holds all things and allows them to be. God is a lap!

In doing this exercise, simply sit and as you do so, work through these levels of sensation, feeling, thought, energy, and spirit, appreciating the power, the freedom, the sovereignty, and the presence emerging from the simple act of forming a lap.

Exercise: Self-Lap
This exercise is a variant expression of the Lap exercise focused on yourself.

- Do the Standing Exercise, feeling your own sovereignty and the power of your individuality.
- Draw that power into yourself and do the Lap Exercise, creating a lap both physically and inwardly as a state of mind and being. Let yourself enter a condition of holding empowered by your sovereignty and individuality.
- Place yourself in your "lap." Hold yourself. Gather all the parts of you that you can think of, including those parts that you may not like so much or feel cause you problems. You are not doing anything to these parts or selves; you are just holding.
- In so doing, pay attention to a felt sense of the life and will of the soul that holds you together, so to speak. There is in each of us that expression of soul which is willing to be incarnate, willing to have parts, willing to have a personality, willing to have a body, willing to create a space that holds all the elements of our lives. How do you experience that? What is the felt sense of it to you? What is the love and the will that holds you?
- There is also in each of us a "body elemental" that is like the collective consciousness of all the cellular and microbial life that constitutes our physical body. It holds all these lives in its embrace, enabling their connectedness. Imagine this presence held in your lap as well, held

in your love, your appreciation, and your wholeness.

- Just let yourself be held and honored by yourself, by your own inner lap.
- When you feel this is complete, just stand up and let your lap dissolve. But remember that you continue to hold yourself. As you go through your day, encountering things in your environment that would snag and pull you apart or things in yourself that would divide you and pull you apart, remember the will that holds. Remember your lap. Remember to hold yourself again in love.

Exercise: The Holding Touch
This is also a variant of the holding (Lap) exercise given above.

- Sit and form a lap. Feel the open space and power of your holding. Feel the love, the acceptance, and the blessing that exists in this holding space before and around you. Imagine the felt sense of this holding space forming a bubble of energy and light that rests in your lap.
- Once you have the felt sense of this bubble of holding space firmly in your mind and body, then imagine this bubble flowing into you and moving down both your arms and splitting into ten smaller "bubbles," each moving into the tip of each finger. Imagine that each finger is like a miniature lap carrying the energy and presence of holding.
- Now get up and move about your room. Touch things. Take a moment with each thing you touch to feel it being held by the loving, holding power at your fingertips. Visualize each touch surrounding that which you are touching with a bubble of blessing, love, and appreciation. Pay attention to the felt sense of this at your fingertips, as well as within your body as a whole. Each "fingercup," each "fingerlap," is empowered by the incarnational power of holding. Each finger's touch awakens the possibility of blessing and spaciousness.
- Once you have in mind the felt sense of this, you can manifest this touch of holding anytime during the day. A simple handshake can become a moment of blessing. Remember that energy is NOT flowing from your hands into another. Instead, your fingers create a space of holding for the other within which their own life, their own Soul, their own beingness and light, can generate a blessing. Nor is energy flowing back into you from whatever or whomever you are touching. Your fingers are helping them to become a cup to hold their own

blessings of their own beings, not being a cup to receive and hold their energies.

- If you feel energy flowing back into you, just see it being held at your fingertips and offered back. This is not an exercise in giving and receiving energy but of holding and creating a space for blessing to emerge. If at any time this activity of holding feels tiresome or uncomfortable, just feel the power of holding moving back up your hand and arms away from your fingers, and back into the core of your being, into the light within you. It will be held there until you wish to extend it again.

Exercise: Holding Life

Blessing is a way of fostering and quickening the life-energy within anything. One way to do this is to hold it in love. This is like an energetic hug. The important thing is that you are not pushing or injecting energy into the object you're holding. You're simply immersing it in a pool of loving potential and allowing it to respond however it will. You do not have to physically hold something to do this. This same exercise could be done with a person by inwardly holding them in your mind and imagination in this pool of loving energy. This exercise is similar to the Touch of Love, but in some ways is simpler.

- Stand in your Sovereignty and Self-Light.
- Pick up an inanimate object you can hold in your hand.
- Take a moment just to acknowledge what it is and to appreciate it. Pay attention to its form, its structure, the substances from which it is made, and its function, if any.
- As you hold it, imagine a pool of love filling your hand, immersing the object which you are holding. This pool of love brings goodwill, appreciation, and vitality to the object, heightening its own life-energies and their evolutionary potentials.
- Hold it for as long as feels comfortable, allowing the object to bathe in this pool of love. Imagine this liquid love penetrating every aspect of this object, touching it inside and out, and allowing this object to absorb as much of this loving energy as it wishes or can.
- When you feel restless or tired or feel complete with this exercise, see the pool of love draining away, leaving the object energized in your hand. Place the object down and leave it be for awhile.
- Finish by standing in your Sovereignty and Self-Light.

Exercise: Holding Another

- Stand in your own Sovereignty and Self-Light.
- Picture the person you wish to hold in your mind. Whatever your usual thoughts and feelings about or towards this person may be, in this moment, you want to see them in a neutral but loving way, a way that honors, appreciates, and supports them simply for being who they are.
- Visualize an oval of Light large enough to enfold this person coming into being in the subtle environment near them. Within this oval is a clear, open, neutral space that is supportive without being invasive or demanding in any way.
- Mentally invite the person's inner being to step into this oval if they wish, explaining that its purpose is simply to hold them in a supportive, empowering way, creating a clear space in which they can be protected and upheld and in which their own soul's purposes may unfold without interference. You are offering them this space, you're not demanding they use it. [NOTE: *If the individual in question has previously asked you for help and given you permission to hold them energetically, then you can skip this step.*]
- If they step into the oval of Light, then send a stream of energy and Light from your being to activate this holding energy field, like inflating a balloon, allowing it to take whatever form and relationship to the individual you are holding that will best enable it to serve him or her, honoring his or her Sovereignty. Turn the maintenance and caretaking of this field over to the individual's own soul and to whatever spiritual allies may naturally be working with or protecting him or her. Release your connection to it.
- If the individual does not respond to your invitation, then simply allow the oval of Light to dissipate.

CHAPTER SIXTEEN
Energy Hygiene

Energy hygiene is about keeping your personal energy field clear and flowing both internally and in relationship to your environment. It's about establishing and maintaining the energetic coherency of your field and removing or transforming anything that might disrupt that coherency. It keeps you energetically "clean" and vital, just as physical hygiene keeps your body clean and in good working order. It is also a way of cleaning your local subtle environment, just as you would clean your home.

Healthy subtle energies are flowing and vibrant and are connected to the wholeness of the cosmos. They bring life, vitality and connection. But subtle energies can become disconnected from the larger whole of which they are a part or obstructed in their flow. When this happens, they can become stagnant or even toxic. Restoring (or maintaining) attunement, connection, circulation, and wholeness of the subtle energies within yourself and within the environment is what energy hygiene is about. (Energy hygiene for places other than the immediate environment or for persons other than oneself falls under the category of *subtle activism,* which we'll discuss in a later chapter.)

Personal Energy Hygiene

All living things put forth elements or "bits" of subtle energy as a result of their natural activity. These energetic "bits" may have a very short life indeed, lasting only seconds, or they can persist for awhile, depending entirely on the amount of energy and intention that went into their creation. The consequence is that the subtle environments through which we move in the course of a day are filled with energetic "particles" vibrating in some particular manner according to the activity that produced them. Our energy fields naturally absorb some of this much as we can pick up dust and lint on our clothes and skin as we go through our day.

If the material we absorb can be integrated into our energy field and made part of our own Sovereignty, our own identity and wholeness, all well and good. But if these "bits" or "vectors of energy" cannot be absorbed and integrated for one reason or another, then, they can become points of agitation in our field, passing on their energy qualities to our field in ways that can affect our own subtle body as well as our thoughts and feelings.

For instance, if someone in my environment is angry or fearful and is radiating these energies, I may pick up energetic "vectors" of anger or fear which, when temporarily lodged in my own subtle body, can create a sympathetic vibration of anger or fear in me. I may not consciously know where this feeling is coming from. Likewise, if someone is depressed, I may take on some of the vibrational vectors of this depression and start to feel low myself, again without knowing why.

Much of this "psychic lint" is easily sloughed off by our energy field, especially if we are in a reasonably healthy and vital condition. But sometimes, if I continue to simply absorb energetic impulses from my environment, they can begin to "clump" in my field like old grease that gets cold and clogs up a pipe and interferes with the proper flow of water through that pipe. In Chapter 3, I called them "coral reefs," and pictured them in Figure 10. Energy hygiene, then, is a way of "melting" that "grease" and flushing it away, allowing a clear and unobstructed flow to resume.

I'm not talking here about truly negative or harmful energies that we might encounter. I'll discuss those in the next chapter. I'm just talking about the natural wear and tear on our energy field as we deal with all the subtle energies that we encounter in the course of a day. Of course, these need not be negative or abrasive. The energetic emanations from others can also be very positive, enhancing the clarity and flow of our own energy field; we could walk into a burst of joyful energy as well as into a cloud of depression. How we are affected, though, depends on how well and in what manner we can integrate such energetic "bits" into our own energetic coherency. Sometimes, depending on our own inner state, it can be as challenging to encounter and integrate joy and love as it is to deal with the energetic effects of anger or fear.

Although there can be many different ways of doing energy hygiene—the simple act of taking a shower or a bath, for instance, can help as water is a powerful cleansing agency for subtle energies—in the end it comes down to affirming and expressing your wholeness and integrity, enhancing circulation and coherency in your field. This means standing in Sovereignty and Self-Light and attuning to your Presence, the active holopoietic function within you, making sure your *systemic* energies are strong. It's through your Interiority that you can attune to your personal flow of life, unfoldment, and wholeness. From this place, you can then take whatever other steps may be necessary to bring about a cleansing of your aura.

Environmental Energy Hygiene

The same principles hold true with the environment as with your personal energy field: healthy subtle energies are those that can circulate and flow and also be connected to a larger spiritual wholeness and to what I've called the systemic energies. They are energies that bring life, vitality and blessing to an environment, providing nourishment and stimulation in support of the beings who are part of that environment. But the energies in a place, particularly in buildings which due to their shape and structure can sometimes inhibit energy flow, can become obstructed or, because of activities that have taken place in that environment, even toxic. In some manner, they have become *aggravated*. This is when energy hygiene is helpful.

Energy hygiene in an environment means standing in your own integrity and wholeness and deliberately attuning to and enhancing those natural subtle energies I described in Chapter 11 that are systemic and organic and that serve the life, the unfoldment, the intentionality, and the wholeness of that environment. You become an agent of the holopoietic spirit within that environment.

In doing energy hygiene for any environment, it's important to remember that any area we wish to work with is itself connected to other areas and exists as part of a larger ecosystem. We need to be as precise as we can be about the energetic boundaries within which we're working as there could be effects beyond what we can see. Of course, this is true with many of our activities, not just those dealing with subtle energies. Any chemicals I may put on my lawn will end up in Puget Sound twenty miles away since all runoff from our neighborhood goes into the many creeks, rivers, and lakes that make up our local ecosystem, all of which in turn empty into the Sound.

Also, the word "space" implies an emptiness that is not true. We don't live in a vacuum either physically or energetically. Just as the air around me is filled with microorganisms, all of which have their own lives and energy fields, so the subtle environment of any area in which I'm working is also filled with living energies. I need to take their presence into account.

This is not a reason not to do subtle energy work; it's just a reason to be aware, careful and respectful.

Generally speaking, I won't do energy work in or around any environment for which I'm not responsible unless I've specifically been invited to do so. I feel perfectly OK about working with the energies of my own home, but I wouldn't just arbitrarily do energy work for my neighbor's yard or house. This is for practical reasons as well as for ethical ones. It's a matter of consistency and consequences. I'll do energy work in my house because I live in it, and I'm consistently present to deal with any consequences of such work. I'm part of the life of my house. But I don't live in my neighbor's house and have no way of consistently dealing there with the consequences of anything I might do to his house's energy field.

However, fields are nestled within fields. I may not be part of the energy field of my neighbor's house but we're both part of the energy field of our neighborhood and share a collective responsibility for the well-being of the neighborhood. There have been times when I've been walking through my neighborhood and have felt a negative vibe coming from a particular house. I can't go into that house and start clearing and cleansing things; I'm not the responsible party within the boundaries of the house. But I can invite a stronger flow of cleansing and healing energy into the neighborhood as a whole. I can offer a kind of general blessing for my neighborhood, which is more like a prayer for everyone's well-being.

How do we go about doing energy hygiene? There are many ways, and it's important in this instance as with all forms of engagement with subtle forces that you use your intuition, wisdom, and common sense to discern what is needed and what you can safely and effectively do. Here are a couple of suggestions. One method is through circulation. Circulation means restoring or enhancing the movement and flow of subtle energies. One of the simplest ways is to move yourself. If it's your own energy field you're working with, then taking a walk can not only get your blood moving but your vital subtle energies as well. It may not do the whole trick, but it's a start. (It's one reason that a number of psychologists prescribe walking as therapy for depression.)

Breathing is also a time-honored method for getting vital energies moving. Rhythmic breathing of some nature has been a foundation of meditation practice since the beginning of such practices, but not only for its calming effect. In the martial arts, breathing is a way of raising chi or vital energy within the body, with the mind then directing it where it needs to go.

If it's an environmental field, such as stagnant energies in a room, then walking about in the room can help to stir things up as well. So can dancing, clapping, singing, and making music, as sound currents are another way to create circulation.

Most of us are familiar with the circulation of heat in a room from a radiator. The radiator heats the air around it which then flows outward into the cooler air of the room. The cooler air, displaced, moves towards the radiator, where it is in turn heated, continuing the circulatory cycle. Something similar happens in the subtle realms. If I heighten my own energy with love or with whatever positive qualities I want to bring into the environment—or simply by attuning to my own Interiority or standing in an inner condition of blessing—an energy differential can be created between my energy field and that of the space in which I'm working, just as there's an energy differential between the warm air near the radiator and the cool air in the rest of the room. This sets up a flow of energy within the local subtle environment.

I can enhance this flow with my intention to bless the environment. Energy does follow directed thought and imagination, so if I visualize the energy state I wish to create in the local environment and see this state flowing out from me, there will be a response. This may be all that an environment needs. Providing a presence of energy may jump start the flow of energy, like jumping a car where the battery has died.

However, you can also work with the systemic energies of the environment by attuning to forces of life, emergence, and holopoiesis which are always present even if obscured by toxic, stagnant or disconnected energies in that environment. In effect, you align your Interiority—the place in you where these energies are most active—with the Interiority of the environment, which may in fact be part of the life and energy of Gaia itself. In such a case, you are seeking to draw forth and enhance the natural potential for holistic and flowing energies within the environment itself, letting those forces then do the work of energy hygiene.

In addition to enhancing circulation, another method could be called transubstantiation. Transubstantiation means simply the changing of one substance into another. In Christian theology, it's the changing of the substance of the bread and wine into the body and blood of the Christ through the consecration of the Eucharist. In what might be thought of as a "Eucharist of life", green plants do something equally magical. Through the process of photosynthesis, they transform the pure energy of sunlight into the physical form of a sugar molecule. Plants turn energy into matter.

This ability to change one thing into another can be used when clearing and cleansing subtle energies, though it should be applied only with care and skill, and with adequate attention to your own boundaries and Sovereignty. In this case, instead of sunlight, you are using your Self-Light and the wholeness of your Interiority to attune to and draw to yourself transpersonal energies or forces from your soul level or beyond, which you then transform into embodied spiritual forces within yourself. In a way, you create "sugar molecules" of joy, love, serenity, and so forth within your heart and mind which you can then radiate out into the environment or into your own energy field. In this way, you become a transformer, "stepping down" a more powerful energy into a form that can positively affect and be easily assimilated by the local subtle environment.

There is a reverse process by which you can take in negative or imbalance energies from the environment into your own field and "transubstantiate" them into positive, transpersonal energies through your own attunement, but it obviously has risks. It's a technique that can be very powerful but requires skill and knowledge and great care in its execution. Just taking in imbalanced or negative energies without knowing how to properly transmute them is a recipe for disaster and can cause you harm. I've had two friends, both skilled workers with subtle energies, who attempted this, only to end up very ill as a consequence, one of them fatally so. Unless you know what you're doing and have experience and skill in working with subtle forces and in self-protection and self-cleansing—or you are working in partnership under the protection and guidance of a transpersonal being who does have such experience and skill—don't try to draw negative energies into yourself for transmutation.

The Ethics of Energy Hygiene

A friend of mine and I once ran a weekend workshop in a very old building that had at one time been a monastery but had been turned into a school. Arriving early to check out the rooms we would be using, we were dismayed to discover how dismal and lifeless the energies were and how dark the rooms. The whole atmosphere—inner and outer—was depressing. We knew that it would be very hard to have a successful workshop in these surroundings if we didn't do some thorough cleansing and heightening first. It was not our building; the rooms we were using didn't belong to us, though we were renting them. But we were responsible for the quality of the experience that the people coming to the workshop would have; we were responsible to the well-being of their energy fields. So, asking permission of the spirits of the place and explaining what we were going to do and why, we set about doing a major job of subtle energy cleansing.

The way we did it, though, was fun. We explained what the situation was to the workshop attendees, and we spent the first morning physically cleaning down the place while energetic music played in the background. Physical cleaning is one of the best ways to alter the energies in a room, and we all went at it with mops and sponges, washing walls and windows, the floor, the furniture. We laughed a lot (always a good way to get energy moving), we danced some, we sang along with the music, and we put elbow grease into that old room. We also took time to meditate to focus our subtle energies in blessing ways. We called forth to the systemic, life-giving energies in the stones and plaster, the paint and wallpaper, and all the other materials that made up the rooms in which we were holding our program. We gave the whole place a transformation. Needless to say, after this, the workshop was a great success and taught some valuable lessons in cleansing a space.

The rooms in which we worked had clear, discernible boundaries, and we were clearly responsible for the quality of subtle energy that would encompass the workshop, but this is not necessarily true for natural spaces. Once when visiting a friend of mine, she asked me to come with her to a particular spot in a local road. It was a sharp bend, and over the years, there had been a number of accidents there with lives lost. What prompted her to invite me to see it was that in a space of two weeks, there had been three major accidents, one of which had killed a young woman. My friend wondered if a negative energy vortex had developed in this spot, one that might be attracting accidents.

When I stood in this bend in the road where the accidents had occurred, I could feel that the psychic atmosphere was distressed and turbulent due, I felt, to the deaths that had happened there. There were the remains of several bouquets of flowers that people had left there in memory of at least one of the people who had died. Walking around this area was like stepping into a low pressure area where a storm front had formed. I didn't feel any negative forces, such as angry beings or lost souls, but I did feel a heightening of the possibilities that an accident would occur at this spot. A pattern I can only call a "habit" had developed in the energy around this bend in the road. It had the feel of an accident waiting to happen.

It was hard to discern how far this effect extended. What I did feel was that in some way a pocket of energy had formed that was not connected to the surrounding land. I couldn't tell how big it was, but I could feel its disconnectedness.

This spot was on public land. As a member of the public, I certainly had a right to bless the area and to do energy work. However, what I didn't know and, given my particular skills at the time, wasn't sure I could find out, was whether the cause of this negative patch of energy was due to the accidents or whether the accidents were due to the negative energies being there as a result of some other cause that wasn't immediately apparent. For instance, the building of the road itself in this area might have cut across some subtle line of energy that was causing a "short-circuit" which in turn caused the negative patch. I couldn't undo the road, and I didn't have the knowledge or skill to realign a broken etheric line of energy.

So, while I was sure I could clear away the immediate cloud of negativity, I wasn't sure that it wouldn't come right back. Even if the cause lay in the accidents and in particular the deaths, the cleansing might have to be repeated over a period of time to have a lasting effect. This wasn't something I could do as I didn't live in the area.

In the end, I decided that even though I might have a right to act, I didn't have enough information or understanding of the deeper causes to know how to act properly. I didn't want to just treat the symptom and not the cause. And not living nearby, I felt I probably wasn't the right person anyway as I didn't have the opportunity to consistently work with this bit of land as it might need. I didn't want to start something and then leave it unfinished. That could just make things worse.

What I ended up doing was asking a generic blessing for this damaged spot, surrounding it with love, and then asking the local nature spirits to do what they could to heal this area and reconnect it with the larger wholeness of the land around them. This may have worked as the last I heard, my friend said there had been no more accidents.

Doing energy hygiene in particular environments raises important questions that you need to consider. Here are some examples:

- Are you responsible? Can you act freely and with authority in this situation? In the case of the workshop, my friend and I could answer yes.
- Do you know what is needed? With the workshop, we did, but with the road where the accidents had occurred, I did not, at least not in the deep way I felt was required for a successful act of energy hygiene.
- Can you supply what is needed with care and skill? My friend and I knew what we were doing in cleansing the rooms we were using in the old monastery. I was not sure I had the right skills for cleansing the road.
- Can you avoid doing harm or making a situation worse? I could not answer in the affirmative with the road, so it was better to do nothing directly.
- Can you stand in an attunement that allows you to be a partner in co-creating wholeness. The answer in both cases for me was yes, but with the road, I used this attunement to give blessings to the local subtle beings who I felt were in a better position than I to do something positive about the situation.
- Can you follow through if necessary? With the monastery, we weren't trying to cleanse and vivify its energies throughout the building for all time; we were working with specific boundaries in time and space. What we did was only for certain rooms for three days. No follow-through was necessary. With the road, though, part of what led me to decide to do nothing in the way of direct energy hygiene was that I was a visitor, only there for a day. I had no way of following up on the inner work should it be needed.

Afterthoughts

Imagine going to a doctor and having her say to you, "I know what's best for you. I'm in charge here, and you need to do what I say." How would that approach make you feel? What if she said instead, "I want to be your partner. You are in charge of your body and your health, and I'd like to use my skill and knowledge to help you heal yourself." How would that approach make you feel? In one, you are disempowered, while in another you are empowered.

Although subtle energies don't have emotions, they are sentient and alive. They will respond to being shaped by will but they will respond even more to a cooperative approach that engages them as partners in achieving wholeness and health. Just as you might respond with resistance to the first doctor's approach, for few people like to be bossed about, you are more likely to respond with openness and cooperation to the second approach. Subtle energies are really no different. Coming on to them like gangbusters or like a powerful wizard demanding they obey your commands is likely to generate a backlash of resistance.

In a way, this is the larger lesson for our species. We've had an attitude of dominating nature and telling it what to do, and we can see in the growing ecological disruption and climate change that this approach isn't working all that well. It's time to try partnership, and this is true in the subtle domains as well.

You will notice that I haven't talked much about working with subtle beings and spiritual allies in doing subtle energy work. Particularly with clearing and cleansing, engaging (as a partner!) with a subtle ally can be very effective and powerful. For instance, if I want to clean up jagged or stagnant energies in a particular place, I could call upon the spirit of the place, the *genus loci*, which in nature might be a local Deva or for a room in a building could be an angel overlighting that building or neighborhood—or the town as a whole. In fact, this was my approach in dealing with the cloud of negative energy on the road in my story.

Partnering with subtle beings is a topic of its own that is, as I have said, the focus of the third book in my Subtle Worlds trilogy. What I want to focus on here is the art of working with subtle energies using your own subtle energy field and your Interiority as your primary tools. If you have a solid foundation in working with subtle energies, collaborating with subtle beings will come more easily and be more successful.

EXERCISES FOR CHAPTER SIXTEEN

An Important Caveat

The exercises I offer here are fairly simple and are designed for everyday energy hygiene. They are the equivalent of taking a shower or a bath. Bathing your body is a good, hygienic thing to do to get rid of the day's accumulation of dirt and grime on a physical level, and the same is true on an energetic level. But there are situations that require more than this. To change the metaphor, if you've been badly injured, you may need a doctor to deal with the wound and the trauma. Simple home remedies or first aid solutions aren't enough.

In using these exercises, please use discernment to know if you may be facing something that is beyond the scope of these simple techniques. Simple energy hygiene can be helpful with everyday feelings of depression, low energy, irritation, and the like brought on by temporary turbulence in your energy field. But they are NOT designed to substitute for the deeper work that therapy can provide. If you are experiencing turmoil in your subtle energy field, it may be coming from experiences and trauma lodged in the psyche and requiring some form of psychotherapeutic or somatic therapy. It may be caused by a purely physical condition which is best treated by bodywork or medical intervention.

We are complex beings. Energy hygiene as I present it here is a useful technique but it only goes so far. You can do a lot with loving treatment of your own energy field, but some things really do require the help of a trained professional.

Exercise: Energy Hygiene for the Personal Energy Field

- Stand in your Sovereignty, in Self-Light, and in Presence: i.e. in the felt sense of your wholeness as a person.
- Imagine yourself standing in the middle of an oval or "egg" of energy that surrounds you completely and extends above your head and below your feet.
- Above your head at the top of this oval of energy, imagine a point of Light; imagine a similar point of Light at the bottom of this oval under your feet. Imagine and feel a circular flow of energy between these two points, down the front of you and up behind you. This movement creates a flow of Self-Light throughout your field.
- Imagine and feel the transpersonal Light of your soul radiating out into your subtle field from your Interiority. As it does so, its Light becomes part of the circulation of Self-Light flowing around within your field, heightening and intensifying it, enhancing its connectedness to your wholeness and integrity. This creates an internal environment in which any energetic material, whether taken

in from the environment or arising from your own psyche, that is disconnected from your Sovereignty, your wholeness, and your vital spirit takes up the Light of your being and is either transformed into material you can assimilate and integrate or it is swept out of your field into larger fields of wholeness and Light where it can be properly assimilated and transmuted.

- Take as long as you wish to feel this process of cleansing as your Self-Light circulates in your field, instilling in all the aspects of your energy field an attunement to the integrity, wholeness and health of your incarnate beingness. When you feel complete, take a moment to thank all parts of you for their participation in this process. Finish by standing in your Sovereignty.

Exercise: Energy Hygiene for the Subtle Environment

Overview

When clearing your own energy field, you are the responsible party and thus the authority. After all, it is your energy field! You are working basically with your own subtle energies, though you can certainly draw upon help from sources outside yourself. When working to clear an environmental field, such as that within a room or around a particular landscape, you are engaging with more than just your own being, so a partnering, collaborative approach works best.

Working with an environment, it's not always so clear where the negative energy and psychic "lint" is coming from or how deep the problem runs. It's one thing to clean out a pond of water that's had dirt and mud thrown into it and something else to clean a pond that is being fed by an ongoing polluted stream coming, say, from a factory runoff. Cleaning the muddy pond may be totally within your capabilities but trying to clean up a situation of industrial pollution may be more than you can undertake on your own. You need to be discerning.

There are two kinds of environments: "built" ones like buildings and rooms in buildings, and natural ones. Although they can pose different challenges and have different characteristics, in both cases you are dealing with an ecology. A room in a building is part of the whole energy field of the building, and sources of negativity can be located outside the room in other parts of the building where you do not have access. This is certainly the case when dealing with a natural environment outdoors. I might want to work with the subtle energies in my backyard, for instance, but my yard is part of the whole ecosystem where I live which includes hundreds of other houses in our subdivision, a nearby lake, surrounding mountains, and so on.

So as I said in Chapter 9, I need to establish boundaries for the clearing and cleansing work I want to do. This is the first step. If it's a room, then the walls, floor and ceiling of the room will provide those boundaries. If it's outdoors, then I have to deliberately establish mental and energetic boundaries and clearly designate the area which I want to affect and where I will be working.

The second step is to establish an "anchor." An "anchor" is simply something within the environment to which you can anchor your energy work and which acts as focal point. So, for instance, an anchor ally might be a piece of furniture in a room whereas outdoors it might be a stone or a bush. The use of the anchor is to tie your energy work specifically within the boundaries and the space with which you will be working. In a way, you are such an anchor point, but something that is naturally part of the space can extend and ground your energetic presence. It's a way of further focusing your work in the midst of a larger energetic ecology.

The third step is to align with natural systemic currents of nourishing, cleansing and healing energies in the local environment, as I discussed in Chapter 10. On a physical level, sunlight and wind can be very cleansing (as can rain). Sometimes the simplest way to clear stagnant subtle energy in a room is to open the windows and let in sunlight and breezes. The point is that you don't have to supply all the energy from your own self, though you can trigger and direct it. You provide the focusing lens and Nature provides the oomph!

With these things in mind, here are two exercises, one for indoors and one for outdoors.

Indoors

- Stand in your Sovereignty, Self-Light and Presence, making sure your own energy is clear, flowing, grounded and in balance.
- Be aware of the boundaries of the space with which you are about to work, which most likely will be the walls, ceiling and floor. If you are working with a space within a room but not filling the whole room, then in your imagination, be clear where the boundaries are and hold that as an image in your mind.
- Greet the life—the living energies—within the space with loving respect, telling it what you are going to do and why and inviting its cooperation.
- Imagine the larger context of the world within which this space exists. Be aware of the flow of forces of life, wholeness, and Light flowing through the world as a whole, a circulation of vital energies. Whatever the condition of the subtle energies in the space with which

you are working, the space as a whole is still part of and embedded within this larger flow. Attune to this flow of circulating energies in the larger environment as if you were stepping into a flowing river of Light and life.

- Identify an object in the room to be your "anchor", inviting it to be your partner in the act of cleansing. Embrace and hold this object in the flow of circulating energies moving through you. You are connecting this object with this larger flow so that through your attention and agency, you are making it part of this flow as well.

- Now from this anchor point, visualize and feel the flow of circulating, cleansing, healing, reconnecting energies radiating out into the space with which this object is connected, into the room of which it is a part. In your mind's eye, see the boundaries of this space being filled with Light and this Light circulating through the space to draw all parts of it into harmony. See any stuck or disconnected energies, any negativity of any kind, either being transformed into a healthy, connected state or being swept cleanly out of the room by the circulatory flow for which you and your anchor object are the lens and the focal point.

- Hold this flow—and this image of cleansing—as long as feels comfortable or until you feel tired. Then, step out of the circulatory flow that you have been drawing into the space. Give thanks for its assistance and for the cooperation of the living energies of the space itself.

- Standing in Sovereignty, grounding yourself wholly in your body in whatever way is appropriate to you. Then go about your normal business.

Outdoors

- Stand in your Sovereignty, Self-Light and Presence, making sure your own energy is clear, flowing, grounded and in balance.

- Be aware of the boundaries of the space with which you are about to work. Outdoors, you are in the midst of a variety of spaces, each nested within the other, so you need to clearly delineate the boundaries of the particular space you wish to clear. Either mark these boundaries in some manner or identify the edges of the space using the natural landmarks, objects and plants around you. Because you can't "cleanse" all of Nature, it's important to be specific about the area where you are focusing your efforts.

- Greet the life—the living energies—within this designated space with loving respect, telling it what you are going to do and why and inviting its cooperation.

- Imagine the larger context of the world within which this space exists. Be aware of the flow of forces of life, wholeness, and Light flowing through the world around you as a whole, a circulation of vital energies. Whatever the condition of the subtle energies in the space with which you are working, it is still part of the larger environment within which forces of circulation and energy flow are at work. Attune to this flow of circulating energies in the larger environment as if you were stepping into a flowing river of Light and life.

- Identify an object in the immediate environment to be your "anchor", inviting it to be your partner in the act of cleansing. Embrace and hold this object in the flow of circulating energies moving through you. You are connecting this object with this larger flow so that through your attention and agency, you are making it an agent of this flow as well.

- Now from this anchor point, visualize and feel the flow of circulating, cleansing, healing, reconnecting energies radiating out into the space with which this object is connected, into the immediate, local environment of which it is a part. In your mind's eye, see the boundaries of this space being filled with Light and this Light flowing inward into the space to circulate and draw all parts of it into harmony. See any stuck or disconnected energies, any negativity of any kind, either being transformed into a healthy, connected state or being swept cleanly away by the circulatory flow for which you and your anchor object are the lens and the focal point.

- Hold this flow—and this image of cleansing—as long as feels comfortable or until you feel tired. Then, step out of the circulatory flow that you have been drawing into the space. Give thanks for its assistance and for the cooperation of the living energies of the space itself.

- Standing in Sovereignty, grounding yourself wholly in your body in whatever way is appropriate to you. Then go about your normal business

CHAPTER SEVENTEEN
Protection

Protection is a special form of energy hygiene, one that deals with aggravated subtle energies. Before examining these energies in more detail, let's see what we have in the form of innate subtle protection, our inner immune system, if you will.

To understand the nature of protection, I want to remind you that generally speaking, your subtle body perceives its environment by resonating or blending with what it encounters. Think of a calm lake where the water responds with waves and ripples to the breezes that blow against it. In a manner of speaking, as I have said in previous chapters, this is "perception through becoming." As the outer surface of your subtle field ripples and responds to the play of subtle energies upon it, it sends a signal to the mind about what it is sensing. But unlike a similar sensory signal from your physical environment that tells you that what you see, hear or touch is "out there," this subtle sensory signal can feel as if it is saying, "This is 'in here;' I am this sensation I'm feeling; this is who I am." In other words, it feels subjectively rather than objectively. It takes some practice and discernment to distinguish between a sensation that actually arises from within you—one that is truly subjective—and one inspired and instigated by something in your objective subtle environment.

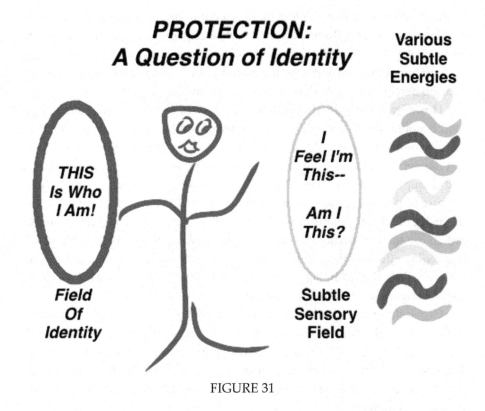

FIGURE 31

In a manner of speaking, as suggested in Figure 31, subtle perception begins with a question: "Am I this?" This is quickly resolved by the coherency and presence of our identity, our inner sense of who we are. In effect, there is part of us that knows "This is who I am!" On a physical level, this knowing is held in our DNA; in the subtle dimensions, it's held in the "field of identity" that is created by our soul and by our Sovereignty. This field manifests as the integrity and coherency of our overall energy field. It gives a unique and signature "spin" or vector to our subtle energies. Note that this field of identity is an energy phenomenon; it is not necessarily the same, nor is it dependent upon, our psychological sense of self, in exactly the same way that our genetic identity is not dependent upon who we think we are in our autobiographical musings. Our energetic identity is a felt sense that embraces physical, psychological, and spiritual components of our being. It is part of the energetic boundary of who we are, differentiating us energetically from the surrounding environment. It is part of the identity encoded in our subtle body.

In physical perception, our brain evaluates the signals coming from our various sensory organs and compares them to what it already knows. This allows me to look at a coffee cup and know it's a coffee cup or to look at a tree and know it's a tree. Unless there is a pathology that makes this process dysfunctional, I can tell a book from a bush, a car from a dog, an airplane from an artichoke. There is a similar process of discernment and identification going on with our subtle sensing with the added layer that not only identifies what is being perceived but also distinguishes it from who we are.

However, if our field of identity is weakened in some manner or our energy field is not coherent enough for the presence and knowledge of our identity to fully permeate that field, then this process becomes dysfunctional. This can happen because of trauma—an experience that weakens our boundaries and disrupts the internal development of a sense of selfhood. It can happen because of psychological difficulties (for example, I can weaken myself from the inside out through constant self-judgment, criticism, disparagement, and so on). It can happen because of drugs and alcohol which can have a boundary-weakening effect on the subtle body. However this occurs, when it happens we are vulnerable to being over-influenced or affected by subtle energies, particularly those of an aggravated nature.

Generally speaking, those elements in the subtle environment that can harm us do so through a kind of "identity theft." Energetically speaking, "identity" is in part a "spin"; it is a signature characteristic of how a particular energetic "particle" or "wave" is vibrating, moving and aligning itself. If an energy phenomenon has its "spin" changed, then it becomes a different phenomenon. Its identity changes.

What I've called "aggravated energies"—energies that are "smoggy," "jagged," or malicious and predatory—harm us by hijacking our energetic and psychic identities in some manner (they cannot harm our spiritual identity anchored in the soul). Protection is a matter of empowering or restoring our native identity, preventing or healing energetic identity theft.

Boundaries

An important concept when discussing protection is that of boundaries. When we talk about boundaries in the subtle world, we are not necessarily talking about a membrane or a barrier in the same way our skin is a boundary on the physical level. We are really talking about a zone of interaction in which the energies of our identity encounter and blend with energies from the subtle environment. In a way, we perceive by becoming that which we perceive. I might call this "perception through becoming." I illustrate this in Figure 32.

Imagine that there are three zones of subtle energies. On one side is the zone of our identity, our "I" zone, so to speak. This constitutes the energies of our subtle being that are clearly aligned with and expressive of who we are as spiritual, mental, emotional, physical, and energetic identities. On the other side is the "zone" of the subtle environment itself, the "They" zone, composed of all that is not-us and their respective energies. In-between is a zone that is a "We" zone, a blend of our "I energies" and the world's "they energies." This "We" zone is our subtle boundary.

Obviously this is not a wall or even a hard line of demarcation in the way our skin is. It is a dynamic zone of activity and interaction within which our subtle body is participating in the energetic life of the world around us. The kind of participation that takes place determines how protected we are. The more the "We" zone reflects the energetic "spin" or character of our "I" zone, the more we can engage with the world without having our energetic identity threatened or hijacked.

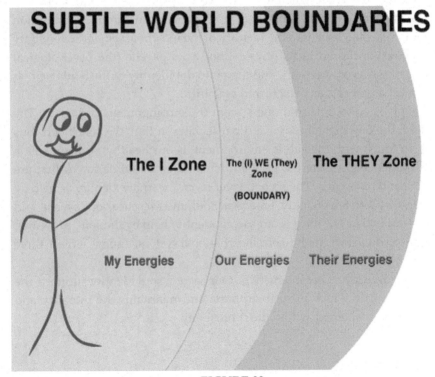

SUBTLE WORLD BOUNDARIES

The I Zone   The (I) WE (They) Zone   The THEY Zone

(BOUNDARY)

My Energies   Our Energies   Their Energies

FIGURE 32

In this context, we can see that "boundary" reflects and is an expression of the clarity, strength, integrity, stability, and robustness of the energetic "spin" that expresses our identity. How difficult is it for our energy to have its spin changed (and thus its identity changed) by an outside force? The stronger the boundary, the more difficult such a change is.

On the other hand, a boundary should not isolate us. As you can see, boundaries are there not just to protect and identify but also to enable engagement and connection. They are a "We" zone for a reason, to allow interaction and perception to take place. For this reason, the surface layer of an energy field such as our subtle body possesses a "mutable identity;" it can take up the spin of energies it encounters in order to blend with them and thus come to perceive and to know them. This means that the "We zone," which in essence is the sensory layer or sensory organ of the subtle body, is very fluid and "wears" its core identity lightly. It can easily change "shape" to configure to the environment around it. What is important is if it can quickly reassert its core shape or spin, that it doesn't forget who it is in the process of conveying information through becoming something else. In effect, the "I" component of the "We zone" is not overwhelmed or replaced by the "they" component.

A healthy and coherent subtle body is one that has an unbroken connection of identity reaching back into the identity of the incarnate self, its Sovereignty and Presence anchored in its physical body, its psyche (the psychological structure of our everyday self), and then into the identity of the Soul itself. It knows itself as energy, as person, and as spirit.

This gives our subtle immune system three components or layers. The first layer, the one that supports and participates in the "We zone" and thus is most in touch with the subtle environment, is our healthy, resilient subtle body experiencing a coherent flow and circulation of subtle forces that are vitalizing and renewing. The second layer is our incarnate identity as held by our Interiority (our Sovereignty, Emergent Soul, and Presence), our psyche, and our physical body. The third is our sacred identity held by the soul, providing a flow of spiritual energies into our incarnational system. I suggest these three layers in Figure 33.

These three layers are interactive. Our sacred, soul identity supports the incarnate identity which in turn supports and maintains the integrity and coherent flow of energies within the subtle body.

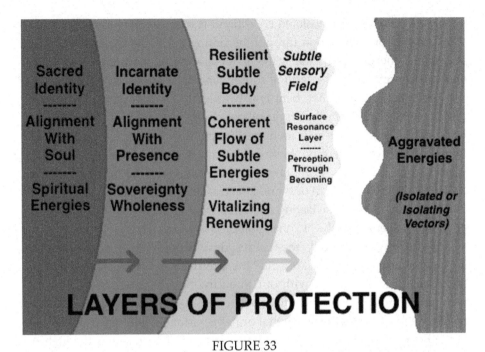

FIGURE 33

With this in mind, we can see that for the most part, protection is a matter of maintaining and manifesting the integrity and coherency of identity throughout our incarnate system and its various fields of energy; it's an expression of Sovereignty and wholeness expressed through inner connectedness. It's when these three layers of ourselves become disconnected and out of alignment that we become more vulnerable, for then our innate inner immune system becomes less resilient and functional.

Principle of Protection

When we do need subtle protection, what are we protecting ourselves from?

Healthy energies and healthy identities have an internal coherency and flow and they are connected to larger fields of life and being. A healthy identity is not isolated or alienated from the world around it; at least energetically, it takes part in a connective, circulatory flow of living energies. We are all part of a greater whole.

However, for various reasons, subtle energies can become cut off and disconnected, and when this happens, they can become what I called in Chapter 11 *aggravated energies*. Their main characteristic is that in some manner and to some degree they are expressing a "vector" that is isolated or isolating.

When we encounter such energies, the surface layer of our subtle body senses and takes on this isolated condition. It may do this passively as part of its process of "perception through becoming." On the other hand, if the aggravated energy is particularly intense or aggressive, it can force its "shape" onto our energy field with varying consequences.

The effect of this is that, temporarily at least, a part of our field becomes disconnected itself from the larger whole of our identity. More precisely, it begins to express an energetic identity different from our own which attempts to make itself "our" identity. In this, it functions similarly to a physical virus which, when it invades a cell, takes over the DNA-making processes of that cell and uses them to churn out viral DNA. If this process is contained within the "We zone," it has little lasting effect; it's when it invades our deeper levels of energetic identity in the "I zone" that problems arise.

In a healthy subtle body, the first response is simply to erase the isolating impression and organically "re-spin" the affected parts of our field, bringing them back into alignment with our integrity, Sovereignty, coherency, and identity. A metaphor for this might be an Etch-A-Sketch. The aggravated or negative energy is like the pencil that draws a particular pattern on the surface of the Etch-A-Sketch, but this image disappears and is erased as the Etch-A-Sketch is shaken, restoring it to its clear, pristine condition. Taking cognizance of the negative energy and its effect and conveying that information to our inner mind, our subtle field then flushes that pattern away.

But sometimes, for reasons I'll soon discuss, this isn't enough. The pattern is engraved more deeply on the Etch-A-Sketch surface of the subtle body; the "spin" in your "We zone" becomes more "They" than "I," and not in a good way. If the impression is deep enough, it may begin to affect the energy vectors of the deeper layers of your subtle body. If it continues to affect you, it begins to affect your psyche; that is, the effect ceases to be purely energetic and is translated into your thoughts and feelings. For instance, the aggravated energy might be one of anger which moves from being an angry vibration in your energy field to stimulating angry feelings and thoughts in your psyche. If you identify with these thoughts and feelings, personalizing them and making them your own, then the aggravated energy is turning you into someone who reflects and generates those angry energies in turn. Your identity has been hijacked by the anger.

The basic principle of protection is to reverse this process and to project your own identity more forcefully and fully into your own subtle field and then out into the subtle environment. So, for instance, in the example of encountering angry subtle energies, rather than taking them in and becoming angry yourself, you deliberately and powerfully stand in your Sovereignty and affirm your calmness, your lovingness, your compassion as the dominant elements of your identity. You refuse to identify with the anger.

If you have difficulty doing this, then the next step is to go deeper into your Interiority and its connection with your soul. You want to attune to and invoke your soul presence and its spiritual energy, affirming your sacred identity. This may also take the form of invoking spiritual allies or attuning to sacred figures who can inspire you with Light and vitalize the sense of spiritual identity within you.

In each of these steps, you are not simply being defensive. You are also expressing a level of energy that can withstand the negative and disconnecting effects of the aggravated energies and begin to "re-spin" them, breaking down their isolated condition and restoring them to a healthy and proper flow and connectedness with the larger wholeness of life. In effect, the principle of protection always incorporates the possibility of healing and redemption of the aggravated energies and a transformation of their disconnected condition. If the healthy flow of your subtle body is not sufficient to do this, then you draw upon deeper and higher inner resources until you can embody and express a condition of being that makes it difficult for the negative energies to remain in your vicinity without becoming transformed. Figure 34 illustrates this process, using the model suggested in Figure 32:

In other words, the basic principle of protection, at whatever level of identity can deal with the problem, is that you attune to that level and empower it, express it, and allow its characteristic "spin" and nature to fill your being and manifest itself as both boundary and identity. In a manner of speaking, you push the most effective level of identity in the moment—whether than of spirit and soul, thought and emotion, or subtle energy—into your subtle body and its "We" zone, so that that boundary becomes resonantly and strongly expressive of the "I" component in contrast to the "They" component.

You are establishing who is the energetic master of your subtle house.

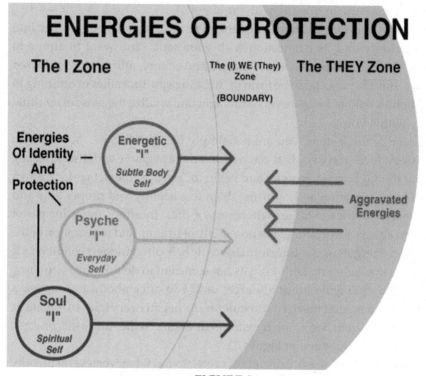

FIGURE 34

With this in mind, an important element of protection is managing your own internal energy field and the impact of your thoughts and feelings upon it. If you consistently express anger, hatred, depression, fear, or other negative psychological states, your energy field reflects this. Since the subtle worlds generally operate through resonance—a "like attracts like" quality—this means that a habitual build up of aggravated energies in your own psyche and subtle field—that is, in your "I zone"—makes you more vulnerable to the effects of aggravated energies that enter your "We zone" from your subtle environment. It's why moral and spiritual development needs to go hand in hand with psychic or subtle development. The more powerful you become in working with subtle energies and the more sensitive your field becomes as a consequence, the more important it is that you are able to maintain a calm, loving, balanced character to your personal energy field. Any of us can have a momentary experience of fear or anger, but if the natural characteristic of your inner life is one of harmony, your subtle body can easily absorb and "re-spin" any negative energies you may temporarily produce. But if you have made negative thoughts and feelings towards others or towards yourself a habit, then your subtle body will not necessarily automatically transmute these energies, creating a vulnerability within you to such aggravated energies in the world around you.

Coupling

Subtle energies, like any organism, do not exist in a vacuum. Even when they are disconnected and isolated, they still have to position themselves in an environment that can allow this condition to exist. All organisms, subtle and physical, are *coupled* with their environment. Change the environment, and the organism will have to change and adapt as well, or it will remove itself and find an environment that is more compatible to its existence.

An aggravated energy by its very nature is partially or entirely cut off from the life-giving and life-sustaining flow of the larger whole. So it has to find a way to maintain its existence. It needs an environment that will not challenge its existence, and it needs to find a source of energy to replace what it would ordinarily have received by participating in a larger whole. One way to do this is to parasitically draw upon and use the living energies of others. Like a virus, to do this, it has to change the identity of the other at least sufficiently that it can live within that other's field and draw upon its energy. It has to change the energy environment of the system it's parasitizing so that some degree of coupling can occur.

As I mentioned above, this environment doesn't have to be outside of us. It can be within us, in our subtle energy field. If we regularly and habitually indulge in thoughts and emotions that generate fear, anger, lust, hate, greed, selfishness, and so on, we are creating an inner environment that can be compatible to all kinds of aggravated subtle energies. It is much harder to gain an energetic foothold in us if we have a regular practice of attuning to and filling our energy field with love, compassion, forgiveness, and joy.

In other words, if our incarnate identity is already feeling disconnected and injured, it not only can become a source of aggravated, negative energies in itself, but it actively creates a subtle environment both within itself and around itself that can feed and sustain such energies whether they arise from oneself or from others.

For this reason, protection involves more than just dealing with a particular aggravated energy. It also includes energy hygiene, actions to change the inner and outer subtle environments so that such energies have a harder time maintaining themselves and their disconnected state. Introducing beauty, life, joy, and laughter into one's environment can be an effective and important adjunct to other protective measures. Break the coupling between an aggravated energy and your inner and outer environment, making those environments energetically inhospitable to negative states, and you've won half the battle.

This is not always possible. For one reason or another, the environment itself may have become so energetically toxic and aggravated that de-coupling isn't possible, at least not in the short term or with the resources available to you. An example might be a place where pain, anger and hatred have persisted over a long enough period of time or have been intense enough to deeply warp the energies of a place. A battlefield where many have suffered and lost their lives could be an example or a concentration camp where people have been tortured and abused, though the causes of such a condition need not have been so dramatic; they simply have to have been of persistence and long duration. Cleansing, healing, and transmuting such an environment may well be beyond the ability of any one person or may take time and patience.

Sometimes when faced with aggravated energies arising from and coupled with a deeply traumatized environment, from the standpoint of your protection rather than energy hygiene, the best and most effective response may be simply to leave that environment. Aggravated energies cannot affect you if you are not in their presence or exposed to them. This doesn't "cure" or "heal" the situation, but it gets you out of harm's way. You need to discern whether you have the skills and the energy to deal with what's confronting you, and if you feel you don't, then distance yourself from the situation if you can. If not, then you must be vigilant and persistent in your energy hygiene and in maintaining the full complement of your protective capacities.

Aggravated Energies

I've been talking about aggravated subtle energies as a general concept. Now we need to examine them more particularly. You'll remember from Chapter 11 that I separated aggravated energies into three categories: "smoggy," "jagged," and "malicious." In exploring these different categories, we need to exercise some imagination and metaphoric license. Subtle energies are not like physical energies. To describe them as "particles," "bits," or "waves" is merely a convenience, not a precise description. If anything, they are more akin to quanta of light in quantum mechanics, possessing qualities of both particles and waves yet transcending both. Still, for rhetorical purposes, I'll refer to "particles of subtle energy." I illustrate four possible states of such particles in Figure 35.

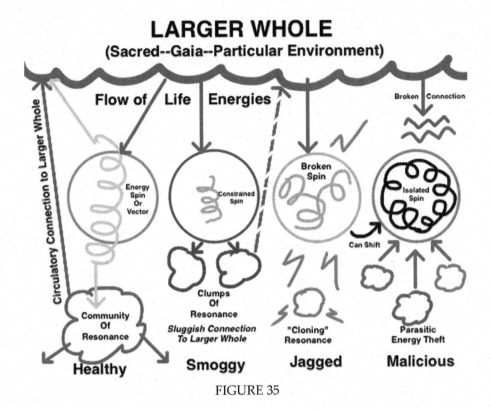

FIGURE 35

Healthy and positive subtle energies, as I've described before, exist in a state of flowing connection to some larger whole. Ultimately that larger whole is the Sacred, the Life-Source of the universe, but here on our world, it might also be Gaia, the Planetary Soul, or some other particular environmental field which possesses an internal coherency and identity.

The four different energy states illustrated in Figure 35 are differentiated by "spin" and "connectedness." Spin is a direct manifestation, at least in the human world, of the mental and emotional qualities and the type and clarity of intent put into setting these energies into motion. There are other factors that can come into play, as well, but I wish to focus upon intentionality and connectedness, for these are also the tools that act both to protect and to redeem and heal broken energies. The specifics depend on where they fall on a spectrum from mildly "smoggy" to virulently malicious, but the overall principles are the same: reconnect the energies and give them a different and healthier spin or identity. Remember, in describing this that I am using concrete imagery to describe non-physical, energetic phenomena. Figure 35 is a metaphor. Subtle energies don't come in discrete little bubbles with hard boundaries like I've drawn them, they are more fluid and interpenetrating than that. But I hope my drawing can give us useful insights for working with disturbed and aggravated energies.

As shown in Figure 35, a healthy subtle energy "particle" is part of a larger whole from which it receives a flow of life energies. It has an energy spin that defines its nature and identity, that is, what kind of energy is it and the nature of its source and the intent behind it. I call this spin its "vector." This vector is dynamic and is in resonance with all other subtle energies that are part of the whole, participating in what we could call a "community of resonance" in which there is a freedom of circulation and communion. There is also a circulatory connection back to the larger whole. We have here an energy cycle from Whole to Particle and back to Whole again. It's this circulatory connection that helps define healthy and beneficial subtle energies.

Some subtle energies, however, have a constrained spin. Their energy is more inward turned, so to speak. This makes the energy particle "sluggish"; it has low energy. An example might be the energy generated by states of depression or anxiety. Its connection to the larger whole is there but "slow" and wavering. Its energy is not very dynamic. It tends to form "clumps of resonance" with other energy particles similar to itself, like cold grease accumulating in a pipe. This can create a cloud-like effect within a particular environment, one that can be seen clairvoyantly or felt as it touches one's subtle body.

The challenge of these "smoggy" subtle energies primarily lies in their inertia and in the way they "clump" and accumulate, gaining strength both to resist change and to affect their environment through their collective "mass." These are the kinds of psychic conditions that can develop in a place that rarely receives any kind of energy hygiene; it is a place where the natural flow of living currents of energy has in some manner become restricted or blocked, preventing the normal process of cleansing and revitalization from taking place.

Usually, I have found, this condition is found in rooms and buildings that are cut off from the rejuvenating currents that are organically part of most natural landscapes. It is a condition that may have accumulated over time like dust piling up in an old house that has gone unused for years, or it may have been produced by a specific and intense generation of negative energies, metaphorically like a cloud of pollution suddenly bursting forth from a factory smokestack. An outburst of anger and conflict in a room, particularly if sustained over time, can result in smoggy energies in that room. But such subtle conditions can arise as well simply from a lack of vitality in the space. For example, a meeting room with no windows, sealed off from the outside, where boring meetings regularly take place that people resent having to attend, may never see a sudden outburst of anger or passion, but the resistance to being there and the lack of meaningful interaction can create a "sinkhole" of wearying and depressive energies. For me, a wonderful example of this kind of environment is shown in the beginning of the movie *Joe vs the Volcano*, with Tom Hanks and Meg Ryan. The building and the room in which Joe works are exaggeratedly bleak and soul-deadening, but they do represent exactly the kind of environment in which smoggy aggravated energies develop and accumulate.

The danger of smoggy energies is largely that through the pressure of their inertia and psychic mass, they can transfer their qualities to your field. You are not being psychically "attacked" as such. But their presence can wear away at you, as if in such an environment, you are carrying a weight all the time—which in an energetic sense you are as your subtle body continually has to cope with the effects of such a psychic cloud. There is a constant pull for your energy field to begin vibrating at the frequency of the cloud, and the very mass of the smoggy energies can cut you off from currents of energy that would otherwise be vitalizing and refreshing. You can find yourself emotionally and mentally taking on the character of these stuck energies. Their "spin" starts to become your energetic "spin" through the pressure of their presence.

There are two main approaches to dealing with smoggy subtle energies. The first is to prevent your own subtle field from being affected by them. Keep your own energy high and flowing. Don't take on the identity or "spin" of the cloudy energies. Make sure your own subtle energies and your mental and emotional states are balanced, harmonious, and vital. Being an energetic presence in the midst of smoggy energies is one way to counteract the inertia and begin to break up the psychic cloud. Draw upon spiritual energies such as joy, love, and compassion; one of your greatest allies in such a situation is laughter. Humor that isn't mean or damaging to oneself or another can definitely heighten the subtle energies in an environment.

The second approach is through energy hygiene to break up the "clumps" of energy and expose the cloud of smoggy energies to a renewed flow of vitalizing currents. You want to change their "spin," and to do so, you will need to overcome their inertia. Here are some suggestions:

If you can, clean the affected area. A good physical housecleaning is a wonderful way to break up accumulated smoggy energies, especially if you invoke circulating energies as you do so. In other words, apply principles of energy hygiene. If the aggravated energies have built up over time and their inertia is great, then you may have to do this more than once to fully break up and "re-spin" the patterns.

Bring things into the area that are naturally energy-boosters and that enhance circulation. Plants are excellent for this as long as they are taken care of and kept vital. If possible, music can help a great deal, as can color or paintings that lift your spirit. There's been a great deal of research on the psychological effects of color; if you can surround yourself with colors that empower and energize you, then you are adding to your ability to change the energies of your environment.

If you find yourself in a situation where you have little authority to affect or change the environment—for example, you are one of many people working in a large office—then establish an area, like your desk, where you can make changes or where you can control the space. Visualize this space vibrating with energy and love; give it your appreciation and honor as an ally. If you can have things there of your choosing that will enhance your energy and psychological state, such as pictures, then add those things to your space. Just bringing in a fresh flower everyday can have a powerful effect on the energy of a space. If you are unable to do any of these things, then you will need to do the necessary work inwardly. Have something on your person that helps you feel connected to higher frequencies and to a vitalizing flow of spirit, the energy of which you can then share with your surroundings. For instance, you can make yourself an identity pouch as described in Chapter 6 and wear it under your clothing.

As I've said, healthy energies are moving, flowing energies for the most part. If your work is sedentary and you are in a place where energies tend to stagnate or clump, get up and move about periodically. Not only does the physical exercise help get energies moving within you, the fact that you are moving through the space can set environmental energies in motion, too, at least for a time. Every little bit helps!

Smoggy energies develop through habit and repetition. They don't even have to be "negative" in the usual sense of the term, just stuck. Changing your habits or the way you perform an activity or set up a space may help to break up this stuckness by allowing energies to move in a different way. For instance, if you arrange your desk in a particular way and have done so for some time, changing things around may help revitalize the energies around your desk. Sometimes, of course, it's important to keep things set in a certain pattern as repetition can provide energetic stability and strength, but if things seem to be feeling stagnant around you, then experimenting with change is one way to liven things up.

However, the "spins" of some subtle energies are so intense and hurtful that they "break," sending out a jaggedness to the surrounding environment. Such broken energies can be hurtful to encounter. Rage is a good example of such an energy. Rather than bonding through resonance, it acts in the environment to "clone" itself, creating more waves of angry energy. If we take such energy "particles" into our own subtle body, we can find it replicating anger in us, which, if we identify with it, may seem like our own anger. This is one way destructive and angry moods can spread quickly through a group of people as the broken energy continues to clone itself in one subtle body after another.

I call these "jagged" energies because that's how I experience them. Where a normal subtle body feels smooth to me, one that's vibrating to intense and negative emotional and mental energies like anger, hatred, terror, and the like takes on a porcupine-like aspect, filled with jagged, sharp "quills" of energy that can shoot out at where the anger or hatred is directed.

However they are experienced, these subtle energies can be intense and carry a lot of force, unlike the more smoggy, sluggish type. Their brokenness is at the level of their connectedness. They still are part of the flow of life energies from the larger whole, but their intensity and "jagged" vectors disrupt their ability to connect through resonance. They can clone themselves, but they don't easily participate in any community (or "clump") of resonance.

In all acts of protection, the main thing to do is to bring forward the strength and stability of your identity and Presence, as suggested in Figure 34. Jagged subtle energies will in effect "bounce off" your energy field if it is itself radiating strongly with Sovereignty and Self-Light. You can feel them, but they can't penetrate. They can't hijack your own energy and clone themselves.

However, if the jagged energies feel particularly strong or invasive, you can also shield yourself by visualizing yourself surrounded by a protective barrier of subtle energy, as if you were standing inside a radiant wall of Light. I find shielding is most effective, though, when this wall is not rigid but it partakes of the flowing, organic nature of a healthy subtle field. Normally, I don't try to put up an energetic wall between myself and negative energies because the wall itself can become constricting. So if I feel a need to shield, I visualize a flowing barrier, like a waterfall, around me, carrying away any jagged energies the way a swiftly flowing river carries away ice floes.

However, in most cases the best protection is to make oneself "transparent" to the aggravated energies, allowing them to pass through you. This doesn't mean not confronting such energies if such a confrontation is necessary to protect others or acquiescing in their activity. It means altering the frequency and vibration of your own field so nothing in you resists the aggravated energies or causes them to "stick" to you. It's a posture of being non-adversarial in your energetic makeup.

To do this, you need to draw upon your Interiority, upon the loving, joyful, and transcendent energies of the soul which can embrace without confronting. In this way, you don't create a friction by resistance which only adds to the aggravated energies and in some cases feeds them and makes the situation worse. Allow the negative energies to pass through you without reacting to them. If you do not react, such energies cannot use you to sustain themselves but instead find themselves in the presence of a loving environment and presence that can "re-spin" and "re-align" them, restoring them to wholeness.

This kind of non-adversarial, loving response needs practice as your psyche—your thoughts and feelings—can automatically respond defensively to what you perceive as a threat. Standing in your Sovereignty, in your Presence, in your loving core nature is not always the immediate habitual response that our adversarial culture develops in us, but it's the most powerful thing you can do to protect yourself. In effect, you lift yourself out of vibrational resonance with the aggravated energies.

This has the added effect of beginning to alter the subtle environment around you. Remember the principle of coupling. All subtle energies are environment-dependent to some degree. Alter the energetic nature of that environment, and you create a condition in which aggravated energies, certainly of the smoggy or jagged kind, cannot maintain themselves. Of course, how easily and effectively this can be done depends on the circumstances, but it's still a principle to remember.

The intensity and lack of connectedness can lead jagged energies to burn themselves out and dissipate quickly, losing their force and becoming reabsorbed back into the whole, especially when you do not put up resistance. On the other hand, they can shift into an even more broken state, becoming a "malicious" energy.

A malicious energy is one whose "spin" has become isolated within itself; in a way, it's as if it's collapsed into a metaphorical "black hole" state, one that is truly cut off, alienated within its boundaries. In this state, it has lost connection to any larger wholeness; it is out of any circulatory energy loop. It is now existing by itself for itself.

The key characteristic of such subtle energies is that they become parasitic. Cut off from the normal flow of life energies that would come if they were connected to a larger whole, they must seek out and drain or feed on whatever life energies they can find in places or, particularly, in living beings. They seek to break the normal "spin" of healthy energies in order to draw them into an equivalent self-contained and isolated state, making them disconnected in turn and vulnerable to being absorbed.

This is why I call these energies "malicious." They depend on the destruction and absorption of other subtle energies to feed their own existence. They may be passive in doing so, attacking whatever comes into their vicinity, or they may become predatory and active, seeking out ways to prolong their existence and expand their influence. It depends entirely on the kind of intent and spin that was given to them by the source that created them. These are energies that spring for the most part from the darker impulses within the human mind, destructive impulses of violence, abuse, hatred, contempt, and rage, particularly when these impulses are given expression through hurtful actions that deliberately inflict suffering. They draw their identity from these destructive impulses and seek to use the energy in their environment to maintain and replicate themselves.

You protect yourself against such malicious energies in the same way you do with jagged energies but with added strength and mindfulness. These are subtle forces that have an intent to hurt and to damage, so you need to not give them an entry into your own energetic system. Fear is the primary entry point as well as seeking out points of resonance in your own psyche. For instance, if the malicious energy is one of hatred, can it find seeds of hatred in you to which it can attune as an entry into your energy field?

While shields may be an effective response, transparency and not becoming adversarial may actually work better. These kinds of energies seek out resistance as conflict generates sustenance for them. Facing such forces with love, courage, and a clear stance of Sovereignty and resonance with your soul identity prevents them from gaining any kind of traction with your energy and weakens them.

As in the case of other aggravated energies, if you can alter the surrounding energy environment in which they are existing, you can make it inhospitable to malicious forces, setting up a situation in which they must leave or be transmuted. A powerful burst of Light emanating from your own Interiority directed not at the malicious energies per se but into the environment may disrupt the connections such energies have formed in their surroundings, making them vulnerable to banishment or transformation. Such a shock of radiance would then need to be followed up with energy hygiene to truly cleanse and realign that environment.

Dealing with malicious energies requires skill, balance, courage, and inner coherency and presence. If confronting dangerous people in physical life, the best course of action may be to dial 911 and call for the police who are trained and equipped to handle such situations. Similarly, the best course to dealing with malicious aggravated energies may be to call upon the Sacred and upon spiritual, non-physical allies who may well be in a better position than you as a physical person to contain and transmute such forces. Working with such allies is the theme of the third book in this trilogy, *Collaborating with Subtle Worlds*, and is beyond the scope of this book.

Summing Up

On the whole, it's been my experience that the subtle realms are not dangerous places or filled with dangerous forces or beings; like any environment anywhere, you want to approach them mindfully, lovingly, and with some common sense and respect for what is present. Nevertheless, there are times and there are places where aggravated energies of one kind or another may arise, congregate, or become entrenched, just as there are places in the physical world where toxic materials become concentrated, largely due to human actions. If you should run into such energies, here are the basic principles for your protection:

- Leave the environment if you can.
- If you can't, stand in your Sovereignty and Presence and strengthen the coherency and flow of your subtle field; strengthen your boundaries.
- If you feel the need, surround yourself with a flowing shield of Light.
- If the aggravated energies persist, make yourself transparent to them through non-resistance and a non-adversarial attitude and energetic posture. Attune to love and to joy.
- If you are able, radiate your Self-Light, love and blessings in ways that can alter the energetic identity and atmosphere of the environment so that it cannot be a source of "food" or sustenance for the aggravated energies.
- If you are still feeling threatened or overwhelmed or feel the situation is beyond your ability to cope, then call upon the Sacred and upon spiritual allies in whatever way is appropriate to you, but even as you do, maintain your stance of Sovereignty and coherency of Identity.

Remember, there is a difference between protection and energy hygiene, even though they both are responses to unbalanced or aggravated subtle energies. If you had to enter a toxic physical environment such as a pond polluted with sewage, you would wear protective covering to avoid being harmed. That's the protection side. Cleaning up that pool to remove the sewage and restore the water to a pure state, that's energy hygiene. They work hand in hand, but sometimes the opportunity or ability to perform energy hygiene may not be present, yet you still have to protect yourself from the toxicity in a particular environment. Knowing how to distinguish between these two activities is part of the wisdom of working with subtle energies.

Being Protective

There is one final thing to be said about protection: learn to be protective of others. It's an unfortunate habit in our culture to project our anger and even our hatred upon others, particularly upon public figures such as our politicians or media celebrities. We may not agree with them or support what they are doing, and this is our right. But if we want to align with protective energies, we cannot attack them with our own thoughts and feelings.

Imagine if you are in the public eye and are a focus for the subtle energies and projections, both positive and negative, from thousands or millions of people, especially with the added energy given such focus by modern social media. Also remember that in the energy world we are all profoundly interconnected. Our thoughts and feelings have a wider outreach and effect than we may realize. If I am angry with the person who is President of the United States, for instance, and I think and project unloving, hurtful thoughts and feelings towards him or her, in the subtle realms that can be as damaging as if I tried to attack that person physically. If that is my intent, then in the process, I sabotage my own protection by enhancing my own vulnerability to aggravated energies.

Protecting another energetically means holding them and their energy field in a supportive, enhancing, and protective way. I discussed this in Chapter 15. You're not trying to do something to them; you're not projecting or injecting energy into their incarnational system. Instead, you are surrounding them in a field of Light that honors and empowers their own Sovereignty, identity and integrity, supporting a space around them within which they can work out their own destiny without interference from others. Mostly, you are refusing to impact them with your own mental and emotional projections.

This doesn't mean we can't get upset with people in the public limelight if they are doing something that goes against our values; it does mean that if we are serious about working with subtle energies, we cannot turn those feelings into energies of attack, projecting our anger or hatred at those people. We don't have to agree with them or support them, but energetically we need to realize they are part of the same wholeness we are, and we need to hold them in love.

This is simply acknowledging that we need to be responsible for the quality and kind of "spin" we put on the subtle energies we radiate into the world. This is true whether we're talking about a famous celebrity, a co-worker, a neighbor, or someone we just see in passing on the street. If we want to help heal the world of the many aggravated energies that do exist and accumulate, then we have to be careful not to add to them. We want to commit to not doing energetic harm ourselves. In the context of protection, the philosophy behind the martial art of Aikido applies here: to defend oneself in a way that, as much as possible, doesn't injure either the attacker or oneself.

If I want to be protected, I need to be protective. Learning this simple truth is a major step towards learning to work effectively and skillfully with subtle energies.

Attuning to Interiority

An old saying is that the time to repair a leaky roof is when the sun is shining. Similarly, practicing the skill of attuning to your Interiority—to your Sovereignty, Self-Light, Coherency, Soul-Connection, Identity and Presence —is when you are not being pressured or threatened by external forces. Many of the exercises I've presented in this book, like the Standing Exercise, are designed to help you with this practice; they are "Interiority-oriented." When you need to protect yourself is not the time to wonder just what your Interiority feels like or how to attune to it. You want to know automatically the felt sense of your Interiority and how to draw upon it in the moment. Beyond any technique, this is really the first step, the foundation of any protective work.

To remind you of the elements that make up your Interiority, as I discussed in Chapter 7, here is Figure 36.

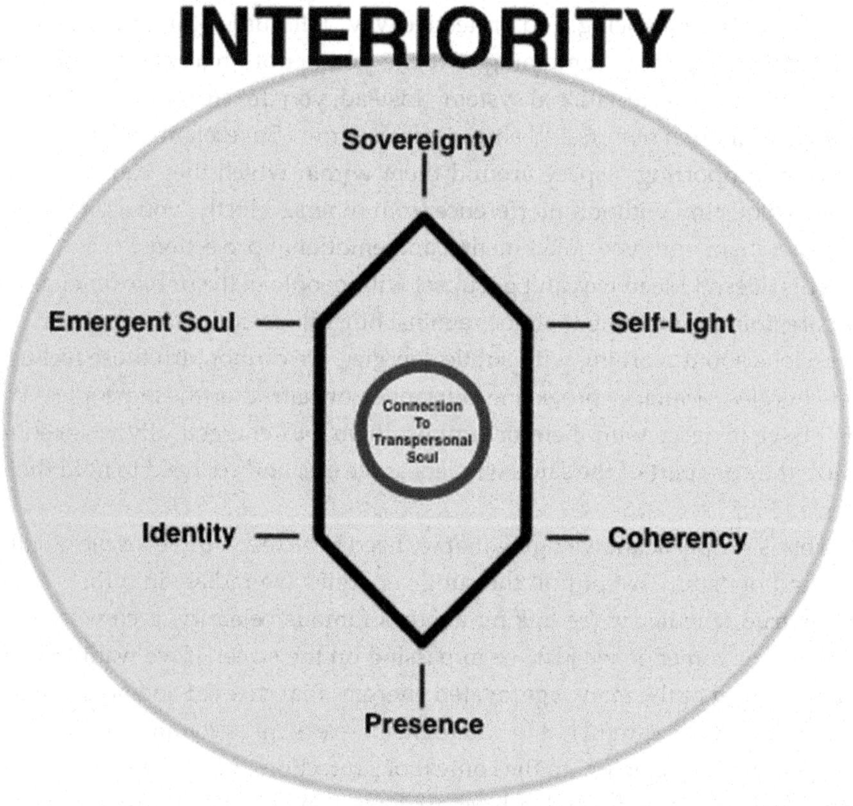

INTERIORITY

Sovereignty

Emergent Soul — — **Self-Light**

Connection
To
Transpersonal
Soul

Identity — — **Coherency**

Presence

FIGURE 36

Remember that your Interiority is not something separate from you. It's just a way of talking about and representing those elements that express your wholeness. Its power manifests through your whole incarnational "system," which also includes your body, your psyche (which most of us experience as our everyday self), and your subtle energy field. Each of these elements needs to be honored and embraced; they are all partners to each other as I remind us in Figure 37.

THE INCARNATIONAL PARTNERSHIP

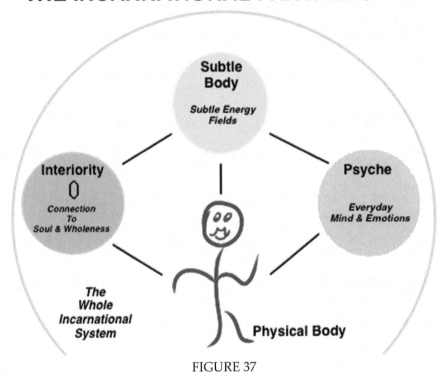

FIGURE 37

Ultimately, your subtle energetic protection rests on and arises from the wholeness of this incarnational system and partnership. Each partner is important and needs to be honored. But the forces that actively maintain and nurture this wholeness come from your Interiority. That is its function, and it is the mainstay of your innate subtle immune system.

With this whole system and partnership in mind, attuning to your Interiority is vitally important, and it is more than just attuning to your soul or to that which is transpersonal or transcendent within you. It also means attuning to the Sovereignty, the Self-Light, the Identity, the Presence found in your physical body, in your everyday self and personality as expressed through your psyche, and in your subtle energy field, your subtle body. It's a practice of honoring and embracing your entire incarnate state, your embodied presence here in a world that is both physical and non-physical in its expression.

However you choose to do so, come to know the felt sense of your incarnate wholeness and of your Interiority so that when you need to, whatever subtle energies or environments you may be encountering, you can confidently call upon it and stand in your wholeness as an integrated and coherent Identity and Presence connected to your soul. Being able to do this is more than half the game when it comes to protection, as well as for any other form of working with subtle energies.

EXERCISES FOR CHAPTER SEVENTEEN

Exercise: Strengthening Boundaries

In this exercise, you want to combine the Stance, as discussed in Chapter 11, with your Interiority and incarnational partnership as illustrated in Figure 36. You strengthen your boundaries not by building a wall around them but by increasing their organic connection to the forces of identity, connectedness, and wholeness within you.

- Standing in Sovereignty, attune to the forces of wholeness within your Interiority, the forces of your Self-Light, your Presence, and your connection to soul, both the Emergent Soul of your incarnate life and the transcendent Soul of your spiritual nature.
- Extend the Self-Light radiating from your Interiority into your physical body, blessing and honoring all the cellular life that makes up that body. Extend this Self-Light and Presence into your thoughts and feelings, into your psyche, honoring and loving your everyday self. Extend this Self-Light and love into your subtle body and surrounding subtle energy field.
- Connect to the Earth beneath you and to the surrounding environment and the life around you with appreciation and honor. You are poised and ready to act with the power of love and joy to engage the subtle environment around you in whatever way is appropriate and needed.
- Attune to this connectedness with self, soul, and other (Earth and environment). Feel its coherency and wholeness, its strength and balance. Feel the flow of subtle energy circulating through your being and around you as a result of this connectedness. Feel the confidence and poise that comes from this state of being.
- Feel this flow of subtle energy, arising from your Interiority, the partnership of your incarnational system, and your connections to the earth and the environment around you, filling and strengthening the outermost layers of your subtle energy field, giving your boundaries definition, resilience, cohesion, and presence. Know that nothing can pass through these boundaries that is not in harmony and resonance with the wholeness of your being, the harmony of your incarnational partnership, and the Light of your Interiority. Know that your boundaries are your presence and identity in loving engagement with the world.

Exercise: Flowing Protection

If you feel the need for some kind of shielding in the moment, then here is one way to create a shield that is more dynamic than just a wall. I prefer this image of a cascading flow of energy circulating around me than one of a static shield of Light. For me, energy is always in motion. Working with subtle forces in this way "goes with the flow", which is an advantage.

- Stand in your Sovereignty, drawing upon the Self-Light and Presence of your Interiority.

- Imagine a point of energy like a small star above your head. Out of this point, energy cascades down like a sheet of flowing water over and through your energy field in front of you. As it does so, it flows under your feet to blend with the life and vitality of the Earth. It then rises like a flowing sheet of water up the back of your energy field and back through the star above your head, flowing back down again.

- As this energy circulates around you, it flushes away any negative or unwanted subtle energies that may be in the environment or attempting to affect your energy field.

- Once you have a felt sense of this flowing cycle of energy up and around and down your energy field, attune to your Interiority, drawing on the Light of your Soul and of the Sacred. Let this Light radiate out into the circulating energy around you, providing a deep layer of safety, love and joy moving through your energy field.

- Anything unwanted or negative, touching this circulating flow, simply drains away into the earth or is transformed and transmuted and drawn into the Light of the Transpersonal. However, any and all healthy and wholeness-creating energies within the environment have no difficulty connecting with you in appropriate and life-enhancing ways. This flow doesn't cut you off from the world; it simply washes away what would obstruct or distort your wholeness and your connections with the world.

- There is no strain upon you to keep this flow in motion. It is the natural state of your healthy energy field to be in motion. Just imagine this circulation of flowing Light around you and radiating from you and let it go about the business of protecting you.

Exercise: Shock and Awesomeness

Under most circumstances I do not advocate being adversarial or "attacking" aggravated energies in one's environment as this can set up a reaction that only makes things worse. However, there are times when a "blast of Light" may be just the ticket for shaking loose, banishing, or otherwise disrupting such energies so that there is a greater opportunity and space to do energy hygiene and effect a healing or transformation of the subtle environment. Here is one way to produce such a blast of "shock and awesomeness."

- Stand in your Sovereignty and attune to your Interiority.
- Attune to your Self-Light and to your generative power as a presence of embodied Light. In your mind's eye, see this Self-Light growing as a ball of fiery Light within your heart.
- In your Interiority, attune to your Soul and to the Light that comes from transpersonal and transcendent sources, i.e. from the spiritual worlds. Feel this Light flowing into and adding to your Self-Light as it glows within your heart.
- Standing in Sovereignty and anchored in the Stance of connectedness, stoke this fiery Light within your heart as much as you can, feeling it grow brighter and brighter. When you feel ready, let this Light flow into your entire subtle body, turning you into a fiery presence of Light.
- With an act of will, release this Light as an explosion of radiance into the surrounding subtle energy environment, illuminating all dark and shadowy areas, bathing the entire subtle environment with Self-Light and Soul-Light, insisting that the Light of the Sacred be made manifest in all things around you and that anything not able to stand in that Light either transform so it may do so or be banished from the environment. Honor and bless all that remains with love.
- Draw the Light back into yourself and take a moment to stand again in the fullness of your Sovereignty, your Self-Light, and your wholeness. Then proceed with whatever further energy work seems appropriate to do.

CHAPTER EIGHTEEN
Fostering

Attuning to Gaia

Gaia is the term I use for the World Soul, the animating Presence for whom the Earth itself is its incarnation. The idea that the Earth is a living being and has its own soul is an ancient one. What we think of as subtle energies and the subtle environment are largely expressions of the subtle body of this planetary presence. So when we are working with subtle energies, we are usually working with the living energies of Gaia.

For many kinds of subtle energy work, attuning to Gaia enhances whatever it is we are doing. After all, we are working with subtle energies that are part of Gaia's own life; to engage with the world soul as a partner and to build our Gaian connections cannot help but add to whatever we are seeking to do.

To connect with Gaia, it's common in many spiritual and metaphysical traditions to attune to the earth for purposes of grounding, balance, healing, and so forth. However, this attunement is usually presented using the same vertical perspective that can turn us from a whole being into a layer cake of stacked levels of life. In other words, the common tendency is to see the "earth" as "down there" below our feet as the location and source of Gaian energies, and thus to draw energy "up" from the earth (or project our energy downward into Gaia like roots from a tree).

What this view doesn't take into account is that we don't live on the earth; we live inside the earth—not inside the physical earth like cavern dwellers but inside the living field of Gaia. Thus Gaia isn't "below" us; it's all around us. If I want to attune to the earth, it's only convenience that leads me to direct my attention to the land under my feet. I could just as easily attune "upward" to the sky or "outward" into the environment around me since Gaia, the soul of Earth, surrounds me in all directions. I am immersed and embedded in Gaia; I don't just walk upon its surface.

To attune to Gaia, I don't just think about what's under my feet. I attune to all that's around me. When I think of attuning to transpersonal or spiritual realms, many of these realms are in effect the transpersonal aspects of Gaia. In other words, the "transpersonal Earth" is not simply "up" but "all around" as well.

I want to begin thinking spherically rather than just vertically or horizontally. To attune to the world soul, I visualize that soul as surrounding me, and I expand out into Gaia in all directions, not just downward or upward or outward. In this manner, I create around myself a sphere of energy attuned to the subtle and the transpersonal or spiritual energies of the planet. I illustrate this in Figure 38.

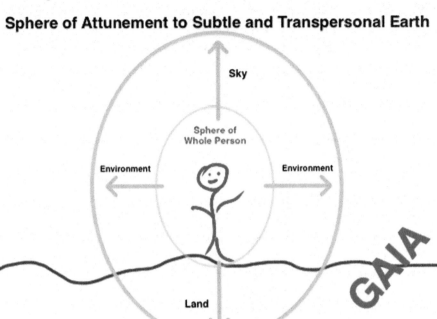

FIGURE 38

Fostering

One thing is very clear about Gaia: it fosters and supports life. We see this in abundant evidence here in the physical world. Life exists from the smallest microbe to the largest whale and the tallest redwood. This is equally true in the subtle realms where non-physical life can range from atom-sized elementals all the way to vast planetary angels and Devas whose auras or life-fields span entire continents, if not the globe itself. Life is ubiquitous, and it includes all those objects we choose to classify as inorganic and non-living. There is nothing in the world that is non-living. As I've said before, all subtle energies are themselves alive and sentient, even if the nature of the life and sentiency is nothing like that possessed by a human being. The basic principle is this: **working with subtle energies is working with life**.

One phenomenon in the subtle worlds is the presence of specific energies that are generated by a being to support the functions and potentials of life itself. Thus, I often feel subtle energies coming from the Devas overlighting the nearby mountains or from the spirit of a nearby lake; or on a smaller scale, the energies coming from the particular nature spirits who tend to the trees, bushes, and creatures living in my back yard. You might say these are "custodial" or "stewardship" energies. They are directed from one set of beings to nourish the life, unfoldment, and wholeness of another set of beings, and as far as I can tell, this is a process that is repeated throughout the chain of life from the most complex and vast cosmic entities right down to the faeries in the garden and the elementals working with those lives at the very beginning of a particular evolutionary stream. I call this fostering. It's a process of "each one teach one" as more advanced beings assist those that are less developed (or differently developed).

There are beings in the subtle worlds whose spiritual presence and life-energy is far beyond our own. We may look to such beings for blessing and help in our own spiritual evolution. In my own experience, such vast beings are usually happy to provide such help in ways that are appropriate to us, for they serve the overall Gaian impulse to foster life and to aid all living things in their development and evolution.

What we don't usually think of is that we are as advanced in consciousness and energy over many of the subtle lives that surround us in the world as such more evolved beings are over us. If there are great beings who foster and aid our human development, there are lesser beings for whom we can do the same. In our generative and loving capacities, we can be "fosterers" to the environments in which we live. A unique feature of the human being is that we can attune to and hold within our subtle energy fields a wide range or spectrum of spiritual energies from the "higher" or more complex soul levels right into the physical vibrations of matter, which gives us a powerful ability to bless and foster and to tailor our blessings to an equally wide range of lives and consciousnesses. To use our subtle energies in such a way is to resonate with the intent and life of Gaia. It's a powerful form of Gaian attunement.

This is particularly true within the "built" environment—i.e. in the midst of our human civilization with its buildings, cities, and so on, filled with various artifacts of our construction from the simplicity of my coffee cup to the complexity of my computer or the technology of the Internet. For various reasons, parts of the built environment, at least as I understand it, are less directly available to the fostering energies of Angels, Devas and nature spirits.

This is not to say there are not angels overlighting and seeking to bless cities, neighborhoods, buildings, and various forms of human activity, for there are. But humanity has a way at the moment of disrupting connections along which energy can flow freely and in a healthy manner, and we definitely have a propensity right now for generating energetic pollution and toxic, aggravated energies that are anything but fostering in nature. Undertaking fostering as a deliberate way of using our subtle energies contributes to the healing and transformation of this situation as well as directly benefitting the living energies in the things that surround us.

The most powerful fostering and life-nurturing quality is love. To give love to anything is to quicken its life-force. Love can take many forms besides just affection. It can manifest as honor, respect, appreciation, even at times just as a simple acknowledgement that says to someone or something, "I see you. I know you are there. You're not invisible or inconsequential. I acknowledge your presence and value."

The opportunities for fostering are all around us every day. The things we use—the coffee cup we drink from, the chair we sit in, the table we put things on, the things we put on the table, the computer we use for our work, the earrings in our ears or the jacket we're wearing—are all filled with living energies that are themselves evolving. When we mindfully embrace these things with our love and our fostering energy, we are acting as Gaia does towards us.

We need to be realistic about this. Much of the life that surrounds us is very slow in its evolution. We may not feel or see any difference. For that matter, a transcendent being may love and bless and give us energy for years without seeing a lot of difference in how we behave either! But nothing is lost, and a difference *is* made.

What is most important is that when we act toward the things around us as we would want greater beings to act towards us, we are doing what Gaia does. This is an important form of working with subtle energies for it adds to the overall wholeness of the world. In some ways, it may be the most significant thing we do energetically. While I may not immediately see an evolutionary shift in my coffee cup as a result of my loving it and holding it in an appreciative and fostering energy, I can definitely feel a shift in me and in my relationship with the world when I do so.

The nice thing is that this way of working with subtle energies is easy to do. It begins with the simple act of acknowledging the life in the world around you, including the energy of life in all those things that we in our culture don't believe or see as "living". As you go through your day, if you radiate appreciation, love, and acknowledgment to the things in your life, no matter how mundane or non-living they may seem, you are enhancing the fostering work of Gaia, as well as expressing a fostering energy yourself. You become a mini-Gaia to the things embraced in your personal energy field. While this isn't the reason to do so, given the principle of resonance at work in the subtle worlds, if you are a fostering presence to the life around you, it enhances the fostering energies flowing to you for your benefit.

EXERCISES FOR CHAPTER EIGHTEEN

Exercise: Being a Fostering Presence
• Begin by standing in Sovereignty, Self-Light, and Presence, that is, in your Interiority.
• Shift your attention and awareness from your body to your subtle field, using your body-mapping capacities of your proprioceptive sense. In effect, "map" your body to your surrounding subtle field.
• With your awareness and attention "standing" in the subtle field surrounding your physical form, fill your subtle field with love. Imagine your own surrounding field becoming heightened and energized with a presence of love.
• Now, imagine your subtle energy field expanding and touching the surrounding energies in the space in which you are. Allow this loving, heightening, fostering energy to flow out from your energy field into the surrounding subtle field, touching, enfolding and blessing everything within this field.
•   Do this as long as feels comfortable; then, when you feel tired, restless, or complete, imagine your personal energy field drawing back around you. Stand or sit for a moment, allowing the love to bless your own field. Then allow that energy of fostering love to diffuse throughout your body.
•   Take a moment to stand in and reaffirm your Sovereignty.

Exercise: Holding Life
The simplest way to foster and quicken the life-energy within anything is to hold it in love. This exercise is similar to the Touch of Love, but in some ways is simpler.

• Take a moment to stand in your Sovereignty and Self-Light.
• Pick up an inanimate object you can hold in your hand.
• Take a moment just to acknowledge what it is and to appreciate it. Pay attention to its form, its structure, the substances from which it is made, and its function, if any.
• As you hold it, imagine a pool of love filling your hand, immersing the object which you are holding. This pool of love brings goodwill, appreciation, and vitality to the object, heightening its own life-energies and their evolutionary potentials.

CHAPTER NINETEEN
Subtle Activism

Subtle Activism

Subtle Activism is energy hygiene at a distance. The basic principles involved are the same as those we've been studying when working with subtle energies in your personal field or in your immediate local subtle environment. The primary difference is the use of imaginal attunement to transfer your energy work to a place distant from where you are physically located.

Subtle activism is not a substitute for taking action and doing good in wise and compassionate ways in the physical world, but it is an important complement to outer activism. Physical activism is necessary, for we live in a world where pain and suffering, hunger and disease, oppression and injustice, pollution and environmental degradation have real physical manifestations and consequences. Subtle activism is not instead of but in addition to work and effort to heal the world and ourselves.

When a subtle environment in a particular area is turbulent and filled with aggravated negative or disconnected energies, perhaps due to a natural disaster like an earthquake or a human-created one such as a war zone, the effects of such toxic subtle energies can hinder and diminish outer efforts at helping in a situation. Conversely, when a subtle environment is filled with positive, flowing, vital energies, its effects can support and enhance the good efforts and positive results of physical activists working in that area.

What are situations in which you might use subtle activism? Well, theoretically, you could use it in almost any situation where energy hygiene—i.e. the heightening, blessing, clearing, and cleansing of subtle energies—could be useful to support positive outcomes that enhance wholeness in the world. It can be used to support opportunities and creative efforts, such as doing subtle activism on behalf of those who are researching a cure for cancer or to promote peace. It can also be used to respond to natural disasters, such as an earthquake or a tsunami, a tornado or a flood, in which many lives are lost and there is suffering.

Imagine the difference between walking through mud and walking on firm, solid ground or on a paved road. The former takes more energy than the latter. If the subtle environment is roiled and turbulent for some reason, filled with disconnected and negative energies, then for our subtle body, it can be like moving through mud would be for the physical body. A negative subtle environment, one filled with fear, anger, suffering, and violence, is draining; it takes vital energies from us and bombards our own personal field with negative impacts.

Subtle activism is an act of performing energy hygiene in such situations to diminish the negative effects of out-of-control collective energies, helping to restore peace, Sovereignty, and wholeness to the situation. It is also a means of supporting the vital energies of physical activists working in the midst of a tumultuous situation, as in the aftereffects of an earthquake or other natural disaster, so that their subtle bodies are better able to draw on positive, vital energies that can in turn support their physical efforts. When subtle energies are clear and flowing in an environment, the odds can be tilted towards positive outcomes or at least towards making connections that can lead to such outcomes, thereby creating synchronicities and "coincidences". Subtle activism that heightens the healthy flow of subtle energies in a place where suffering has taken place can enhance the emergence of creative and positive possibilities.

Seven Rules

In working with subtle activism, there are important considerations or "rules" to keep in mind. There are seven of them that I follow:

1. Don't Impose
2. Partner with Stakeholders
3. Be Connected
4. Stay Grounded and Aligned
5. Be Inclusive
6. Honor the Specific
7. Be What You Send

We each have our own personal energies, our own opinions and ideas about how the world should be and how people should live for their highest good. We resent it when someone else tries to impose their way of being, thinking, and doing upon us, particularly if it's very different from our own. When we are in trouble, we may need help, but we resist being thought of as something to be "fixed." We want and need help in a form that honors and respects our own sovereignty, that empowers us to develop our own capacities, that helps us to grow, and enables us as much as possible to find our own solutions to the problems. We want assistance but we want empowerment as well.

This is true in any situation. The subtle activist doesn't seek to impose his or her "way" or energies upon a situation but seeks to create openness for the innate spirit, health, and wisdom within people to emerge and express in a manner unique to them and appropriate to the situation.

With this in mind, a subtle activist wants to identify the "stakeholders" in the situation, that is, who is being affected or will be affected by the outcomes of the situation. In doing inner work, he or she wants to connect and collaborate energetically with the spirit of those involved, or at least be aware that the work is done on their behalf. This also helps the subtle activist remember that the work is one of partnership with the forces, people, and beings involved and not one of acting alone.

Dealing with the psychic pollution and negative subtle energies of the world is not something any person can do on his or her own, any more than one person could clear away all the rubble and rescue all the survivors in a town devastated by an earthquake. We need allies. We need to be connected to the larger spirit of wholeness in the earth. We need to be aligned and connected with the Sacred and, through our Sovereignty, Self-Light and Presence, with the Light of our own soul. If we don't have any physical allies to work with, we can seek out allies of a spiritual nature who themselves live and work within the realms of subtle energy. And as I said, we need to work with the souls and energies of those whom we seek to help.

In this process we want to be sure that we are grounded. I mean this in three ways. We want to be grounded in our own Sovereignty, identity and personhood, feeling whole and good about ourselves. We don't want to bring our inner conflicts into our subtle activism. We want to be energetically grounded in our immediate, local environment, our subtle energy connected to and anchored in the energy fields around us: in the earth, in the things around us, the nature around us, and so forth. And we want to be grounded in and aligned with the spirit of the Sacred, the Ground of All Being. It is from this spirit that we draw the holopoietic power of creating wholeness.

Sometimes, a person drawn to subtle activism sees himself or herself as a "warrior of Light" going forth to do battle with "forces of darkness." It's easy to frame a situation so that there are "friends" to help and "enemies" to combat. But subtle activism is not spiritual combat. It is an act of healing, which is inclusive by its nature. There are no enemies in subtle activism, only conditions to be understood, held in love and positive energies, and transformed. When we are aligned with sacredness, we feel this inclusiveness more powerfully.

Attuning to the Sacred is for most of us akin to attuning to the universal and the transpersonal. But we want to be attuned to the specific as well, to the particular conditions that define the situation for which we are doing subtle activism. Such a situation involves specific people in a specific place meeting specific challenges which will have specific consequences. Our work as subtle activists is to bring the wholeness and spirit of the universal into connection and engagement with all these specificities. We need to honor the specific.

One way we do this is to embody in ourselves the spirit and energy that we wish to bring to the situation or the outcome that we would like to help promote. If it is a situation of conflict, for instance, then we want to embody peacefulness, calm, and the wisdom to resolve that conflict. We don't simply "project" peace and hope (or insist) that whoever is involved picks up on that quality and embodies it; we're not telling others "you must be peaceful." Instead, we embody these qualities in the specificity of our own being and place ourselves energetically in the situation where we can be an energetic presence around which the subtle energies of that environment can configure. We must be whatever it is that we "send."

There are many techniques of subtle activism, many different ways in which individuals and groups can participate in this endeavor. But at its core, subtle activism is a process of enhancing the flow of organic and systemic energies that foster wholeness. Not imposing, partnering the stakeholders, being grounded, forming connections, being collaborative, being inclusive, and honoring the specific are all simply ways of doing so.

Subtle Neighborliness

Sometimes the idea of being an "activist" can convey a more forceful approach to this inner work than is intended, particularly when the word "activist" is associated in our minds with civil protest and other forms of opposition. There is nothing adversarial about proper subtle activism. As I said above, it's not about being a "warrior of Light" or some such fantasy.

For this reason, I often think of subtle activism as a form of neighborliness, a "subtle neighborliness" that works to make the planetary neighborhood in which we all live a better place. In this context, the technique of subtle activism can be explained using the metaphor of helping a neighbor. Here are the steps that I can use:

1. **Anchoring:** This is the preparatory step. It's what I do in "my house" before attempting to help my neighbor. This is the work I do to stand in my Sovereignty and Self-Light and to make sure the energies in my personal field are balanced, calm, integrated, and loving.

2. **Shaping:** This step is putting together the "package of aid" I intend to take to my neighbor. I am invoking and shaping within myself the subtle energies and qualities I wish to bring to help another person or a situation. It is the step of creating the energetic and physical "felt sense" of what I wish to offer. In terms of the "rules" I listed above, it's being that which I wish to bring into the situation. For instance, if I want to bring an energy of calm and peacefulness, then I want to establish a felt sense of peace and calm within my own energy field.

3. **Attunement and Resonance:** This step is when I travel next door to my neighbor's house. This is the step of using my imagination and intention to attune to and energetically enter the subtle environment of the person or situation I wish to help.

4. **Allies:** This step is optional but can be very helpful. It's like asking friends to come with me to my neighbor's house to help and asking those living in my neighbor's house to help as well. It's the invocation of or alignment with subtle and spiritual allies that can help in the process.

5. **Holding:** This step is what I do in my neighbor's house to fulfill the reason for going there. Basically it's holding within my own energy field the qualities and energies I wish to introduce to the subtle environment I'm seeking to help, allowing them to radiate out and become part of that environment in their own organic way.

6. **Closure:** This step is leaving my neighbor's house, shutting the door behind me and coming back into my own home. This is the step of closing down the connections with the subtle environment with which I've been working and letting go of the energies I've invoked, creating closure for the process.

7. **Being Home:** This step is attuning to being back in my own home and appreciating its unique environment and how it nurtures and supports me. In this step, I take a moment to stand in my own Sovereignty again, honoring and blessing my own energy field and that of my personal environment, grounding myself back home in my body and surroundings.

Other Sources

Subtle activism is becoming recognized as a powerful and valid form of spiritual practice in its own right. Many people are exploring it. One source you could investigate if you are interested is www.gaiafield.net. There you will find articles on subtle activism and a variety of related activities. Another source is www.gratefulness.org. Though not explicitly about subtle activism, it deals with the underlying spiritual attitudes that go into it and into creating wholeness in our world.

There is also a Subtle Activism resource page on the Lorian website, www.Lorian.org, where you can find both articles and exercises for further exploration into this topic. There also are both the recording and the transcript of an interview between myself and David Nicol on subtle activism in which I go into in some detail a method for doing subtle activism. (David Nicol, by the way, is the individual who coined the phrase "subtle activism" and is the author of *Subtle Activism: The Inner Dimension of Social and Planetary Transformation* published by SUNY Press.)

What is most important, though, is that you realize that you are a source of blessing and healthy subtle energies. Subtle activism is a relationship you form with the world. It's a relationship based on love and caring, compassion and concern; it's a relationship based on a willingness to take actions that create wholeness in both the inner and outer worlds. For this reason, how you perform subtle activism will emerge in part from your uniqueness, from who you are as an individual and how you relate to the world. In learning how others do subtle activism, don't neglect discovering how you do it and what works for you.

EXERCISES FOR CHAPTER NINETEEN

Exercise: A Subtle Activism Algorithm

An algorithm is a procedure for doing something such as accomplishing a task. The following is a suggestion for a general procedure for performing an act of subtle activism (or subtle neighborliness).

1. Stand in your Sovereignty and Self-Light, filling your heart, mind, and your energy field with love and honor for who you are and for your connection to the wonder and joy of creation.
2. Take a moment to connect with love and honor to the subtle life energy within your immediate local environment and the things in it. Invite its support and participation in what you are about to do.
3. Be clear about what the situation is to which you are going to attune and what you wish to bring to it. Be sure that you can engage this situation with clarity and calm and with a loving energy.
4. Create your "aid package." Fill your heart, mind and energy field with the felt sense of those qualities and energies you wish to bring to the situation and people you wish to help. Become the living presence of these qualities.
5. Using the best information available to you, picture the situation to which you are attuning, where it is, what is happening, and who may be involved, so that you can clearly imagine yourself energetically and spiritually present in that situation. Imagine an inner door opening, and you step through it into the midst of the situation you're seeking to help.
6. Imagine a field of assistance—like an inner First Aid tent—overlighting the area. Connect to this field by directing your thoughts towards it. Offer it your "aid package," the qualities and energies you are embodying. This field is there to support and nourish all those who are actively seeking on both physical and non-physical levels to assist the situation, to help any who may be suffering, to encourage and give hope, and generally to gather up and heal broken energies. Just as you might donate money to an organization giving aid in a disaster, in this case, you're donating your energy and presence.
7. Hold your presence and energy in connection with this field of assistance as long as feels comfortable. When you begin to feel restless, tired, or uncomfortable, allow this connection to end. Turn your thoughts completely away from the situation you've been attuned to and back towards your body. Step back through the inner

door you opened into your own environment, closing the door firmly behind you. Bring your attention and consciousness fully back into your body.

8. Take a moment to appreciate and honor your body. Center yourself within it. Stand in your Sovereignty and Self-Light, honoring and loving your unique incarnate self. Give thanks to your local environment for its support. Let love flow to all the parts of you and to the physical and subtle environment around you, then go about your everyday business.

Exercise: Webmaking
Overview

Here is a very simple form of subtle activism which can be performed anywhere at any time. I call it Webmaking as you are contributing to a web of Light. The overall intent is similar to that of the exercise I just presented, but the approach is different.

The brain has been discovered to be "plastic," always changing in dynamic ways as we respond and adapt to our environment. In the developing science of neuroplasticity, it has been demonstrated that the twin powers of intention and attention when directed in certain ways can result in lasting changes in brain structure. As we change our brain structure, so we change our behavior and our capacities. In other words, the power of thinking can have a more profound physical effect than science had previously suspected.

There is a similar phenomenon at work in the non-physical or subtle environment of the world, the environment in which subtle activism takes place. We are constantly forming energetic connections between ourselves and others and between ourselves and our surroundings. Even simple acts of perception and recognition can do this. The quality and nature of these connections depend on the kind of subtle energies we weave into them. If they are negative in nature, it results in one kind of subtle connection and structure; if they are positive, it results in a different one. Further, the intensity and intentionality behind our thinking and feeling determines how long these connections and this subtle structure may last. Most dissolve immediately as our attention shifts and moves about, but some can persist and eventually stabilize into a long-lasting configuration of subtle energies.

One of the tasks of subtle activism is to shift the subtle structure of the world away from being stuck in violent, hateful and negative configurations towards patterns and flows of energy that are healthy, holistic, loving, caring, and nurturing. It is a work of generating a structure, a "web" of positive qualities and energies that can support and bless individuals, attune them to the loving inclusiveness of the Sacred, and foster goodwill and collaborative behavior that creates wholeness in the world. If this is done on a regular basis, then patterns develop that persist within the subtle world.

This exercise is something we can do "on the run," as we go about our daily lives. Think of a spider spinning a web. It anchors a strand of silk on something solid and then swings out to connect with something else where it attaches the other end of that strand. In Webmaking, you are making a connection between an individual and the Sacred, a connection that is a strand of blessing.

By "Sacred" here, I don't mean any particular religious image of God, though you can certainly use whatever image of deity is important to you and in which you believe. What I mean is a universal and inclusive source of life, wholeness and love, the Ground of All Being, which seeks to bless each individual life according to its uniqueness and its needs, enabling it to fulfill in optimal ways its potentials.

Webmaking is something you can do with anyone you meet during your day. As per the rules of subtle activism, you are not imposing anything, nor are you projecting a particular energy to anyone. You are, however, establishing a connection of a particular nature—the strand of the web. You can even do this with objects in your environment and certainly with animals and plants as well. This web of Light and lovingness ultimately connects all to all.

We could say that there already is a universal Web—the Sacred itself—that connects everything to everything else, and we would be right. But operationally in our lives and in the life of the earth this universal Web is often more potential than realized. We have but to watch the evening news to see how fully and tragically humanity falls short of implementing it. Further, the activities of disconnection and violence, fear and anger in which humanity does participate creates a very different kind of subtle energy structure, one that breaks the sacred Web and prevents it from manifesting. Our collective "brain" is badly wired, creating habits of separation and violence that only make that faulty wiring more persistent.

The good news is that the subtle environment, like our brain, is very plastic and can change, often very quickly. We can create inner structures and configurations of energy that support and promote wholeness. What is needed for this to happen, though, is for us to make those changes through the power of our intentionality and our attention. We have to intend goodwill, intend love, intend collaboration, intend understanding and then we must give those intentions our attention and focus, particularly where those qualities don't exist or are being undermined in a given situation. So while the universal Web of connection, life and love is there, we can't simply take it for granted. It's up to us to participate in its expression and to do what we can to manifest it.

In Webmaking, then, there are three steps in doing this. The first step is to make a connection with another individual, to "spin a strand" in his or her direction. The second step is to connect that strand to the Sacred. The third step is to further connect that strand to a larger, evolving web that you are part of co-creating. Let's look at each of these in more detail with some examples.

Part 1: Spinning a Strand

When you see an individual—it doesn't matter whether you know them or not—imagine a ribbon or strand of Light between you and that person. This strand is NOT tying or binding you two together in anyway; it is simply a carrier of your goodwill, love, and blessings to that person. In effect, you are affirming a universal truth: "We are connected in the love and blessings of the Sacred; we are connected in the universal web of life that seeks to manifest wholeness on the earth. Between us there is no violence or separation, only goodwill and mutual support." With your strand, you are activating and expressing this truth.

You can do this with anyone. For example, while driving, you can spin strands to other drivers around you. While shopping, you can spin a strand to other shoppers or to the clerks that serve you. In a restaurant, you can spin a strand to other diners and to the waitpersons who bring you your food. And you can spin strands to plants, animals and objects as well. The possibilities are endless.

Part 2: Connecting to the Sacred

Imagine this strand of light and blessing that you've spun between yourself and another and extend it through and beyond yourself into the Sacred, however you imagine that Presence. This is important. You are spinning the strand, not anchoring it in yourself. You are carrying it deeper into your Interiority, into your connection with your transpersonal soul and from this into Light itself, anchoring the thread in your felt sense of the Sacred, in the Beloved of All Beings, the Ground of all existence. This prevents unwanted psychic links from coming into being between you and another, assuming that the link lasted anytime at all. The Sacred is the universal anchor for the web of life.

If this is the case, why have the first step at all? Why not directly see the individual as connected to the Sacred and leave out yourself as a middle person? There are several reasons. For one, there is a benefit to your personal expression of caring and goodwill; this is good for you and it's good for the recipient. For another, you and the other individual (or plant, animal or object) have a natural resonance already by virtue of being part of this physical world. You can form a connection along this natural resonance that then becomes a "carrier wave" for the deeper connection with the Sacred. You provide the specific connection that then can be connected to the Universal.

It's not that you don't wish to acknowledge or empower your connectedness to the other; it's that you don't want to anchor that connectedness in yourself. Once the connection is recognized and affirmed through your intentionality and attention, you then want its "end point" to be established within a larger, universal field that embraces both of you. That larger field is the Sacred.

Part 3: Connecting to a web

The next time you "spin a strand" of light and blessing between yourself and another and connect it to the Sacred, think back to the previous such strands you've "spun." Visualize this new strand connecting to them, forming a web. See this web filled with the Light of the Sacred and vibrating to its loving and supportive presence. You don't have to remember each separate strand, each connection you've made as you've gone through your day but do remember and visualize the wholeness of the growing web itself. See this web that you're spinning as connected to and reflecting the universal Web that is the underlying wholeness and life within all things.

In performing these three steps, don't forget that you have a personal strand yourself between yourself and the Sacred. Be sure to think of this from time to time to renew your own connections and participation in the larger Web.

What makes this exercise work is the intention behind the Webmaking and the attention you bring to it. Each strand you spin and send out to connect a person to the universal Web needs to have your clear and clean intention behind it. Part of that intention is your intent that that person (or animal, plant, or object) be blessed and, through connection with the Sacred, empowered in the expression of his, her, or its unique identity and soul's purpose. It is an intention of goodwill and love made impersonally and in a way that places no binding on the individual, no imposition upon his or her sovereignty and personal energy. You are not insisting that something happen. You are only augmenting the will of his or her soul and innate sacredness to unfold the highest of which he or she is capable.

To give power to this intention, you must give attention to that person (or thing, if it's not a person). This can be very brief, no more than a few seconds, but in that moment—however short—your whole attention is on that person and their wellbeing and connectedness to wholeness.

In short, in Webmaking, you have to mean it. It's not something you do idly or wishfully. It need not take much time or energy, only a second or two, but it needs to be sincere. For the three steps to work there needs to be intention and attention behind them.

If you practice this, you will find, however, that the growing strength and vitality of the web you're creating and its attunement to the universal Web will empower your ability to spin your strands. A deeper part of you, knowing what you intend and that you're sincere in following through, will take over and greatly augment the process, so it becomes almost automatic for you (though never taken for granted).

In this way, you become an agent for shaping the subtle environment of the world, drawing into manifestation the energies and patterns of the universal Web of wholeness. This is a powerful act of subtle activism. It means that when the individuals whose connections to that universal Web you have empowered encounter situations that may cause them to react in a negative way, they have something positive and life-affirming to respond to other than the habits of mental, emotional and physical violence engraved into the subtle fields of the earth. The function of all subtle activism is to bring new options into play and create loving alternatives to habitual action. That is what your Webmaking can help bring about.

Exercise: The Home "Ley Lines"

One form of service to the world that our ancestors engaged in and which a number of modern people are rediscovering involves working with lines of flowing earth energy called ley lines or power lines.

The following exercise is a miniaturization of this and was suggested by an inner contact of mine as a way in which individuals could begin working with the planetary energy grid. The idea is analogous to installing solar panels in a home to generate electricity for the house and then selling back to the regional power company whatever excess energy is produced, which is then channeled into the local power grid. In this exercise, you are creating a "personal home energy grid"—that is to say, ley lines within your house or apartment—which you can cultivate and then send the energy that is generated out from your home to connect with the planetary grid. Through this practice, you are turning your home into a spiritual power station, generating positive subtle energies to "feed into" the planetary energy grid, the "meridians" of Gaia's flowing life.

I drew a little picture to illustrate this:

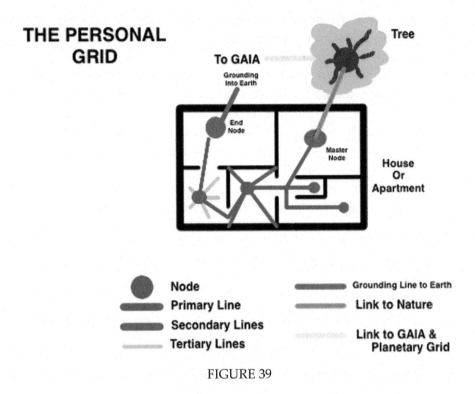

FIGURE 39

CREATING THE PERSONAL HOME ENERGY GRID

Part I

- You can start in any room of your home. This room will contain the initial or "master" power node (though you can change this later if you wish or circumstances dictate). This node can be anchored in a physical object if you wish or it can simply be a point of energy that you focus upon within the energy field of the room itself.
- In doing this gridwork, feel free to call upon any allies you wish. Include the overlighting *Genus Loci* (Spirit of the Place) of your home.
- Begin by Standing in Sovereignty, Self-Light, and Presence. Attune to the room, feeling what its energy is like. Attune to the life within the room. Use the Grail Space practice to establish a collaborative energy space that fills the room, drawing all within it into a circle of connection. State clearly your objective to create an energy node in this room. If you are anchoring this node to an object, identify the object and, if possible, hold it up. Visualize the collective life energy

of the room, gathered into collaboration by Grail Space, focusing upon this object, or if there is no physical object, upon a place in the room. Focus your own Self-Light into this focal point as well. Imagine a small star of radiance coming into being at this focal point and dedicate this star to the wholeness and well-being of this room, of the house or apartment as a whole, and to the world as a whole outside your home. Through the power of the Grail Space, align and connect this star with the Sacred in whatever way is meaningful to you. This is now your Master Node.

- When you feel complete with this, thank your Grail Space partners in the room and invite them to return to their usual state. You, however, are now going to create the Primary Line of your personal energy grid.

- Walk into the next adjoining room, drawing a line of energy with you like a thread from the Master Node you have just created. Attune to this room and create Grail Space within it. Create another node in this room as you did before. You may anchor it to a physical object or not at your discretion. When this is done, connect the thread of energy and Light from the Master Node to it. See these two nodes vibrating in resonance with each other, a line of radiance connecting between them.

- Repeat this process with the next room. Do this until you have entered all the rooms of your home. As you do, you are extending the Primary Line from one room to the next until it runs throughout your home.

- In the last room you enter, once you have created the node and linked it to the Primary Line, state clearly that this is a "Closed Node", that is, it is the end point where the Primary Line grounds itself. Visualize the Primary Line extending down into the Earth where it is linked to the protective and grounding power of the planet. This is exactly the same as you would do if you were grounding an electrical wire into the ground. The purpose is to not leave any open ends of an energy line waving about where energy could leak out or something unwanted could enter. Ask your allies to see that this grounding is secure.

Part 2

- Once you have your Primary Line laid down (and you may need to do Part 1 of this exercise more than once to fully establish this), then it's time to lay down the Secondary Lines. These are lines of energy unique to each room. Consider them the Primary Lines of the room's own energy grid.
- Go to each room as before. Attune to the Node that's there and to the Primary Line running through it. Then visualize four radiant lines of energy extending from this Node to the corners (or the walls) of the room, connecting to the structure of the house or apartment and filling the room with their blessing. You are wiring the room itself, drawing on the Primary Line as a source of energy. When you are done, give thanks to the spirit of the room for its assistance. (Again, call upon any allies you wish, including the overlighting spirit or angel of your home.)
- When you have done all the rooms, go back to the Master Node and attune to it. Visualize and bless the whole personal energy grid, the Primary Line linking all the rooms together and the Secondary Lines carrying the energy of the Primary Line into each room and integrating it into that room in its own unique way.

Part 3

- Once you have the Primary and Secondary Lines established of your personal energy grid, it's time to link it up with the planetary grid.
- Go to your Master Node and attune to it. Draw a line of energy from it into your own subtle energy field. Go outside.
- Outside your home, identify a plant (trees work very well for this) to be a connecting point. Go to this plant and inform it what you wish to do and that you would like it to be the connecting point between the personal power grid within your home and the larger Gaian grid of life and energy that encompasses the planet. Your intent is to channel the Light, the blessings, the energy that your personal grid produces into the planetary grid for the blessing of all. Ask the plant if it's willing to be your partner in this and a conduit for connecting your personal grid's energy to that of Gaia. (Never assume cooperation; always ask.) If you get a sense of "Yes", then draw the line of energy that connects to the Master Node and that you've been carrying in your own subtle field and offer it to the plant, connecting it with its

energy field which in turn is attuned to the planetary field as well as, through its roots, with the earth itself (providing another important form of grounding). Again, invite the assistance of any appropriate inner ally in this process.

- When you feel complete with this, thank the plant and return to your home. Go to the Master Node and attune to it again, this time visualizing the connection with your new partner outside. In this way, you connect your power grid to that of the planet.
- At this point, you have an energy grid that is completely accessible to you and one you can work with in your home, attuning to it, giving it blessing, keeping it charged with Light, and in so doing, you are generating energies of life and blessing that now flow out to become part of the planetary grid itself.

Once you have your own personal set of "home ley lines" active and connected to the larger world outdoors, you can then nourish and connect with this "home energy grid" through blessing, through meditation, through whatever energy work seems appropriate to you to send positive spiritual forces and qualities flowing into and through these miniature ley lines within your home. By heightening it and making it a living part of the energy system of your home, this home energy grid becomes a conduit for these good energies to flow out into the energy grid of the world. You can in whatever way you wish invoke and draw down higher energies of Soul and other transpersonal sources to flow into your Master Node. If you do this daily as a practice, it will become an automatic blessing, and you may well find the Master Node itself drawing down what it needs to keep your home energy grid alive and flowing and radiant with blessings.

CHAPTER TWENTY
Final Thoughts

Throughout the writing of this book, I've been aware, at times painfully so, of the need to simplify, especially in my drawings, what are complex and dynamic realities. What may be lost at times, I fear, in my descriptions is a sense of the livingness, even the "dancing-ness" of subtle energies and of the worlds, invisible to our physical senses, in which they operate. Even more, I think I am unable to do justice to the nature and beauty of our own subtle beingness. By necessity, I've had to describe immaterial realities in material ways, using words and concepts best suited to our physical surroundings. A poet or an artist might have done a much better job.

Here's an example of what I mean. In describing the way our subtle bodies perceive their energetic environments, I've used phrases like "perception by becoming" or "participatory perception." Such a description is true as far as it goes, but it doesn't go far enough. It would be more precise to say that our own subtle fields reach out and embrace the subtle world in a dance that is grounded in love and intended to generate beauty. It's not so much that we become what we see in the inner realms as that the act of perception is really an act of co-creativity and mutual sharing, the result of which is not simply an awareness of "what's out there" but a revelation of the sacredness that is at the heart of all things. It is perception as an act of mutual celebration of life and of the presence of a universal Beloved. The challenge with what I've called "aggravated energies" is that they resist this co-creative dance; they resist being drawn into the revelation of wholeness. It's like reaching out to a dancing partner who pushes you away or struggles in your embrace, stepping on your feet in the process. The result is awkwardness and a loss of grace at best, and a harmful disruption of harmony and possibility at worst.

This is the thing: all healthy, non-aggravated interactions in the subtle realms support the emergence of possibility to some degree. They enhance life. They are moments and actions of joy. We can taste this in the physical when we see something in the world that thrills us with its beauty and for a moment we feel grateful and joyous to be part of a world in which such a thing can exist.

I began this book talking about the fact that we are part of a living universe. I cannot emphasize this enough. Discussing subtle "energies" can lead us to think in terms of blind, unthinking forces, the way we usually think of electricity, for instance, or electromagnetism in general. We forget that these forces operate through living relationships; they are living, sentient manifestations. As a non-physical being once told me, "there is no healing 'power,' only healing relationships." This is a profound vision if we think about it, one that reveals the heart of the world in which we live. It is why all forms of working with subtle energies possess a moral dimension, just as any relationship does with another living being.

This is why I don't approach the subtle realms or the energies (or beings) of those realms as a magician or a "warrior of Light," determined to impose my will and desires upon my surroundings. I am not a dictator but a collaborator. In the process, I learn about my own inner Self and its sacredness as I seek to uphold and reveal the sacredness in the world around me.

Working with subtle energies can be summed up in two principles. The first is to honor and be ourselves, standing proudly in our incarnate, human state, connected both to spirit and the earth. The second is to engage the subtle worlds with love and respect and a willingness to partner.

Why Bother?

Why bother working with subtle energies? Millions of people live perfectly good lives without ever dealing directly with the subtle dimensions of the world. The fact is, though, that the subtle dimensions do exist. They are the planet's other half. And we ourselves, like the earth, possess a two-fold nature, partly physical, partly non-physical. Even while embodied, we still inhabit the earth's other, subtle half as well. To discover and express our own wholeness as well as to contribute to the world's wholeness, we need to learn how to properly and successfully engage with these subtle parts.

This is not something that can be learned from a single book or a single class. It's a lifetime endeavor because it's life itself. And, as I said at the beginning, this book is not a comprehensive encyclopedia of the subtle realms or of all the ways we might engage with subtle energies and forces. Much of the way you will need to learn for yourself because many, if not most, of your relationships to the subtle worlds are the result of ways of partnering that are unique and individual to you.

However, I do hope this book provides a solid foundation from which you can take your own steps into coming to know your own subtle self in your unique way and in the process becoming a citizen of the whole world, not just of its physical dimension.

REFERENCES

At different times throughout this book, I've made reference to books by other authors that I think you might find interesting or helpful in this area of working with subtle energies. For your convenience, I thought I would repeat that information here so that it's easy for you to find should you wish to do so. I've also added some other favorite books of mine that bear on this topic in one way or another. They can serve as places to start exploring if you wish to do so.

I've arranged the books by topics correlated with chapters or topics in the book.

Felt Sense

The Power of Focusing, by Ann Weiser Cornell

Subtle Worlds

Subtle Worlds: An Explorer's Field Notes, by David Spangler
Collaboration with Subtle Worlds, by David Spangler

Subtle Body

The Subtle Body: An Encyclopedia of your Energetic Anatomy, by Cyndi Dale

Sensory and Somatic Awareness

Reclaiming Vitality and Presence: Sensory Awareness as a Practice for Life, edited by Richard Lowe and Stefan Laeng-Gilliatt

Subtle Awareness

Meditation as Contemplative Inquiry, by Arthur Zajonc

Imagination

The Three Only Things: Tapping the Power of Dreams, Coincidence, & Imagination, by Robert Moss

Presence

Kything: The Art of Spiritual Presence, by Louis M. Savary and Patricia H. Berne
Full Body Presence: Learning to Listen to Your Body's Wisdom, by Suzanne Scurlock-Durana

Sensing
Second Sight, by Judith Orloff

Blessing
Blessing: The Art and the Practice, by David Spangler

Protection
Feeling Safe, by William Bloom
Psychic Protection, by William Bloom
Psychic Shield, by Caitlin Matthews

Healing
The Encyclopedia of Energy Medicine, by Linnie Thomas and Carrie Obry

Subtle Activism
Subtle Activism: The Inner Dimension of Social and Planetary Transformation, by David Nicol

ABOUT THE PUBLISHER

Lorian Press is a private, for profit business which publishes works approved by the Lorian Association. Current titles can be found on the Lorian website www.lorian.org. Our address is:

Lorian Press
6592 Peninsula Dr.
Traverse City, MI 49686

The Lorian Association is a not-for-profit educational organization. Its work is to help people bring the joy, healing, and blessing of their personal spirituality into their everyday lives. This spirituality unfolds out of their unique lives and relationships to Spirit, by whatever name or in whatever form that Spirit is recognized. The address is:

The Lorian Association
PO Box 1368
Issaquah, WA 98027

For more information, go to www.lorian.org
or www.lorianassociation.com

CPSIA information can be obtained
at www.ICGtesting.com
Printed in the USA
LVOW06s0222271017
553708LV00014BA/639/P